Inclusive Dualism

Critical Frontiers of Theory, Research, and Policy in International Development Studies

Series Editors: Andrew Fischer, Uma Kothari, and Giles Mohan

Critical Frontiers of Theory, Research, and Policy in International Development Studies is the official book series of the Development Studies Association of the UK and Ireland (DSA).

The series profiles research monographs that will shape the theory, practice, and teaching of international development for a new generation of scholars, students, and practitioners. The objective is to set high quality standards within the field of development studies to nurture and advance the field, as is the central mandate of the DSA. Critical scholarship is especially encouraged, within the spirit of development studies as an interdisciplinary and applied field, with a classical focus on national and global processes of accumulation and structural transformation, and associated political, social, and cultural change. In this manner, the series seeks to promote a range of applied theory and empirics based on the analysis of historical development experiences, as was the methodological and epistemological strength of classical development studies.

Also in this series:

The Aid Lab: Understanding Bangladesh's Unexpected Success
Naomi Hossain

Taken for a Ride: Grounded Neoliberalism, Precarious Labour, and Public Transport in an African Metropolis
Matteo Rizzo

Inclusive Dualism

Labour-intensive development, decent work, and surplus labour in Southern Africa

Nicoli Nattrass and Jeremy Seekings

OXFORD
UNIVERSITY PRESS

OXFORD
UNIVERSITY PRESS

Great Clarendon Street, Oxford, OX2 6DP,
United Kingdom

Oxford University Press is a department of the University of Oxford.
It furthers the University's objective of excellence in research, scholarship,
and education by publishing worldwide. Oxford is a registered trade mark of
Oxford University Press in the UK and in certain other countries

First Edition published in 2019

Impression: 1

Published in the United States of America by Oxford University Press
198 Madison Avenue, New York, NY 10016, United States of America

British Library Cataloguing in Publication Data
Data available

Library of Congress Control Number: 2018965986

ISBN 978–0–19–884146–3

Printed and bound by
CPI Group (UK) Ltd, Croydon, CR0 4YY

In honour of W. Arthur Lewis and Leon Deetlefs: Lewis showed the importance of labour-intensive manufacturing for development; Deetlefs, after years of helping to shut down labour-intensive clothing manufacturers in South Africa for failing to comply with rising minimum wages, resigned and subsequently helped workers to establish co-operatives to save their jobs.

Acknowledgements

Our research on the clothing industry in South Africa was made possible by the kind assistance of many employers, workers and the National Bargaining Council for the Clothing Manufacturing Industry. We are especially grateful to Alex Liu, Michael Chang, Robert Han, Ferdie Alberts, Johan Baard, the Simunye workers' co-operative and the late Leon Deetlefs. The research benefitted from funding from the Millennium Trust, the support of the Centre for Social Science Research (CSSR) at the University of Cape Town, and research assistance from Liang Xu, Gareth Olds, and Lingxiu Zhang.

We are grateful for comments provided by reviewers, and from participants in seminars, workshops and conferences at Oxford University, Yale University, Harvard University, the University of Cape Town, the University of the Witwatersrand, Rhodes University, the University of the Western Cape, and the Centre for Development and Enterprise. We have benefitted especially from discussions with Anthony Altbeker, Anthony Black, Sam Bowles, Mike Morris, Nebahat Tokatli and Liang Xu.

Earlier versions of some chapters have been published elsewhere. An early version of Chapter 3 was published as 'Employment and Labour Productivity in High Unemployment Countries', *Development Policy Review*, 36, S2 (2018). An earlier version of Chapter 4 was published as 'Trajectories of Development and the Global Clothing Industry', *Competition and Change*, 22, 3 (2018). Chapter 5 uses some material published previously in 'Setting the Level of a National Minimum Wage: What can South Africa Learn from Other Countries' Experiences?', *Transformation*, 92 (2016) and 'Institutions, Wage Differentiation and the Structure of Employment in South Africa', in A. Black (ed.), *Towards Employment Intensive Growth in South Africa* (Cape Town: Juta, 2016). An earlier version of Chapter 6 was published as 'Job Destruction in Newcastle: Minimum Wage Setting and Low-Wage Employment in the South African Clothing Industry', *Transformation*, 84 (2014). An earlier version of Chapter 7 was published as 'Trade Unions, the State and Casino Capitalism in South Africa's Clothing Industry', *Review of African Political Economy*, 43, 167 (2016).

Contents

List of Figures

List of Tables

List of Abbreviations

AGOA	African Growth and Opportunities Act
AMSA	Apparel Manufacturers of South Africa
ANC	African National Congress
AU	African Union
BEE	Black Economic Empowerment
BIG	Basic Income Grant
COSATU	Congress of South African Trade Unions
DTI	Department of Trade and Industry
EPWP	Expanded Public Works Programme
FAO	Food and Agricultural Organization
GATT	General Agreement on Tariffs and Trade
GDP	Gross Domestic Product
GPN	Global Production Network
GVC	Global Value Chain
HCI	Hosken Consolidated Investments
IDC	Industrial Development Corporation
ILO	International Labour Organization
LSM	Living Standard Measure
MFA	Multi-Fibre Agreement/Arrangement
NASL	National Anti-Sweating League
NBC	National Bargaining Council for the Clothing Manufacturing Industry
SACTWU	Southern African Clothing and Textile Workers Union
UNCTAD	United Nations Conference on Trade and Development
UNECA	United Nations Economic Commission on Africa
UNIDO	United Nations Industrial Development Organization
VAT	Value-Added Tax
WD	Wage Determination

1

Introduction

Southern Africa has the highest unemployment rate of any region in the world. Yet, especially in South Africa, the economic powerhouse of the region, the capacity to generate new jobs out of economic growth steadily worsened in the late twentieth and early twenty-first centuries. Not only have South African governments failed to expand labour-intensive sectors, but they have also actively undermined them. This is clear in the case of the clothing manufacturing sector, which is the most important of the labour-intensive industrial sectors. In 1994, when Nelson Mandela became President of the newly democratic country, South Africa's clothing manufacturing industry produced for both the domestic and export markets and accounted for almost 10 per cent of manufacturing employment. More than twenty years later, less than a quarter of those jobs remained. Meanwhile, the number of jobless people reporting that they wanted work more than doubled between 1995 and 2018, rising from 3.6 million to 8.9 million.

Whilst growing international competition (especially from China) contributed to the collapse of South Africa's last remaining labour-intensive manufacturing industry, government policies also undermined the competitiveness of South African producers. Notably, rising institutionally driven labour costs placed additional pressure on clothing manufacturing firms and many factories were shut down for failing to comply with fast-rising minimum wages. Industrial policies did assist some of the more skill- and capital-intensive compliant firms—that is, compliant with wage regulations—to 'upgrade' their technologies, raise labour productivity, accommodate rising wages for more skilled workers and remain competitive. But this typically came at the cost of mechanization and the shedding of less skilled jobs.

This trend was reflected across the manufacturing sector where the employment elasticity of growth was *negative*, meaning that employment fell as output rose.[1] Labour productivity (output per worker) increased—but at the cost of net job destruction—a spectacular failure for a country, which as of September 2018, had an official unemployment rate of 27.5 per cent (counting only active jobseekers), or 35.3 per cent if discouraged work-seekers are also included.

Unemployment is a major cause of poverty and inequality in South Africa (Seekings and Nattrass 2005, 2016; Leibbrandt et al., 2012) which is why labour-intensive growth and a rising employment elasticity of growth is essential for inclusive development. The case of South Africa reveals the dangers for countries with high unemployment of development strategies that increase labour productivity by closing off opportunities for labour-intensive growth. Improving labour productivity can be developmental in that it facilitates higher wages for those with jobs and potentially generates resources that can be invested or redistributed. When labour markets are tight, that is, the demand for labour is close to the supply, then any workers who lose their jobs through mechanization and labour process restructuring (the typical components of rising labour productivity) should be able to find work quickly elsewhere, perhaps with some retraining. But when unemployment is high, rising labour productivity implies a growth path that is increasingly expensive in terms of additional output and the capital required to generate much-needed new jobs. Such a growth path is likely to benefit an insider class of predominantly skilled workers whilst exacerbating unemployment and inequality. A more differentiated or 'dualist' approach, which also facilitates the expansion of labour-intensive jobs, would be more inclusive.

W. Arthur Lewis, the only economist of African descent to win the Nobel Prize for economics, famously depicted low-wage industrialization as a route to development for countries with large supplies of under-utilized ('surplus') labour (Lewis, 1954; discussed further in Chapter 2). The 'Asian tigers' (Hong Kong, Singapore, South Korea, Taiwan) subsequently demonstrated (from the 1960s into the 1980s) how Lewis-like export-oriented labour-intensive manufacturing could draw labour out of subsistence agriculture at low wages until such rural labour supplies dried up, which then placed upward pressure on wages and pushed their economies in more capital-intensive directions (Braude and Menashe, 2011).

[1] Using data from the South African Reserve Bank based on firm-level surveys, between 1995 and 2017, real manufacturing output expanded at 1.9 per cent per annum whereas employment contracted by 1.3 per cent per annum, resulting in an employment elasticity of growth of –0.7. Using data from labour force surveys, available only from 2000, manufacturing employment fell (at –0.02 per cent per annum) between 2000 and 2017, whereas output expanded by 1.8 per cent per annum, resulting in an employment elasticity of growth of –0.01.

Lewis's conception of 'dualist' development took as a stylized fact that developing economies were highly differentiated both between 'subsistence' and 'capitalist' sectors and within the capitalist (or modern) sector itself:

> What we have is not one island of expanding capitalist employment, surrounded by a vast sea of subsistence workers, but rather a number of such tiny islands . . . We find a few industries highly capitalized, such as mining and electric power, side by side with the most primitive techniques; a few high-class shops, surrounded by masses of old style traders; a few highly capitalized plantations, surrounded by a sea of peasants . . . There is the same contrast even between people; between the few highly westernized, trousered, natives, educated in western universities, speaking western languages, and glorying in Beethoven, Mill, Marx or Einstein, and the great mass of their countrymen who live in quite other worlds. (1954: 147)

Lewis's model of development with 'unlimited' supplies of labour reflected what he saw in the cases of Egypt, India and Jamaica. Labour-intensive industrialization, he argued, was an affordable means of expanding the modern sector beyond its few 'islands' of relatively capital-intensive, high-paid work. Such a growth path offered a route out of poverty for many because even relatively low-wage industrial jobs were more productive and hence provided higher earnings than subsistence activities. Labour-intensive growth posed no threat to the existing islands of relatively high-wage work, but rather benefitted them by creating an expanding base of consumers for their products and services.

Subsequent development discourse became more suspicious of labour-intensive activities. Lewis's dualist perspective has been overshadowed by a development narrative that sees relatively low-wage work as a competitive threat to the islands of high-paid jobs. In this narrative, labour-intensive growth is portrayed as a 'low-road' trajectory, promising nothing but a 'race to the bottom'. Whereas Lewis saw dualism as the ladders of improved welfare, the new narrative saw it as the snakes of impoverishment. Dualism and differentiation has morphed from being a taken-for-granted characteristic of developing countries into a problem needing elimination through regulatory action. This is evident in both the arguments put forward by the International Labour Organization (ILO) and in much of the industrial policy literature. Middle-income countries in particular are advised against labour-intensive development because of strong competition from China and other countries already on the Lewis growth trajectory. They are advised instead to focus on improving skills and labour productivity in order to expand the more skill- and capital-intensive islands of high-paid work.

Lewis's framing of the capitalist sector in developing economies as encompassing a range of coexisting production technologies (and associated wage rates) has accordingly been overtaken by an 'upgrade or die' policy discourse.

The fact that there are choices of technique, whose economic optimality depends in large part on factor prices (notably labour), has been pushed to the side. Instead, rapid technological innovation (especially digital—the so-called 'fourth industrial revolution') is emphasized as implying that sustainable development necessarily depends on moving towards the 'cutting edge', even if this means becoming increasingly skill- and capital-intensive in the presence of large supplies of unskilled labour. This narrative of development dovetails with the negative framing of labour-intensive industry (especially in clothing production) as 'sweatshops', to create a policy discourse that justifies the neglect of, and even active job destruction in, labour-intensive firms and sectors.

Such developmental narratives can be politically appealing, especially in middle-income developing country contexts where organized business and labour have an interest in expanding the skill- and capital-intensive sectors of the economy. Yet, some of these countries are also home to millions of poor, relatively unskilled, people. Some of these countries, especially in Southern Africa, face high and rising unemployment. Pushing labour-intensive growth out of the frame of acceptable policies in such contexts severely constrains the potential for inclusive development.

Fourth industrial revolution digital technologies are changing the world and will continue to move the technological frontier forward, even for labour-intensive firms. In the clothing manufacturing sector, new technologies have meant that some jobs have been mechanized. Automation in manufacturing is a pressing issue primarily in the advanced capitalist countries where wages are high. Developing countries can expect disruptions, but with a time lag, because their lower wages enable them to remain competitive using more labour-intensive technologies (World Bank, 2016: 130–1). The clothing manufacturing sector is an example of a sector with relatively limited scope for automation. The basic technology—the sewing machine—has changed little over time. In developing countries, therefore, more labour-intensive firms can continue to exist alongside more capital- and skill-intensive firms and sectors, offering job opportunities for the masses of unemployed people who, as in Lewis's day, continue to live in quite other worlds.

The impact of the fourth industrial revolution and the urgent requirement to keep global growth within the limits posed by our increasingly environmentally stressed planet poses challenges for development and distribution both locally and globally (Raworth, 2017). More can be done to promote family planning to help slow population growth (De Silva and Tenreyro, 2017) and new job opportunities will hopefully arise in emerging green industries such as recycling, retrofitting homes to be more energy efficient, etc. Twenty-first-century growth, if it is to be sustainable, will be very different from the fossil-fuelled, mass consumerism of the twentieth century. This raises questions about the potential for export-led development, although for basic wage goods such as clothing, international demand is likely to persist, thereby providing ongoing opportunities for Lewis-like growth in the developing world. Most labour-intensive manufacturing uses relatively less energy per unit of output than capital-intensive industries, and sectors such as clothing manufacturing can form part of a desirable green industrial policy (Altenburg and Assmann, 2017).

This book argues that labour-intensive development industries can and should form part of a more differentiated development strategy, especially for developing countries with high unemployment. We argue, using the clothing manufacturing industry as a lens, that Lewis's notion of dualism as differentiation and coexistence of firms using a range of technologies remains relevant. The Manichean binary between 'high' and 'low' road trajectories in contemporary development narratives is overplayed. Relatively high- and low-wage firms use different technologies and often target different product markets, meaning that a race to the bottom between sectors, or even within domestic clothing industries, is far from inevitable. As Lewis emphasized more than half a century ago, profitable production is possible using different technologies and associated wage rates—which is how highly capitalized, relatively high-wage firms were able to exist 'side by side with the most primitive techniques' (Lewis, 1954: 147). International competition from low-wage countries certainly poses challenges for producers in middle-income countries but does not necessarily imply they cannot compete by exploiting differences in factor prices, productivity and industrial policies, as well as by seizing shifting opportunities for profitable production within national and international value chains.

Domestic policy matters in shaping national development trajectories. The history of the South African clothing manufacturing industry shows that, with modest protective tariffs, labour-intensive clothing producers remained able to compete with imports from China until rapidly rising minimum wages sparked job losses. This policy-induced structural adjustment towards more capital-intensive production was justified by the dominant employer organizations, policymakers and organized labour as necessary for 'social upgrading' (or promoting 'decent work'), and 'economic upgrading' (raising labour productivity) to improve competitiveness. Imposing rapid increases in minimum wages in poor, more rural areas was presented as a means to 'level the playing field' between higher-wage firms in the main metropolitan areas and the lower-wage firms outside of them. In practice, however, the imposition of rapid increases in minimum wages for the most labour-intensive end of the industry did little if anything to assist higher-wage firms that were using different technologies and mostly competing in different product lines.

Figure 1.1 Abandoned clothing factories in rural Eastern Cape and KwaZulu-Natal

The result was an unnecessary destruction of jobs in an economy with millions of poor, unemployed people.

Abandoned clothing factories in rural South Africa (Figure 1.1) are testimony not only to the policy-induced destruction of labour-intensive jobs in areas that desperately need them, but also to a development strategy that exacerbates rather than alleviates inequality.

Successive national development strategies hoped that rising productivity would generate sufficiently rapid growth to absorb the unemployed. This manifestly failed. As noted above, the employment elasticity of manufacturing growth was negative in the post-apartheid period. From the turn of the twenty-first century to 2017, the South African economy grew by only 2.8 per cent per annum and total employment (that is, including all formal, informal, full- or part-time jobs as measured by labour force surveys) grew at a paltry 1.6 per cent per annum—insufficient to absorb new entrants into the labour market, let alone reduce unemployment.

The title of this book, 'Inclusive Dualism', emphasizes that Lewis's notion of dualism as differentiation is both an ongoing economic reality and an opportunity for inclusive development, especially in surplus labour countries. A dualist industrial policy is one that serves employment objectives by assisting firms in improving competitiveness across a range of labour- and capital-intensive technologies whilst prioritizing the development of labour-intensive firms and sectors most likely to benefit the poor. Only in a tight labour market should policymakers seek to destroy low-productivity jobs through regulation and upgrading. Inclusive dualism in a surplus labour economy entails labour and industrial policies that support firms across the technological spectrum because a differentiated economy is desirable and enables the development of capabilities necessary for the rapid expansion of higher-productivity sectors once labour markets have tightened.

Rising productivity is essential for sustainable development, but the appropriate measure of productivity depends on the context. Where labour is plentiful relative to capital, labour-intensive technologies are well placed to maximize employment growth per unit of additional capital and hence it makes sense to focus on raising the productivity of capital (output per unit of capital) rather than labour productivity (output per worker). Where the supply of labour is plentiful relative to the demand for labour, that is, when unemployment is high, it is appropriate to consider the productivity of the entire labour force—that is, of available labour including the unemployed as well as employed workers. When unemployment is high, generating new jobs through the expansion of labour-intensive work lowers average labour productivity (an arithmetic artefact of dividing rising output by faster rising employment) but raises the productivity of both capital and the labour force as previously unemployed people (who contribute nothing to output) become productive workers. Development policies that prioritize raising the labour productivity of the employed workforce under all circumstances either assume that unemployment does not exist or ignore it. This is blind to the plight of developing countries with high unemployment including most of Southern Africa.

Ours is not an argument for unregulated capitalism, nor is it 'neo-liberal' in any meaningful sense of the term. Inclusive dualism is consistent with improving workplace health and safety standards and with the setting of minimum wages. The challenge is to confront potential trade-offs between wages and employment and to craft a growth path that is sustainable, environmentally friendly, pro-poor, and inclusive.

1.1 Unemployment, Decent Work, and Inclusive Dualism

South Africa was not alone in emphasizing productivity growth over labour-intensive development. Indeed, by the turn of the twenty-first century, the historically widespread developmental path through labour-intensive manufacturing had become distinctly unfashionable in international development circles. From 1999, when Juan Somavia became Director General, the ILO developed its 'decent work' agenda. This presented better-quality and better-paid jobs, social protection, and workers' rights not simply as desirable social objectives, but as essential for development under all circumstances (ILO, 2005: 4). In this new framing of the relationship between growth and employment, relatively low-wage, labour-intensive jobs were portrayed as morally suspect and as a threat to sustainable development. The ILO's preferred alternative was to advocate universally for improved skills, technology, and management to sustain competitiveness whilst facilitating higher wages, and to strengthen regulations to protect workers against the disadvantages of informality and ensure 'decent' incomes (ibid.: 5).

The World Commission on Social Dimensions of Globalization, a United Nations initiative reporting in 2004, followed suit by constructing low-wage work and informal employment in developing countries as not only developmentally dangerous, but as indicative, emblematic, and at the heart of what was unfair in the international economic order. To promote development and human dignity, countries were advised to emphasize skills development, labour productivity growth, and the expansion of worker protection—including by bringing the informal (unregulated) sector, where incomes were lower, into the regulatory net (WCSDG, 2004: 61). This utopian vision of a universal 'high road' to growth reflected the optimism of the mid-2000s rooted in the global economic boom. The implicit assumption was that a rising tide would lift all boats, meaning that rapid growth would ensure that more capital- and skill-intensive economies would also be employment-demanding, providing sufficient good quality jobs to mop up unemployment. Such optimism ended with the 2008 global recession. It is no longer feasible to rely on rapid growth to deliver the necessary jobs: more attention needs to be paid to making the growth path more labour-intensive, especially where unemployment is high.

It is useful to distinguish between 'better work' policies—which are consistent with inclusive dualism—and what we term 'decent work fundamentalism'. Better work policies include: ensuring workplace health and safety; preventing egregious exploitation by employers (setting a minimum wage floor); facilitating greater voice for workers either through collective bargaining at the factory- and industrial-level; and facilitating the growth of workers' co-operatives. Decent work fundamentalism, however, goes one step further to insist on raising wages and labour productivity, even if this comes at the cost of destroying labour-intensive jobs. Decent work fundamentalism can be welfare-enhancing when economies are growing fast, labour markets are tight, and active labour market policies reskill those workers who lose their jobs, enabling them to re-enter employment quickly. But, in developing countries with high unemployment, especially where growth is slow or stagnant, decent work fundamentalism is likely to be a utopian strategy with dystopic consequences: job losses and rising unemployment rates alongside higher wages for a relatively privileged group of insiders.

Persistently high unemployment poses challenges for how we think about inclusive development. When development economics emerged in the early post-war period as a primarily modernizing project to promote accumulation and growth in 'Third World' countries, the ruling assumption was that poor countries were capital-constrained and caught in a poverty trap. The hope was that foreign finance and aid could provide a 'big push' to facilitate economic 'take-off' (led by a modern, capital-intensive industrial sector), prompting a virtuous cycle of rising living standards, savings, investment and growth. Like these early development models, Lewis assumed full employment (on the reasonable grounds that people were too poor to be openly unemployed) but emphasized that in countries like Jamaica, Egypt, and India, significant 'surplus labour' existed in the form of underemployed people scratching a living in low-productivity work, notably in peasant agriculture but also in personal services and in what later came to be termed the informal sector (see Chapter 2). For Lewis, surplus labour represented an opportunity for industrialization as it could be drawn out of the low-earning sectors for a sustained period at wage rates marginally above subsistence level and at relatively low cost in terms of the capital required.

Lewis's conception of surplus labour was imprecise. As discussed further in Chapter 2, subsequent theoretical extensions of his model differed over whether surplus labour should refer to those whose marginal product was zero (meaning that they contributed nothing to output), or just relatively low. Open unemployment is the clearest case of surplus labour in that jobseekers are not productively employed and hence their marginal product is obviously zero. Creating jobs for unemployed people is unambiguously welfare-enhancing under these conditions because it increases productivity and *per capita* income as it creates employment opportunities for jobseekers otherwise forced to rely on social security (if it exists) or social networks for support. In Chapter 3 we identify a set of thirteen countries with exceptionally high unemployment rates, defined as more than one standard deviation higher than the mean for middle- and low-income countries. These thirteen countries also have relatively low rates of employment—hence we refer to them as 'surplus labour countries'. Aside from occupied Palestine (the West Bank and Gaza), the surplus labour countries fell into three categories: post-communist countries, oil-dependent unfree countries (one in North Africa and the other in West Africa) and six, mostly democratic Southern African countries.

Labour-intensive manufacturing, including the clothing manufacturing industry (discussed in Chapter 4), remains relevant for countries with surplus labour. Clothing production played a central role in the development of manufacturing in almost all industrialized countries. It was the backbone of recent Chinese industrialization and remains a crucial source of employment in developing countries like Bangladesh. Mauritius solved its unemployment problem in the late 1970s by attracting clothing manufacturers from Hong Kong. The South African town of Newcastle adopted a similar strategy in the 1980s, resulting in the creation of thousands of low-wage jobs and the establishment of a vibrant ethnic Chinese community of immigrants from Taiwan, Hong Kong and subsequently mainland China (Chapter 6). More recently, Lesotho and Ethiopia actively courted large export-oriented Asian clothing manufacturing firms as part of a Lewis-like strategy to generate jobs through labour-intensive industrialization.

Yet, despite being an historical 'gateway' for Lewis-like development, the clothing manufacturing industry has a chequered reputation, being something of a lightning-rod for concerns about 'sweatshops' and exploitation, making it appear to be emblematic of the supposed 'low road' to growth (Chapter 5). For example, after a sub-standard building (Rana Plaza) collapsed in Bangladesh in 2013, killing over a thousand people, many of them clothing workers, the ILO's *World of Work* Report observed that the incident 'showed in the grimmest terms the risks entailed when firms take a low-road approach to achieving competitive outcomes' (2014: 75). Rana Plaza was an avoidable tragedy that could and should have been prevented. Inclusive dualism is consistent with improved building safety and better work initiatives, such as the ILO's own Improving Working Conditions in the Ready-Made Garment Sector Programme, which subsequently improved factory safety, strengthened health and safety and improved worker participation/voice in Bangladesh (ILO, 2017). Inclusive dualism is not, however, consistent with the rejection of low-wage, labour-intensive work as morally unacceptable under all circumstances or as necessarily entailing development down a 'low' road to growth.

Decent work fundamentalism is a policy position with serious implications for development. As Schmidt points out, ideas in the political domain '(re)conceptualize interests and values as well as (re)shape institutions' (Schmidt, 2008: 530). The South African case (Chapters 6 and 7) illustrates how the narrative and practice of decent work fundamentalism drove both labour policy and industrial policy, thereby moulding and consolidating a growth path inimical to inclusive development.

As Lewis himself acknowledged, islands of relatively high-paid work are shaped by economic, historical and contingent factors including colonialism, imported technologies best suited to developed countries, and wage pressure from predominantly urban-based trade unions. Development is strongly path-dependent, reflecting and consolidating particular political economies of growth and development. The history of the South African clothing manufacturing industry in the twenty-first century indicates that the dominant employers and especially the trade union were concerned more about harnessing government policy incentives to improve productivity on their (shrinking) islands of relatively high-wage work than they were about expanding labour-intensive employment in the industry. The problem for inclusive development, in this case, was that these organized interests were able to use the wage-setting machinery to destroy labour-intensive jobs—and they were supported in this by government policies.

Promoting inclusive dualism inevitably entails grappling with the political dimensions of current strategy and considering potential levers and opportunities to foster change within political–economic constraints. Recent scholarship on the political deals that shape development (e.g. Pritchett et al., 2018) and on understanding the political and economic incentives facing dominant groups in designing development policy (Levy, 2014; World Bank, 2017a) is relevant in this regard. An appropriate analytical approach to trade unions is thus one that acknowledges that collective bargaining is important for industrial peace and for mitigating power differentials between workers and employers—but is alert also to the fact that trade unions typically represent particular interests (relatively high-wage workers in the formal private economy and public sector) and often have incentives that are not necessarily aligned with generating labour-intensive, sustainable growth.

1.2 Decent Work Fundamentalism and Dystopia: Learning from South Africa

South Africa provides a case study of how decent work fundamentalism can have dystopic consequences for surplus labour countries. When the African National Congress (ANC) came to power after the first democratic elections in 1994, it inherited an economy with already high unemployment (between a fifth and a third of the labour force was unemployed depending on measurement). This was the result of a confluence of factors including rising real wages since the early 1970s, the final collapse of peasant agriculture in the 'bantustans' (that is, apartheid-era territories set aside for people classified as black) and other rural areas, shrinking employment in mining and commercial agriculture, and apartheid-era labour policies and industrial policies that promoted greater capital-intensity (Seekings and Nattrass, 2005, 2016). Labour-intensive development existed at the fringes of the economy, mostly in non-metropolitan and bantustan areas where minimum wages were lower or non-existent. The Natal midlands town of Newcastle, which harnessed regional policy incentives to attract foreign investment into a bourgeoning clothing manufacturing industry, was one of the few success stories.

Tito Mboweni, the new Minister of Labour, inherited a patchwork of apartheid-era wage regimes. Collective bargaining took place between trade unions and employers in recognized industrial councils (later renamed bargaining councils) in manufacturing and the public sector, and on a privately organized basis in the mining industry. Some industrial councils were national in scope, others represented unions and employers at a regional level. Industrial councils could request the Minister of Labour to 'extend' collective agreements to all firms and workers falling within the scope of the industrial council. Non-compliance with such a gazetted agreement constituted a criminal offence irrespective of whether workers were unionized or not, or whether firms belonged to employer organizations (and hence were 'party' to the collective agreement) or not. Workers in firms falling outside of the scope of an industrial council had their minimum wages set by the Wage Board. Under apartheid, firms located in the bantustans were exempt from even these wages.

One of Minister Mboweni's first actions was to instruct the Wage Board to set a new national minimum wage for workers in clothing manufacturing firms that fell outside the scope of existing regional industrial councils—including those in the old bantustans. The Wage Board's challenge was to set new minimum wages without undermining what little employment existed in these very poor parts of South Africa. In 1995, just as the Wage Board began its investigations, one of us (Nicoli Nattrass) was appointed to the South African Labour Market Commission tasked with reviewing South Africa's labour market policies. She visited Phuthaditjhaba, the old capital of the QwaQwa bantustan (now a part of the Free State Province), to see how workers and the (mostly Taiwanese-owned) clothing manufacturing firms there were preparing for the prospect of a new minimum wage.

Her first stop was the office of the Southern African Clothing and Textile Workers Union (SACTWU). The local organizer helped set up interviews with the major firms and then insisted on accompanying her on visits to firms. Nicoli was initially puzzled, but soon realized that the SACTWU organizer was worried that she might inadvertently frighten the firms with talk about minimum wages. His standard introduction went something like this:

> 'This lady from Cape Town wants to talk about the new minimum wages that are coming. But you must not worry! We can talk more later. We are happy to negotiate, to introduce the wage increase slowly, slowly . . .'

This was an exercise in damage control. What kept the local SACTWU organizer awake at night was the thought that the clothing factories might shut up shop and relocate over the nearby border to Lesotho, destroying the bulk of Phuthaditjhaba's formal employment—and almost all the available job opportunities for women.

SACTWU's national leader, Ebrahim Patel, however, took a very different approach. He had been part of organized labour's struggle against apartheid and the process of de-racialization of collective bargaining institutions. From 1979, black trade unions could join industrial councils—and starting in the early 1980s when unions in the metals and textile industries joined industrial councils, they transformed these institutions from instruments to push up predominantly white wages, into mechanisms for raising the wages of all workers (Friedman, 1987: 270, 326–31; Seekings and Nattrass, 2005). The Congress of South African Trade Unions (COSATU), established in 1985, pushed for the establishment of national industrial councils as part of its 'Living Wage' campaign (Baskin, 1991; Godfrey and Macun, 1992: 400). As a founding member of COSATU, Patel was committed to raising minimum wages to address the remaining apartheid wage gaps (between races and regions), seeing this as part of a broader developmental strategy ideally supported by productivity-enhancing industrial policies. Thus, at the same time as SACTWU shop stewards were trying to calm the nerves of jumpy entrepreneurs and forge side deals to save jobs in places like Phuthaditjhaba, he was dismissing Taiwanese clothing factories as 'fly-by-nights', saying he would 'eat them for breakfast' (quoted in Hart, 2002: 166). In Patel's eyes, they were emblematic of the kind of production model that South Africa should avoid, a living embodiment of the apartheid wage gap and an affront to South African aspirations to join the league of industrialized nations.

As organized labour's chief negotiator during the transition to democracy, Patel had been instrumental in including key provisions in the 1995 Labour Relations Act, one of the first pieces of legislation passed by the post-apartheid government. Prior to going to parliament, organized labour and business had bargained over the Act in the National Economic, Development and Labour Council—a new tripartite forum. Whilst generally heralded as an improvement to collective bargaining, the Act controversially strengthened the extension mechanism in that the Act required the Minister of Labour to extend collective agreements if requested to do so by sufficiently representative bargaining councils. Critics contended that this would harm labour-intensive and small businesses (as the bargaining councils are easily dominated by the larger employers) and suggested that the Act be amended to give the Minister more discretion and to consider possible job losses before extending wage agreements.

The Labour Market Commission, comprising members from industry, government, organized labour, academia and some international experts, considered the matter and in 1996 recommended that in order to support the government's 'job creating goals', the Labour Relations Act be amended to give the Minister 'greater discretion in deciding whether or not to extend agreements' (LMC, 1996: chapter 4, para 177). Also in 1996, the national Treasury recommended similar amendments to the extension mechanism to facilitate labour-intensive growth (DOF, 1996). However, COSATU successfully resisted all such proposals, arguing that without the extension mechanism there would be a race to the bottom. The ANC had won the first democratic election with the support of COSATU and it is not surprising that COSATU's decent work fundamentalism prevailed politically and the Labour Relations Act remained unchanged. The extension of collective agreements to all firms in an industry became routine—including in the clothing industry after the establishment of the National Bargaining Council for the Clothing Manufacturing Industry (NBC) from 2003.

Bargaining councils significantly increased the wages of black African workers (Butcher and Rouse, 2001; Bhorat, Goga, and Van der Westhuizen, 2012; Bhorat, Kanbur, and Mayet, 2012) but had adverse effects on employment. Exploiting geographic differences in the coverage of bargaining councils, Magruder (2012) estimated that collective bargaining and associated extensions decreased employment by 8 to 13 per cent with most of the losses occurring in smaller businesses. By preventing the survival or emergence of smaller, low-wage, labour-intensive enterprises, extensions contributed to the rising capital-intensity of production and falling employment-intensity of growth (Moll, 1996; Boccara and Moll, 1997; Nattrass, 2000).

Not all analysts, however, agreed that the extension mechanism undermined employment significantly. Some pointed out that the extension mechanism typically affected only a minority of workers in an industry and that bargaining councils often provided exemptions, especially for small businesses (Godfrey et al., 2006a, 2006b, 2006c, 2010: 114–8; Altman and Valodia, 2006, Roskam, 2007: 4; Bhorat and Van der Westhuizen, 2009: 23). Such arguments, however, failed to grapple with the limited and short-term nature of most exemptions (Nattrass, 2000) and, more importantly, failed to consider the impact of bargaining councils on the dynamic of accumulation, especially in labour-intensive sectors like the clothing industry. Unlike in other developing countries where a large non-compliant/informal sector is tolerated, the NBC in South Africa developed significant capacity to prosecute non-compliant firms. As discussed in Chapter 6, the minimum wage-setting machinery became an instrument to promote decent work by improving both wages and conditions for workers, and by driving out lower-productivity, lower-wage, labour-intensive activities. In the South African case, decent work fundamentalism was institutionalized through these wage-setting mechanisms.

Chapter 6 discusses the origins of national collective bargaining in the South Africa clothing manufacturing industry and how, in 2012, a group of low-wage clothing firms in Newcastle took legal action over the extension mechanism. By then, employment in the South African clothing industry had more than halved since the days of the Labour Market Commission, due to a combination of rising minimum wages and competition from China. None of the low-wage factories that we had visited in Phuthaditjhaba in 1995 survived. The last remaining low-wage labour-intensive factories in places like Newcastle remained in business largely by failing to comply with the rising minimum wages imposed by the NBC (a fraught option often entailing moving operations from one venue to another to keep one step ahead of inspections) or by turning all or part of their businesses into workers' co-operatives (because the NBC minimum wage applied only to wage labourers and not to those sharing profits). Political interventions to provide temporary relief from the NBC's rapid increases in minimum wages helped stem job losses, but uncertainty prevailed, and many clothing firms wound down their businesses.

Post-apartheid industrial policy has been directed towards support for high-productivity firms and sectors, most of which were capital-intensive (Hirsch, 2005; Kaplan, 2007; Black and Roberts, 2009; DTI, 2011; Zalk, 2014; Black and Hasson, 2016). Trade union-aligned policy documents supported this upgrading strategy, presenting rising minimum wages as a means of promoting faster labour productivity growth and as purportedly saving South African firms from a 'low-wage, low-skill, low-productivity vicious circle in which they are out-competed by the second-tier newly industrialising countries' (Joffe et al., 1995: 214). Even the clothing manufacturing industry was advised to become less labour-intensive by 'upgrading' and moving into higher value-added product lines produced by better skilled, higher-wage workers (Altman, 1994).

South Africa's growth strategy was thus framed and rationalized by decent work fundamentalism that promised a 'high road' to growth based on rising minimum wages and labour productivity-promoting industrial policy. SACTWU's Ebrahim Patel, who went on to become the national Minister for Economic Development, was the key ideological architect. In addition to his role in the South African government, he had served on the governing body of the ILO, was global spokesman for organized labour on employment and social policy, and co-drafter of the ILO's global employment agenda and Declaration on Social Justice for a Fair Globalization. He was a key figure behind the ILO's conception of productivity-promoting development through 'decent work' *and* its introduction into a post-apartheid development strategy.

In 2012, South Africa's National Planning Commission highlighted unemployment as the number one challenge but ruled out labour-intensive growth on the grounds that 'the country's cost structure requires an emphasis on productivity, products and logistics' (National Planning Commission, 2012: 147–8). Perhaps if the Commissioners had visited Phuthaditjhaba, or a similar largely defunct industrial area, the sight of abandoned factories in a sea of impoverished households might have encouraged them to grapple with the institutional reasons for South Africa's high-wage 'cost structure' and to reconsider the potential for reforms and policies to promote labour-intensive growth. More likely, however, the Commission simply chose to see the wage structure as a binding constraint given the power of the union movement to frame development thinking about wages, productivity, and development. The cost of this was the rationalization and entrenchment of a growth path that undermined inclusive development by failing to prioritize job creation.

1.3 Chapter Outlines

Chapter 2 discusses the Lewis model of development with surplus labour and the ongoing relevance of his dualist approach. We show, using examples from the South African clothing industry, that relatively high- and low-wage firms exist in the same industry by using different technologies and targeting different product markets. This indicates that there is no necessary race to the bottom and that industrial policy could usefully promote competitiveness across a range of (especially labour-intensive) technologies without undermining firms in more skill- and capital-intensive niches. Chapter 3 focuses on the ILO's decent work agenda, arguing that it is blind to the needs of countries with high unemployment. We identify thirteen developing countries whose unemployment rate in 2016 was over twice the mean for low-and middle-income countries. Most are war-torn, post-communist and unfree. However, for a set of Southern African countries, high unemployment is the consequence of domestic policy within a regional context of relatively limited opportunities for smallholder agriculture and dominated by the strength of the South African economy. We argue that contemporary development policy advice, especially from the ILO, prioritizes labour productivity growth without confronting the need to foster relatively low-productivity employment to provide jobs for large numbers of relatively unskilled people in these countries. We show that rising labour productivity in the surplus labour countries during the 2000s came at the cost of stagnant, and even falling, employment rates. Given inadequate welfare support for the unemployed, such growth paths have undermined rather than facilitated inclusive development in these countries.

Chapters 4 and 5 focus on the most important labour-intensive manufacturing sector: the clothing (or garment or apparel) manufacturing industry. The clothing manufacturing industry is notable not only for the role it played (and continues to play) as a gateway for industrialization and development, but also for the international mobilization against low-wage production, or 'sweatshops'. Chapter 4 provides a history and analysis of development trajectories in the global clothing industry. Trade liberalization (specifically the end of import quotas from January 2005) and the rise of global value chains has changed the nature of the global economy since Lewis's time. We use data from the United Nations Industrial Development Organization (UNIDO) on remuneration, output, and employment to identify post-2004 (when the global system of import quotas for clothing ended) national development trajectories for the clothing industry. We distinguish between various trajectories (summarized in Table 4.4). Upgrading trajectories can be pro-labour (in the sense of manifesting a rising wage share of value-added) or pro-capital (a rising profit share). Pro-labour trajectories can deliver rising average wages and employment (e.g. India and China) or higher average wages for fewer workers (e.g. Sri Lanka). Pro-capital trajectories can also deliver higher average wages and employment growth (e.g. Vietnam) or rising wages for fewer workers (e.g. South Africa). Downgrading trajectories are typically associated with falling average wages but can be associated with rising average wages (as in Turkey). We argue that the desirability of a particular development trajectory depends on the economic context, especially labour market conditions.

Chapter 5 grapples with the moral economy of wages and employment. Labour-intensive industry is of potentially great benefit for poor regions where, as Lewis pointed out, capital is scarce and most people rely on low-earning subsistence activities. Yet labour-intensive manufacturing, and especially the clothing manufacturing industry, is also ripe with the distasteful odour of the 'sweatshop', posing social and ethical challenges almost as old as the industrial revolution itself. Chapter 5 shows that the moral economy of rival positions entails different understandings of the relationship between wages, profits, and employment. Many contemporary arguments reflect those made over a century earlier in Britain and the United States. However, whereas the British Fabian socialists sought (and achieved) the simultaneous expansion of labour protection (minimum wages and safety regulations) *and* welfare support for the unemployed, the contemporary anti-sweatshop movement focuses solely on wages. By the early twentieth century in Britain, those who lost their jobs because of rising minimum wages could expect support from the welfare system. In twenty-first-century surplus labour countries, the unemployed fall through what meagre welfare nets exist. In this context, the potential trade-off between wages and employment matters for poverty and inequality. Chapter 5 also reviews the evidence on the impact of rising minimum wages on employment both internationally and in South Africa. The impact is typically neutral or mildly negative, suggesting that policymakers are generally careful about not raising minimum wages excessively. There is, however, evidence that it is mostly unskilled workers who lose their jobs when job losses occur.

Chapters 6 and 7 comprise the South African case study of institutionally driven adjustment in the post-apartheid clothing manufacturing industry. Chapter 6 begins with a brief history of collective bargaining in the industry. We show that its dualist character (high- and low-productivity firms coexisting) has historical and market-related roots and highlight the role of wage policy during and after apartheid in shaping the regional location of clothing manufacturing firms. The rise of China as a global producer of clothing had a profound impact on the South African clothing industry—but it was the simultaneous introduction of national level collective bargaining and the enforcement of rapidly rising minimum wages on relatively low-wage labour-intensive firms that drove the job losses. We describe the 2010/11 'compliance drive' that resulted in legal action by Chinese entrepreneurs from Newcastle seeking to obtain relief from the imposition of sector-wide minimum wages on their labour-intensive firms. Trade union strategy as well as government policy adapted to some extent in the face of job losses, but minimum wages continued to be extended across the industry.

Proponents of decent work fundamentalism in government and in the trade union movement rely on industrial policy to facilitate a (hopefully employment-demanding) adjustment towards a higher-wage, higher-productivity growth path. Chapter 7 places the spotlight on this strategy which manifestly failed to prevent the collapse of employment in the South African clothing manufacturing industry. We argue that SACTWU's strategy was complicated by its dual role as a trade union and investment manager. Having taken advantage of investment opportunities, provided through the government's 'black economic empowerment policies', to grow substantial financial assets and later also direct investments in the clothing industry, the union, in effect, was both a representative of labour as well as a capitalist in the industry. Its connections with Ebrahim Patel meant that it was well positioned to take advantage of government subsidies and related incentives pertaining to 'up the value chain' industrial policy. The incentives and opportunities facing SACTWU were consistent with a union strategy to have a smaller body of better-paid workers rather than growing its membership of lower-wage workers through labour-intensive job creation. The trend away from inclusive dualism in the clothing manufacturing industry was an extreme example, but nevertheless characteristic, of trends in the economy as a whole.

Pressure from the NBC on labour-intensive clothing manufacturers has, however, encouraged a reshaping of the relationship between labour and capital through the growth of workers' co-operatives. SACTWU is suspicious of these because they were often initiated by previous employers and as members of co-operatives do not fall under the Labour Relations Act, they are outside of the control of the NBC. The extent to which these are 'sham' co-operatives designed solely to avoid minimum wage regulation is moot, but the potential for workers' co-operatives to generate more transparent and inclusive productive and distributional practices is exciting and consistent with inclusive dualism.

Chapter 8 considers the challenge of moving towards inclusive dualism for surplus labour countries. It revisits the relationship between labour market institutions and unemployment, arguing that the connection is negative but weak and dependent on context. Improving the welfare net through cash transfers and public works programmes can help, but labour-intensive development is likely to be the backbone of strategy of inclusive dualism, especially in surplus labour countries. We conclude by emphasizing the growing problem of unemployment in Africa—and the impact of decent work fundamentalist thinking in shaping development strategies. We highlight potential areas for growing labour-intensive jobs and fostering Lewis-like development.

2

Dualism and Development

The concept of development through relatively low-wage industrialization was initially formalized by the Caribbean development economist, W. Arthur Lewis, an achievement for which he obtained the Nobel Prize in economics. In Lewis's model (1954), labour-intensive industrialization raised average labour productivity and earnings by providing employment at wages lower than existing modern sector jobs but higher than subsistence earnings. This engine of growth slowed down when the supply of surplus labour (people underemployed in subsistence agriculture or in casual, informal employment) dried up, forcing manufacturing wages upwards and reducing profitability and investment.

Lewis, who taught the first course on the economics of developing countries at the London School of Economics (Lewis called it 'colonial economics') was both an advisor to, and a thorn in the side of, the Colonial Office through the war years and into the 1950s (Tignor, 2006: 52–78). He argued that social and economic conditions in the colonies were poorly understood within the economics profession (and by colonial administrators) and that historically and contextually informed development planning was necessary. Like many of the young Indian scholars studying in Britain during the war who went on to advance development policy and planning in India, Lewis was influenced by Keynesianism, and by the critics of free-market economics like Robinson and Chamberlain who pointed to the distortionary impact of monopolies and market failures (White, 2012). Lewis's work drew on Nurkse's (1953) ideas of balanced growth and Rosenstein-Rodan's (1943) 'big push' case for development assistance—but he paid more attention to the constraints imposed by social customs, to the need for improved social services (especially education), and to the role of the middle class in fostering entrepreneurship (Tignor, 2006: 101–6).

Lewis departed from neoclassical thinking when he conceptualized developing countries as dualist:

> Most countries in the early stages of economic development have not one economy, but two. They have a high wage economy and a low earnings economy.

> Broadly speaking, in the high wage economy we find people employed by plantations, factories, mines, large-scale transportation and so forth. And in the low earnings economy we find people in family farms, handicrafts, domestic servants, petty traders, casual labour and so on... It is irrelevant to the analysis whether the marginal productivity of labour in this sector is negative, zero, or merely small. So long as it is lower than the wage that is paid in the high wage sector, there will be a surplus in the labour market; that is to say, that at the going wage in the high wage sector capitalists can always get more labour if they so desire. (1958: 42)

Lewis identified dualism within and between sectors, emphasizing that high-wage activities existed alongside lower-wage, lower-productivity activities in the same economic sectors and regions. Lewis's conceptualization was vague and in practice he was referring to different economic and social dynamics at play in different parts of a single economy than to two distinct economies. Yet his dualist approach gained traction because he was putting his finger on a key dimension of developing countries. As Gollin puts it: 'Lewis made the incisive observation that poor countries are not uniformly poor and that even the poorest countries have firms, sectors and locations that operate at high levels of productivity' (2014: 73).

Lewis's thinking about the dynamic relationship between differently endowed sectors of the economy sparked a generation of 'dualist' development models which segmented economic activities into different sectors with different average earnings (Thorbecke, 2007; Wang and Piesse, 2013; Gollin, 2014). These typically distinguished between low-productivity subsistence activities (primarily in agriculture) and (predominantly urban) manufacturing, with theoretical additions to explain the growth of urban unemployment (discussed further below).

Indicators of such dualism are limited by the available national statistics, which focus on the sectoral composition of employment and on whether jobs are agricultural or non-agricultural, formal or informal.[1] Figure 2.1 presents the estimated composition of the working-age population (aged 15 and above) in low- and middle-income countries for which data are available from the World Development Indicators. The data are based on the official definition of unemployment, meaning that only people without work and who are actively seeking it are counted as 'unemployed'. Discouraged work-seekers, that is, those who say they want work but are not actively looking for it, are counted

[1] According to the World Development Indicators, informal employment includes all jobs in unregistered and/or small-scale private unincorporated enterprises that produce goods or services meant for sale or barter. Self-employed street vendors, taxi drivers and home-base workers, regardless of size, are all considered enterprises. However, agricultural and related activities, households producing goods exclusively for their own use (e.g. subsistence farming, domestic housework, care work, and employment of paid domestic workers), and volunteer services rendered to the community are excluded.

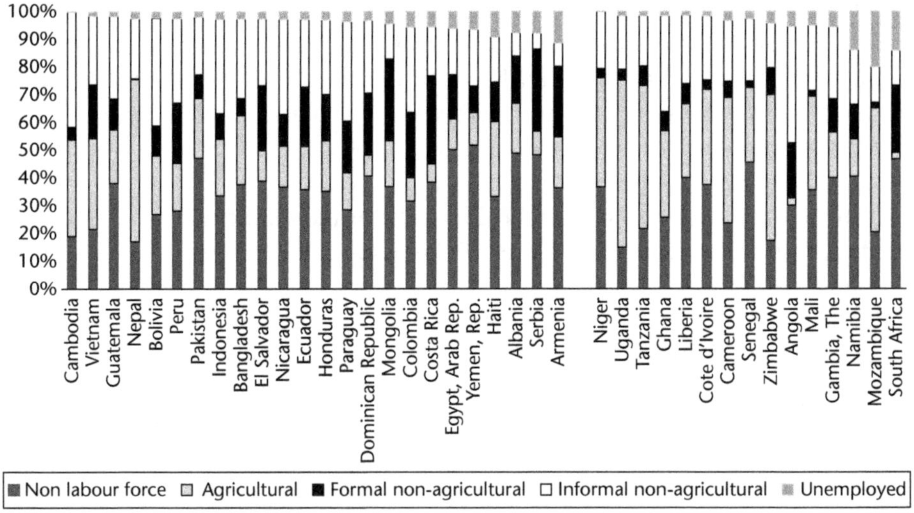

Figure 2.1 Allocation of the working-age population in low- and middle-income countries (2016).

Note: To derive these proportions, employment was obtained by multiplying the World Development Indicator estimate of employment as a share of population aged 15 and above by the population aged 15 and above. The number of unemployed was estimated from the reported unemployment rate and estimated employment (defined above). Non-labour force participants were obtained by subtracting the unemployed and the employed from the population aged 15 and above. Agricultural employment was obtained by multiplying the reported share of employment in agriculture by estimated employment. Non-agricultural employment was estimated by subtracting agricultural employment from estimated employment. Informal non-agricultural employment was estimated by multiplying the reported share of non-agricultural employment that is informal (most recent year available) by non-agricultural employment in 2016 and formal non-agricultural employment was estimated as non-agricultural employment minus informal non-agricultural employment.

Source: Calculated from data in the World Development Indicators (available from https://data.worldbank.org/indicator, accessed 20 May 2018).

amongst the non-labour force participants. Figure 2.1 shows that African countries are less developed in the sense that most have a larger share of the working-age population in agricultural employment. The informal non-agricultural sector varies in importance, ranging from almost half of the working-age population in Angola, to a small fraction in the high-unemployment middle-income countries of South Africa and Namibia. Figure 2.1 also shows how labour force participation rates vary across countries. Where unemployment is high and there is a relatively large share of non-labour force participants (as in South Africa), people outside the labour force probably include many discouraged work-seekers. Under such conditions, 'surplus labour'—in the sense of an available supply of labour for labour-intensive manufacturing—would be found not only amongst the openly unemployed (the active jobseekers), but also in agriculture and the informal sector as well as amongst the non-economically active.

Figure 2.1 suggests that dualist understandings remain relevant for most of Africa in that it paints a picture of a relatively small formal sector and a population reliant on agriculture. The informal sector also appears to act as a cushion against unemployment, notably in Ghana and Angola. In the high-unemployment, middle-income countries of Southern Africa, the informal sector is relatively small. This suggests that there may be economic and/or institutional obstacles to the expansion of informal enterprises, thereby preventing this sector from playing its role as a social safety net of sorts for the unemployed.

Another indicator of dualism focuses on the ratio between manufacturing wages and Gross Domestic Product (GDP) per capita. Golub and Hayat (2014) analyse the available data to show that the ratio is typically higher in sub-Saharan Africa than in East Asia. They conclude that with 'rapidly growing populations, small enclaves of relatively well-paying modern sectors and vast informal economies, Africa resembles the situation described by Arthur Lewis (1954) as "unlimited supply of labour" more so today than at the time Lewis presented his classic analysis' (2014: 12–13). We agree that dualism is a relevant description for Africa today, but distinguish further between the Southern African countries with high open unemployment (and relatively limited informal employment) and other African countries. We also go further to emphasize Lewis's point that dualist outcomes are evident also within economic sectors where firms use different technologies.

Lewis did not believe that there was a large labour surplus in Africa because land-to-labour ratios were high, meaning that people could earn an acceptably good living as livestock or crop farmers rather than enter the industrial labour force. He thus advised newly independent Ghana in the 1950s that industrialization required prior investment to improve agricultural productivity so as to free up a labour supply for industry without compromising food production (Tignor, 2006; Kanbur, 2016). By contrast, he believed there was a significant surplus of underemployed labour in peasant agriculture, personal services, and intermittent informal, casual work in countries such as Egypt, Jamaica, and India. This supply of labour, in his view, could easily be drawn into industry with little if any impact on output—and at wages lower than the wages on offer in high-wage sectors/industries/firms (Lewis, 1954, 1958; see also Fields, 2004; Ranis, 2004).

Lewis did not establish conventional economic micro-foundations for his model, prompting others to specify more formal models showing how dualism might occur and the associated dynamics of growth (see e.g. the review and elaboration in Wang and Piesse, 2013). Scholars differed over whether surplus labour should be conceptualized as having a zero marginal product, in which case pulling workers out of subsistence activities would have zero social or economic costs (Wellisz, 1968: 22) or whether surplus labour had a low marginal product but contributed less to total output than it consumed (Ranis, 2008). Lewis's conceptualization, as we have seen, encompassed both (1954: 141). For Lewis, the key issue was not whether the marginal product of surplus labour was zero, small or even negative, but that surplus labour could be drawn out of subsistence activities without reducing output significantly (1968: 2). Open unemployment is the clearest (and most extreme) form of surplus labour as the marginal product of the unemployed is obviously zero and providing jobs to people otherwise reliant on others for support is clearly output-increasing and welfare-enhancing.

Whether Lewis's model understood wages in the capitalist sector as set by subsistence earnings plus a premium (to cover transport costs etc.) or whether there were institutional forces (trade union bargaining, social customs, minimum wage legislation etc.) pushing up modern sector wages (thereby causing labour market segmentation), was also the subject of confusion and controversy (see e.g. Brown, 2006; Fields, 2006). The issue, however, did not seem to concern Lewis, who at different times pointed to both explanations (Wang and Piesse, 2013). As discussed below, when commenting on the rise of open unemployment, Lewis regarded both institutional features and technology as central.

The Lewis model contributed to subsequent developmental thinking about how labour-intensive manufacturing could potentially serve as a valuable stage in a dynamic process that simultaneously offered a route out of rural poverty and a means of generating profits and savings to finance investment and growth. The model has been criticized for some of its underlying assumptions (see review in Fields, 2004), for focusing on unskilled labour only, and for neglecting the role of existing proto-industrialists (small weavers and the like) in Asian development (e.g. Saito, 2013; Sugihara, 2013). Nevertheless, it remained a useful heuristic for thinking about dualism in developing countries and for describing the potential for relatively low-wage, labour-intensive development to absorb unskilled labour, even if this is only one aspect of a broader (more differentiated) development path.

The surplus labour-absorbing growth dynamic described by Lewis is a stylized fact of post-war Asian export-led development (Chamon and Kremer, 2009: 20; Braude and Menashe, 2011; Lin and Rosenblatt, 2012). The Taiwanese experience of labour-intensive industrialization with stable wages during the 1950s, followed by wage increases in subsequent decades as surplus labour was absorbed and the labour market tightened, is consistent with the growth path he described (Fields, 2004: 730). In Hong Kong, workers were pulled into the low-wage, low-productivity clothing manufacturing industry in the 1960s, 1970s, and 1980s, before moving into higher-productivity, more capital-intensive higher-wage sectors (Chiu et al., 1997; Braude and Menashe, 2011). Similar processes were evident more recently in China, when the drying up of migrant labour out of agriculture underpinned widespread increases in wages in the mid-2000s (Zhang et al., 2011). Labour-intensive growth has been an important means for poverty reduction globally, and in low-income countries like Bangladesh and Ethiopia today (Islam, 2005; Loayza and Raddatz, 2006).

2.1 The Key Role of the Clothing Manufacturing Industry in Lewis-like Growth

The clothing manufacturing industry has been central to labour-intensive growth, as it produces an essential wage good using relatively simple machinery and low-skilled workers. As Robertson puts it, clothing 'often acts as a gateway into manufacturing for countries and workers whose alternatives might be in agriculture, the informal sector, or low-productivity work' (2012: 9). Clothing exports were central to the early stages of Lewis-like development in Asia, forming an important stepping stone on the route to development by generating economies of scale, earning foreign exchange, and developing skills and capacities.

Notably, the production of clothing (garments) and textiles (yarn and material) provided the foundation of Hong Kong's industrialization. By 1960, each of these sectors accounted for almost one-quarter of all manufacturing employment (Chiu et al., 1997). Employment in textiles continued to grow, but slowly (it is more capital-intensive than garment production) and the importance of the sector declined. Employment in clothing manufacturing grew rapidly, however: from 52,000 workers in 1960, to 158,000 in 1970 and 275,000 in 1980 (ibid.: 53). Employment peaked in 1987, at just under 300,000, in just over 10,000 establishments, accounting for 34 per cent of all manufacturing workers in Hong Kong.

Labour-intensive growth eliminated labour surpluses in Lewis-like fashion, and by the 1980s, real wages and labour costs had risen in the face of labour shortages, prompting many Hong Kong clothing manufacturers to relocate across the Chinese border into the Pearl River Delta or to outsource production to Indonesia, Mauritius, Bangladesh, and elsewhere. In the four years between 1987 and 1991, employment in clothing production in Hong Kong dropped by one-quarter. Production work moved, whilst clerical and other more skilled work remained in Hong Kong. Chiu et al. (1997: 3) cite the extreme case of the Yangtzekiang Garment Manufacturing Company Ltd, which employed up to 2,000 workers in the 1980s. By 1994, it employed only 50 production workers and 160 office workers in Hong Kong. Business networking remained crucial to the Hong Kong economy even when production itself was moved to economies with lower labour costs.

Brenton and Hoppe (2007) found that clothing and footwear were the key drivers of export and overall growth for low-income countries: in those countries that graduated out of their low-income position in the period from 1974 to 2004, clothing and footwear exports as a share of total exports grew approximately tenfold; in countries that remained low-income, clothing exports remained low. Collier and Venables (2007) argue that preferential access to the US market enabled African countries such as Kenya, Mauritius, Madagascar, and those in the Southern African Customs Union to grow employment and help develop a more diversified manufacturing sector. The clothing manufacturing industry is widely viewed to be an important stepping stone for development, which is one of the reasons why the US, through its African Growth and Opportunities Act (AGOA) provides enhanced access into US markets for African countries (Williams, 2015: 4).

Bangladesh is an important recent example of Lewis-like growth spearheaded by a strongly export-oriented clothing manufacturing industry. Between 1991 and 2014, the contribution of clothing production to the GDP rose from 3 per cent to 15 per cent to become the second-largest global clothing producer after China, accounting for 82 per cent of Bangladesh's export revenues (Alam et al., 2017: 330). Employment skyrocketed from 40,000 in 1984 to an estimated 4 million by 2012. The clothing manufacturing industry became the driving force of employment growth, accounting for 40 per cent of manufacturing employment, providing jobs to young (predominantly rural) women with three to four years of primary education (ibid.: 336). Analysis based on social accounting matrices estimate that for every additional Taka of garment output, the 'basic needs multiplier' generates an additional 0.76 Taka spending on nutrition (ibid.: 336). The socio-economic significance of these jobs in this poor country is obvious. When the Rana Plaza collapsed in 2013, placing the spotlight on inadequate regulation within this burgeoning sector, the ILO pushed for better working conditions whilst also advocating that buyers worldwide 'stay with Bangladesh' because 'any rush to the exit by international brands would have far reaching consequences for the estimated four million garment workers' (ILO, 2017: 2).

Labour productivity in Bangladesh's clothing manufacturing industry is lower than in other Asian countries (a reflection of its very labour-intensive approach) and the country competes internationally primarily on the basis of its comparatively lower wages (Alam and Natsuda, 2016: 336–7; Alam et al., 2017: 339–40). The industry also benefitted from supportive industrial policies (for example, duty free imports of raw materials for exporters, lines of credit from government-owned banks), preferential access to advanced capitalist country markets, local ownership and its strong relationship with value retailer[2] *Walmart* (Lopez-Acevedo and Robertson, 2012: 213–46). But it was also hampered

[2] A value retailer is a retail outlet where the décor is without frills and prices are relatively cheap.

by corruption, political instability, and inadequate regulation (Alam et al., 2017: 343–7). The Rana Plaza collapse highlighted the dangers not only to workers of unsafe working conditions, but to the entire export industry and the country's growth path. Serious efforts were made to rectify the situation, including the closing down of some factories. The ILO worked with the Bangladesh government to improve working conditions (ILO, 2017). Almost 200 clothing brands/buyers in 20 countries along with local and international trade union organizations signed an 'Accord on Fire and Building Safety in Bangladesh' resulting in inspections and remedial action. According to data reported in Alam et al. (2017), significant progress had been made by 2015 to rectify identified safety hazards, allowing Bangladesh to continue to compete internationally primarily on the basis of its low labour costs, but with improved working conditions.

Labour costs matter profoundly for competitiveness in this highly competitive and globalized industry, yet proximity to (and evolution of) end markets and the architecture of international trade regulations also shaped an increasingly complex set of global value chains (Pickles et al., 2015). Clothing producers are caught up in dynamic global production networks and value chains where the importance of labour costs, quality and turnaround times varies depending on the end-market and product lines—and where regional trade agreements, industrial policy, and various preferential dispensations for low-income countries shape and constrain development potential at country level. We touch on this in more detail in Chapter 4. The point here is simply to note that clothing production has provided an engine for Lewis-like growth in the past—and can continue to do so, but within a structure of opportunities that varies across countries and where the cost of labour is not the only factor affecting competitiveness.

The clothing manufacturing industry is also an instructive illustration of economic dualism in the sense of economic differentiation. As noted earlier, Lewis took for granted that developing economies were characterized by the co-existence of enterprises with vastly different levels of productivity and earnings, both across and within sectors. Low-wage countries have a comparative advantage in the labour-intensive production of basic commodity clothing items, yet even in Bangladesh (the global leader in the production of such products), differentiation is evident between firms as some focus on higher value-added activities and have employed upgrading (of production processes and technologies) to do so, whereas others focus on the more basic commodity items (Alam and Natsuda, 2016; Alam et al., 2017).

The Indian clothing manufacturing industry is similarly characterized by dualism. It has a large, lower-wage, lower-productivity informal sector accounting for the bulk of employment but less than a third of output (Abras, 2012: 109). It is bifurcated between the production of 'low/medium value-added products' by contract workers and homeworkers with 'relatively low skills and low productivity', and the production of higher-value-added products by means of 'capital-intensive technology and a skilled and stable workforce' (Hirway, 2010: 173). Workers in the formal sector are unionized, have access to social security and earn higher wages than their informal sector counterparts (see, e.g. Barrientos et al., 2010).

The South African clothing manufacturing industry illustrates how dualism within a domestic industry can be facilitated through the use of different technologies and business strategies, including the targeting of different product markets. Figure 2.2 illustrates different levels of capital-intensity by comparing two different processes for attaching studs to clothing. The photographs were taken in Newcastle, South Africa, in firms located in the same part of town. In the left photograph, a worker is using electrical and pneumatic technology (compressed air comes down the plastic pipe visible on the right) to fix studs on garments brought to her by a computer-driven overhead rail delivery system. The pictures on the right are of foot presses. The worker in the middle photograph is using a mechanical foot press to attach studs to clothing items delivered to her by a general production worker. She produces fewer fitted studs per hour and earns a lower wage than the worker on the left. Firms that use technologies such as foot presses and manual delivery systems are less capital-intensive and hire more workers per Rand invested in machinery.

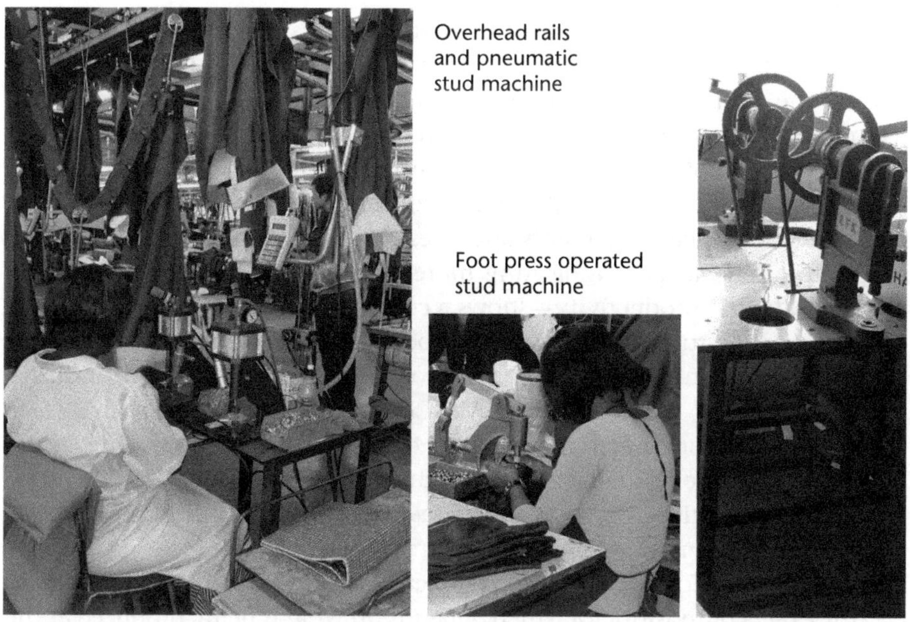

Figure 2.2 More and less capital-intensive processes for attaching studs.

Wages are lower in the labour-intensive firms, but the total wage bill is higher as a share of total revenue than is the case in more capital-intensive enterprises.

It is also worth noting that the workers in Figure 2.2 are producing different products. The worker on the left works for a firm specializing mainly in the niche market for private upmarket school uniforms. According to the production manager, their clients are prepared to pay a premium to obtain good quality, consistently coloured school-wear, and this is what enables the firm to afford the legal minimum wage. The factory has some very sophisticated machinery (some of it purchased with generous government subsidies) ranging from computer-aided design to embroidery machines.

The photograph in the middle panel shows a worker in a small firm owned by a Taiwanese immigrant. The worker is helping to produce a large batch of relatively cheap raincoats for the mass market. The firm is competing with imports from low-wage countries (notably China) and can only survive by paying workers below the legislated minimum wage. The two firms pay different wages, yet the low-wage firm poses no threat to the higher-wage firm because they are competing in different product markets. The existence of the low-wage firm thus poses no 'race to the bottom'-type threat to the higher-wage firm. Indeed, the private school uniform producer benefits from the dualism inherent to the industry in that low-wage firms, like that of the Taiwanese immigrant, provide a ready supply of experienced machinists if they wish to hire more labour.

Figure 2.3 provides a stylized representation of this dualism (in the sense of wage-related, productivity-related, and technologically related differentiation) within the South African clothing manufacturing industry. The image top right—a space indicating firms with relatively high wages and labour productivity—is of the private school uniform producer described above. The overhead rail system and digital management systems allow it to produce short runs of particular garments and sizes in quick succession. The image in the bottom left—a space indicating more labour-intensive firms with lower wages and labour productivity—shows a cut-make-and-trim operation producing a very long run of a single basic product (in this case, sleepwear). That firm paid below minimum wages and was targeted in 2011 by an industry 'compliance drive' (discussed further in Chapter 6). The relatively high wage firm was eligible for government funding to support further upgrading, and it has made good use of the facility to purchase new machinery. The low-wage firm was not eligible because government industrial policy assistance is conditional on complying with minimum wages.

Production in clothing factories is typically organized in 'lines' of machinery, the exact composition of which depends on what is being produced at the time. Each operation is carefully broken down into specific tasks, for example,

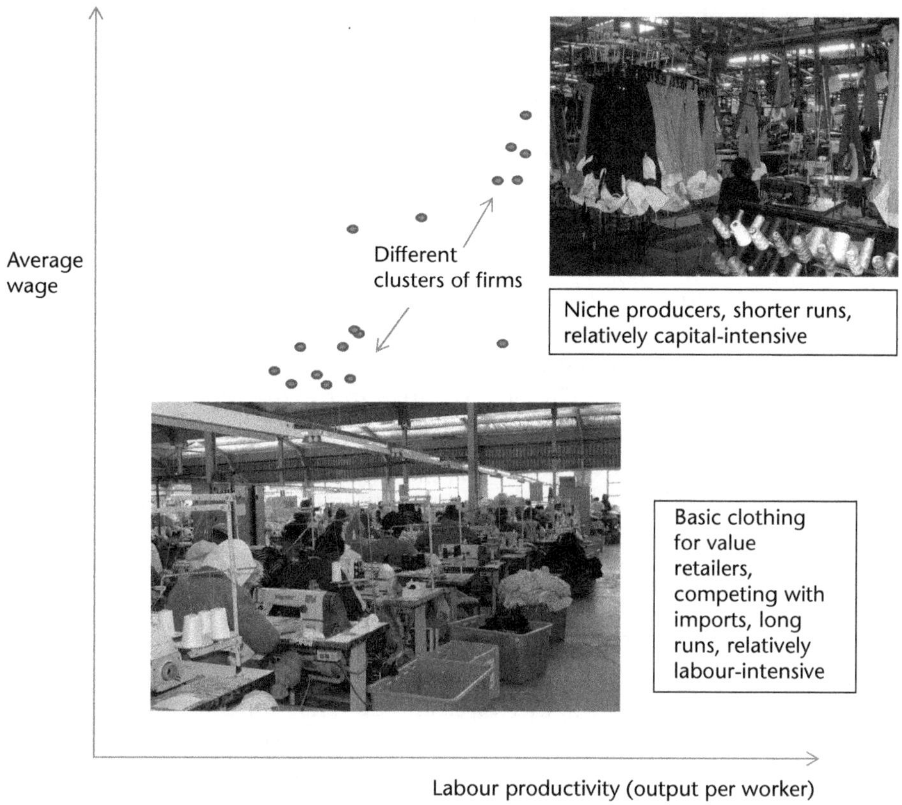

Figure 2.3 Dualism in the South African clothing manufacturing industry (a stylized representation).

laying patterns, cutting pieces, bundling pieces together for assembly and then assembling them in stages linked to particular machines, such as an over-lock machine to create and finish seams, a cover-seam machine for hems, a button-hole machine for button holes etc. In contrast to the overhead rail system depicted in the left photograph in Figure 2.2, and in the top photograph in Figure 2.3, partially completed items of clothing in the very labour-intensive firms are passed down the line manually in plastic containers. This 'bundle' system involves the passing of partially completed bundles of clothing items from machinist to machinist, each of whom has to untie the bundle, complete the task, retie the bundle and pass it on. The finished items are then checked for quality, trimmed, tagged with the final sales price (sales tickets are often provided by the retailer in South Africa), packed and shipped. In the higher-wage firm, the machinists are responsible for trimming (their machinery is better designed for this purpose) and there are fewer workers involved in the final quality control and packing stages.

Factories in places like Newcastle, specializing in cut-make-and-trim, typically produce relatively simple items for the mass market (e.g. t-shirts, sleepwear, knitwear). On factory visits we have seen sales tickets for all the major retail outlets in South Africa ranging from those servicing the low-income end of the market (value retailers such as *Jet* and *PEP Stores*) to retailers targeting predominantly the middle class (*Mr Price*) or middle-class and upper-income consumers (*Edgars, Woolworths, Foschini*). The clothing items produced in Newcastle for higher-income consumers tend to be the relatively simple products required in large quantities.

Dualism within the South African clothing manufacturing industry has a strong regional dimension, largely because of the history of minimum wage-setting (discussed further in Chapter 4). Firms in the metropolitan areas such as Cape Town, pay higher wages, produce for niche markets (e.g. Kevlar vests, high-end children's clothes, relatively small quantities for the fashionable end of the industry). They compete in very different product markets to low-wage firms in places like Newcastle. As Graham Choice, the founder of *Prestige Clothing* (producing fashionable items for the metropolitan domestic market) in Cape Town put it, 'Newcastle is not competing with us, Newcastle is competing with Lesotho'.[3] Buyers from *The Foschini Group* (a fashion producer and retailer that took over *Prestige Clothing* in 2012) reported to us that they sometimes place orders with firms in Newcastle, but that for the most part their order size is too small for the high-volume, low-margin producers in Newcastle.[4] Whilst there are clearly distinct market niches, the clothing manufacturing industry is nevertheless more dynamic than the stylized representation in Figure 2.3 might suggest. Some firms move in and out of different product markets, though industry sources emphasize that this typically happens during slow (off-season) periods when clothing factories are prepared to take orders they would not normally accept when running at full capacity. As reflected by the history of the global clothing manufacturing industry (Chapter 4), no market niche is ever entirely safe. Clothing manufacturers are perpetually subject to challenge as firms in different regions gain additional competencies.

Even relatively high-wage firms producing relatively sophisticated high-end products face potential challenges from small businesses developing new competencies. Figure 2.4 shows a child's fancy dress produced by a small cut-make-and-trim operation in Durban. The work is intricate, complicated and of good quality, yet the owner of this small firm was unable to pay the legal minimum wage for metro producers and was in the process of becoming a workers' co-operative to get around it. Firms hoping to be able to pay higher wages by 'upgrading' into such product markets may well have to contend

[3] Discussion on 21 January 2013.
[4] Discussion with Peter Adams and Selwyn Eagle, 21 January 2013.

Figure 2.4 Child's fancy dress produced by a small cut-make-and-trim operation in Durban.

with such competitors—implying that there are no easy or guaranteed gains from such strategies.

In short, the South African clothing manufacturing industry as a whole is labour-intensive, yet there is a wide range of technological choices in between the extremes pictured in Figures 2.2 and 2.3, and firms sometimes experiment with different options. We encountered firms which use combinations of highly capital-intensive embroidery machines with second-hand overlock machines imported from China. A factory owner near East London (in the Eastern Cape province), producing a range of products including workwear, said he considered the manual delivery system of plastic buckets pushed by machinists and assisted by roving general workers to be the most cost-effective technology for moving garments down the production line. Rising wages could alter that decision, although a factory outside of Ladysmith (in the KwaZulu-Natal province) declined to make the investment in overhead rails, arguing that too much of the stock was caught up in the overhead rail system, violating lean manufacturing principles. *Jonsson Workwear*, a large producer of workwear in South Africa, introduced overhead rails but then removed them.[5] These anecdotes indicate that there is space for a range of production technologies and that what is understood to be 'cutting edge' by some firms, may be regarded as unnecessary capital-investment by others.

Profitability depends on the relationship between wages and productivity and as discussed further in Chapter 4, different 'trajectories' are evident globally. At the level of the firm, managers make judgement calls about whether it is more profitable to employ relatively unskilled 'general' workers to help move items down the production line, or invest in more capital-intensive technologies like overhead rails and retrench the general workers. Dualism, in the sense of differentiation of technology, is highly contextual and dynamic.

[5] Interview with a production manager who used to work for *Jonsson* (19 August 2015).

2.2 Unemployment and Development Strategy

The rise of open unemployment in developing countries posed challenges to development theory and practice. As early as 1958, Lewis observed that urban wages in many developing countries were substantially higher than the premium required to attract labour out of subsistence activities and that this was encouraging a 'drift' of labour to the towns and a rise in open urban unemployment. For Lewis, this large gap between subsistence earnings and the existing 'islands' of high-paid work reflected not only the economic fact of dualism but also the opportunity for industrialization at relatively low wages. As to why modern sector wages were relatively high, Lewis suggested that this was:

> partly because in these days trade unions are effective in the high wage sector and push the wage up all the time; and partly because even in the absence of trade unions it is a habit of capitalists to pass on to the workers in their firms some part of the benefit of high technology and of high capital intensity. So wages tend to rise in the high wage sector as productivity rises in that sector, and the gap between the high wage of that sector and the earnings in the rest of the economy tends to widen. (1958: 43)

Lewis, departing once again from neoclassical economic assumptions, is pointing here to the important institutional and social factors that affect wages. Trade unions enable workers to combine to improve wages and working conditions, but they do so within a broader social context that shapes labour market institutions and employer responses. In the case of South Africa, minimum-wage-setting through collective agreements and the Wage Board was originally framed by a racist discourse and institutional context designed to give white 'civilized' labour a standard of living commensurate with their counterparts in Britain, Australia, and New Zealand (South Africa, 1926). Racial solidarity, coupled with generous government incentives and tariff protection, encouraged and facilitated further wage growth on the part of employers—though this inevitably came at the cost of job losses amongst less skilled black African labour. The modern sector islands of high-paid work in South Africa were thus bolstered by white domination during most of the apartheid period. It was only with the deracialization of industrial councils in the 1980s that (relatively skilled) black African workers could join the club. The widening gap between the relatively high-paid modern capitalist sector and the rest of the economy thus took the form of a widening gap between employed workers and the unemployed (Seekings and Nattrass, 2005).

Lewis did not include unemployment in his formal model of development with unlimited supplies of labour, but subsequent extensions to it showed that it was consistent with urban unemployment as rural migrants 'queued' for jobs (Harris and Todaro, 1970) or swelled the ranks of the urban informal sector as they waited for formal job opportunities in manufacturing (Fields, 1975; Ranis and Stewart, 1999). Open unemployment subsequently served as both impetus and rationale for specific policy interventions to expand the number of labour-intensive jobs (e.g. ILO, 1976). As noted earlier, the state-sponsored development of a local clothing manufacturing industry in Mauritius during the 1970s encouraged entrepreneurs from Hong Kong to set up factories and the policy was so successful at reducing unemployment that, by the 1980s, clothing manufacturing firms were recruiting additional workers from China (Bräutigam, 2009). The South African town of Newcastle similarly encouraged Asian entrepreneurs to the region in the 1980s to combat high unemployment (discussed further in Chapter 6).

The slowdown in global economic growth from the mid-1970s coupled with growing evidence of inequality, persistent poverty, balance-of-payments pressures, indebtedness, and rising unemployment in many developing countries prompted a shift in prevailing development doctrines (Thorbecke, 2007). More attention was paid to structural factors (for example, the opportunities and costs associated with growth centred around the exploitation of natural resources, potential inequities in the terms of trade between agriculture and industry, and the institutional factors shaping the divide between formal and informal sectors). Development theory bifurcated between reformist development economics and radical critics of capitalism. Reformists sought to reorient the objectives of the large donor development agencies to improve living standards of workers and to generate new jobs for the poor (e.g. the ILO's World Employment Programme that was launched in 1969), to assist the growth of small businesses (especially in the informal sector), to pay more attention to poverty alleviation ('basic needs'), and to encourage more equitable growth paths ('redistribution with growth'). Dependency theory and underdevelopment theory drew attention to the unequal nature of trade between the advanced capitalist countries (the 'core') and developing countries (the 'periphery') and the power imbalances between foreign capital and domestic classes (e.g. Amin, 1977; Frank, 1978). Latin American structuralism echoed these concerns, seeing the composition of aggregate demand as dependent on income distribution shaped in turn by power imbalances between contracting parties in factor, input, and product markets and the consequences of exogenously generated technical progress (Di Filippo, 2009: 185; Mahon, 2015). Such approaches supported a more interventionist role for the state and a role for corporatist institutions to shape a process of inward-oriented industrialization in which tariff protection helped compensate employers for higher wage costs.

Whilst Lewis showed that relatively low-wage, labour-intensive development can fuel a dynamic growth path, a rival tradition in development, including Gerschenkron's discussion of Russian economic development, highlighted the potential for the relatively capital-intensive capital goods sector to provide the basis for growth (Gerschenkron, 1962; Elkan, 1973: 84–6). The obvious challenge for any capital-intensive development strategies is obtaining the necessary development finance without borrowing, relying on aid or resorting to coercive strategies (for example, squeezing the agricultural sector as in the Russian case). Galenson and Leibenstein (1955) argued that capital-intensive technologies would ultimately pay for themselves by maximizing the flow of revenues into profits, savings, and investment. They argued that capital-intensive technologies provided the highest 'reinvestment quotient' precisely because the share of income going to labour is small (relatively few workers are employed), leaving the lion's share of income flowing into profits and hence also into investment. Economic growth based on labour-intensive technologies (such as hand looms in the textile industry) might provide more employment in the short-term, but, Galenson and Leibenstein argued, capital-intensive technologies (e.g. mechanized textile mills) were so productive, that, together with the greater profit share they provided for capitalists, they would project the economy onto a more dynamic and sustained growth path that would generate far more jobs in the future. As discussed further in Chapter 3, this idea has once again come to the foreground of development thinking in the guise of arguments for upgrading and the adoption of so-called cutting-edge technologies irrespective of labour market conditions.

Galenson and Leibenstein's capital-intensive approach was criticized at the time for its unrealistic assumptions and its unabashed advocacy of increasing inequality in order to finance savings and investment (e.g. Elkan, 1973: 87–8). Lewis himself was particularly unimpressed with the implications of their position for countries with open unemployment. He noted that their capital-intensive strategy:

> would be feasible only if the labour surplus remained disguised and could therefore be ignored; it is not practicable when the unemployed are roaming the streets and burgling your houses. Most developing countries have to give the highest priority to providing employment now rather than to maximizing consumption or income or employment in ten years' time. (Lewis, 1965: 14)

Lewis's comment remains pertinent as a caution against contemporary development strategies that emphasize labour productivity growth as a means of promoting a more dynamic 'high road' to growth in the presence of high, open unemployment. His famous model assumed that surplus labour took the form predominantly of underemployed labour, yet he was clearly alert to the specific social and development challenges posed by open unemployment and the attendant dangers of prioritizing capital-intensity. Choice of technique matters for distribution, a point often lost in the contemporary development literature (Harriss-White et al., 2011: 94).

2.3 Inequality and Growth

The year after Lewis published his famous model, Simon Kuznets (1955), in another classic of development economics, argued that the kind of growth path sketched by Lewis would display initially rising inequality as rural and urban incomes diverged—the consequences primarily of the expansion of manufacturing jobs. Kuznets over-optimistically posited that the relationship between inequality and development took the shape of an inverted U, initially rising and then falling over time. He attributed the fall in inequality in developed economies to the introduction of 'a variety of protective and supportive legislation, much of it aimed to counteract the worst effects of rapid industrialization and urbanization and to support the claims of the broad masses for more adequate shares of the growing income of the country' (Kuznets, 1955: 17). Kuznets thought that this was more likely to occur in democratic countries (as had been the case with the anti-sweating movement in Britain discussed further in Chapter 5). Yet even in non-democratic China, urban workers have been able to force through improvements in wages and living conditions as industrialization progressed (Chan and Hui, 2014).

Kuznets was not the first to suggest that societal forces would emerge to challenge the distributional consequences of capitalism. In his 1944 classic, *The Great Transformation*, Karl Polanyi argued that society would inevitably introduce regulations to protect against the dangers posed by unfettered markets, notably to save the environment, avoid 'unsettling changes in the price level', and reduce 'the flexibility of wages and the mobility of labour, giving stability to incomes' (Polanyi, 1944: 225). However, Polanyi also warned that these very interventions inevitably 'impaired the self-regulation of the market, disorganized industrial life, and thus endangered society in yet another way' (ibid.: 3). This, in turn, implied that a corrective process of deregulation would follow. In Polanyi's vision, the relationship between society and the market is fundamentally unstable, with the regulation of market forces subject to pendulum-like swings or 'double-movement' of regulation, followed by deregulation, followed by social pressure for re-regulation. One can read the growth of the welfare state in Britain and Europe post the Second World War as a protective movement against the market, and the tax cuts and deregulation in the 1980s in the UK (under Thatcher) and the US (under Reagan) as the subsequent double-movement in the opposite direction. This disrupted Kuznets' predicted path for inequality, allowing it to rise again. Pressure on developing countries from the International Monetary Fund and World Bank to deregulate and open up their economies to international competition can also be seen in Polanyian terms, albeit at a global level (Stewart, 2006). More recent re-regulation of financial markets and calls to reign in the rampant growth in inequality is similarly suggestive of a corrective

Polanyian double-movement to protect society from the dangers posed by unbridled markets.

Different 'varieties of capitalism' have sought to manage the tension between state and market differently, with the more egalitarian and 'co-ordinated market economies' of Europe and Scandinavia displaying greater labour market and related social protection than 'liberal market economies', notably the US and New Zealand (Hall and Soskice, 2001). The forces of globalization have put pressure on welfare systems everywhere, yet social democratic states continue to provide stronger welfare nets than the more liberal market economies. South Africa shares many labour market and welfare features of the European welfare states with the glaring exception of failing to provide any sustained or significant social security for the unemployed (Nattrass, 2014a).

After the end of communism in Eastern Europe and in China, millions of low-wage workers entered the global economy. This placed downward pressure on unskilled wages in the middle- and high-income countries. Competition from China created strong incentives for firms in middle- and high-income countries to shift faster into higher-value-added, more technologically intensive activities, thereby placing a premium on skilled wages. Both developments widened wage inequality, contributing to growing economy-wide inequality (Deaton, 2013; Bourguignon, 2015). In the social democratic countries, increasing international competition accelerated the decline of trade union coverage and encouraged plant-level collective agreements in place of industrial collective agreements (Hayter et al., 2011). Workers in low-wage countries, notably in China and Bangladesh, endured harsh and repressive working conditions, but these jobs offered a route out of poverty for millions of poor people within an increasingly globalized division of labour.

Contrary to Kuznets, inequality worsened within and between countries, a function of both wage inequality and increasingly wealth inequality (Atkinson et al., 2011). Financial speculation by the rich and unsustainable borrowing by poor members of society has been implicated in the 2008 economic crisis (e.g. Wisman, 2013; Stockhammer, 2015) and the 'Occupy Wall Street' campaign and related protests point to widespread disgust with the way in which inadequately regulated financial capitalism endangered society. Thomas Piketty's book *'Capital in the 21st Century'* (2013), which calls for a global tax on wealth, became an international best seller.

There is growing concern that the super-rich have undue political influence in the liberal market economies and that this undermines the role that governments should play in providing basic health care, infrastructure etc. thereby harming society and future economic growth (e.g. Stiglitz, 2012; Deaton, 2013; Bourguignon, 2015). There is also concern that the institutional rules governing the global economy (such as intellectual property rights, non-tariff barriers etc. that protect economic interests in rich countries whilst restricting growth opportunities for developing countries) are exacerbating inequality between countries (Stiglitz, 2002, 2006; Bourguignon, 2015). For anti-globalization protestors, the global trading system itself is the problem. Yet as Bourguignon warns, if globalization and the economic model behind it is brought to a stop 'through various types of protectionist and other interventionist measures... the general benefits brought to a country by globalization would then be lost' (Bourguignon, 2015: 6). The impact on export-led developing countries such as China and Bangladesh would be enormous and disastrous for poverty alleviation.

Bourguignon, like Polanyi, understood that social attempts to rein in markets are understandable and desirable, but that, when done with too much of a heavy hand, they run the risk of endangering society in other ways, by stifling economic dynamism itself. With regard to globalization specifically, Bourguignon warns that protectionist and interventionist measures could undermine the benefits of international trade for all countries and end what Deaton (2013) has called the 'great escape' from poverty. Both Bourguignon and Deaton have pointed out that whilst inequality increased between countries (and within many of them), the world as a whole has become a more equal place as millions of Chinese and Indian workers benefitted from Lewis-like labour-intensive economic growth.

The challenge is to keep drawing people into productive employment through sustainable labour-intensive development and to share the proceeds of development more equally. In Chapter 1 we argued for an approach of 'inclusive dualism' in the sense of tolerating relatively low-wage work and supporting firms with varying labour productivity whilst prioritizing labour-intensive and preferably green employment growth (such as that provided for by the clothing manufacturing industry) for the poor. Keeping the path open for export-oriented growth can help facilitate this, and measures to reduce inequality between rich and poor could further enhance its redistributive impact.

3

Labour Productivity and Employment in Surplus Labour Countries

The predominant contemporary development narrative and related policy discourse portrays labour productivity growth as essential for development (see Chapter 1). Middle-income countries in particular are advised to avoid relatively low-wage, labour-intensive growth (as it promises nothing but a 'race to the bottom') and to pursue 'decent' (higher-wage, more skilled) employment not simply as a normative goal, but as a development strategy. This chapter draws attention to the limits of this approach for developing countries with high open unemployment. Section 3.1 discusses the ILO's decent work agenda (an influential example of this approach), emphasizing how this differs from Lewis's conceptualization of development with surplus labour. Section 3.2 identifies a group of high-unemployment countries (that we term 'surplus labour countries') and shows that rising labour productivity in the surplus labour countries during the 2000s came at the cost of stagnant and even falling employment rates. Given inadequate welfare support for the unemployed, such growth paths undermined inclusive development in these countries.

3.1 The International Labour Organization's Decent Work Agenda

In the 2000s, the International Labour Organization, more than any other development agency, has promoted labour productivity growth and industrial upgrading as a one-size-fits-all strategy for economic development. In a striking reversal of its previous approach, the ILO has paid little, if any, attention to the growing problem of unemployment in many developing countries. During the 1970s, when open unemployment emerged as a serious concern for the development community, the ILO favoured the adoption of labour-intensive technologies in manufacturing and construction as a policy response (see e.g. ILO, 1976). The ILO also proposed greater support for small, informal enterprises, and advocated for the removal of restrictions on informal enterprises (such as cumbersome trading licences) and to put an end to policies that destroyed informal housing and businesses under the guise of slum clearance programmes (ILO, 1972). This approach was consistent with development efforts to promote 'appropriate technology', that is, labour-intensive technologies more suited to developing country contexts than imported capital-intensive technologies developed in high-income contexts where relative factor prices were different (e.g. Lewis, 1958; Stewart, 1977). Yet by the end of the twentieth century, the ILO had come to frame relatively low-wage, labour-intensive jobs as a source of danger, as desirable only in temporary poverty-alleviating projects—and only if implemented in compliance with labour standards and with the support of all social partners, notably organized labour (Tajgman and De Veen, 1998). This latter vision eventually consolidated into a policy discourse, framing labour-intensive manufacturing as a 'low road' to growth. In the ILO's new view, middle-income countries especially risked a 'race to the bottom' against low-wage, low-income countries (e.g. ILO, 2014: 75–6).

The ILO has remained supportive of efforts to facilitate small business development, but increasingly informality was depicted as a problem not only for workers without social protection, but also for workers in formal firms. The ILO's 2015 resolution on the 'transition from the Informal to the Formal economy' depicted formalization as necessary inter alia to 'promote the creation, preservation and sustainability of enterprises and decent jobs in the formal economy'.[1] In other words, the existence of a low-wage, informal sector was cast not as a safety net for the unemployed, but as a source of inferior jobs posing a threat to the sustainability of 'decent', formal jobs. The resolution did recommend that the transition to formality be done in a way that ensures 'opportunities for income security, livelihoods and entrepreneurship'. But aside from this vague formulation, no obvious attention was paid to potential employment consequences of bringing previously informal businesses under the same regulations, including minimum wage regulations, as formal firms. Indeed, those gravitating to an interpretation of this strategy that we term 'decent work fundamentalism' (Chapter 1) were comfortable using enforcement mechanisms to destroy enterprises that failed to adhere with formal minimum wages (Chapter 6).

The ILO has long supported development strategies to accelerate economic transformation away from agriculture and informal activities and towards a greater share of employment in urban manufacturing and services.

[1] http://ilo.org/dyn/normlex/en/f?p=NORMLEXPUB:12100:0::NO::P12100_ILO_CODE:R204.

This is consistent with Lewis's vision of development through structural transformation. The ILO's development strategy has evolved, however, to prioritize (higher-wage) decent work from the outset—irrespective of the labour supply conditions. This diverged from the Lewis growth dynamic, which envisaged manufacturing wages rising only *after* surplus labour had been absorbed (Chapter 2). The ILO's decent work agenda, launched in 1999, placed the spotlight on wages, job quality, worker rights, and social dialogue as essential normative and developmental components of job creation. According to Juan Somavia, then Director General, the decent work agenda marked 'the high road to economic and social development, a road in which employment, income and social protection can be achieved without compromising workers' rights and social standards' (in ILO, 1999, no page number). The suggestion here, developed further in subsequent *World of Work* reports, was that promoting decent work was a development strategy in itself as it helped encourage productivity growth thereby providing the basis for future output and employment growth. Contemporary ILO documents barely mentioned the phrase 'labour-intensive' (presumably because it had become too distasteful and overly burdened with 'low road to growth' connotations). Rather, to the extent that ILO *World of Work* reports mentioned job creation strategies, they favour terms like 'labour-demanding' growth (which could be capital-intensive) or 'employment-intensive' growth (the meaning of which is not obvious; in some contexts it can be read as an anodyne version of 'labour-intensive', but in other contexts refers simply to the expansion of decent jobs).

The concept of decent work was from the outset bedevilled by measurement problems. The ILO failed to come up with a universally applicable methodology to assess it (Burchell et al., 2014). Sehnbruch et al. (2015) argue that this undermined its reach and potential impact. Yet the idea of decent work as a development strategy had political traction irrespective of the inherent difficulties involved in quantifying job quality because it appeared to offer a way of meeting the objectives of organized labour whilst side-stepping the potential trade-off between more jobs and better jobs. Rather than maximizing the number of jobs created per unit of capital invested (as would be the case in labour-intensive development) the decent work agenda held out the prospect of a 'high road' to growth in which the employment rate rises on the back of strong labour productivity growth. This, in turn, is most likely when economic growth is strong. It is no accident that such optimism around development through decent work emerged during the 2000s, before the 2008 financial crisis put an end to the long global boom.

ILO thinking in this regard reflected a broader emphasis in development theory and practice on productivity growth. The business economist Michael Porter was influential in arguing that countries should avoid competing on the basis of 'static comparative advantage' and instead develop 'dynamic competitive advantage' through the promotion of innovation and cutting-edge technologies (Porter, 1985, 1990). Porter argued that government should support and generate 'pressures' for productivity growth through technological 'upgrading' and skills development (Porter, 1990: 87). In his view, 'policies that convey static, short-term cost advantages but unconsciously undermine innovation and dynamism represent the most common and most profound error in government industrial policy' (ibid.). Porter was not necessarily arguing against labour-intensive development. His point was rather that industrial policy should keep a clear eye on developing new capabilities and capacities. There were, nevertheless, distinct echoes in his writing with the argument made more than half a century earlier by Galenson and Leibenstein in favour of capital-intensive growth (Chapter 2).

There is a significant body of Porter-esque policy-oriented research and consultancy work advising middle-income countries on how to help position firms within global value chains, notably by 'upgrading' their technologies, skilling their workers, and shifting into higher-value-added product lines (see e.g. Gereffi and Fernandez-Stark, 2011; Frederick and Staritz, 2012: 50; Cattaneo et al., 2013; Gereffi, 2014: 18–19). In the 'upgrade or die' version of this perspective, 'upgrading is argued to be imperative, not only to capture increasing value within these global industries, but ultimately to survive within the industry' (Psilos and Gereffi, 2011: 3). Low-wage labour-intensive development has thus been constructed discursively in policymaking circles both inside and outside the ILO as an undesirable low road to growth—certainly as compared to the putative alternative high road of rising wages and productivity (e.g. Barrientos et al., 2011a, 2011b; ILO, 2014: 75–6). As noted in Chapter 1, such arguments became hegemonic in South African post-apartheid policymaking (see also Nattrass 2001, 2011). They have a distinct political appeal for organized labour and dovetail with many contemporary interventionist labour and industrial policies.

Various influential development strategists have highlighted the importance of government intervention to improve productivity, boost investment, and to work with business to develop and discover new competencies (Rodrik, 2007; Hausmann et al., 2008; Spence Commission, 2008). But they part company with the ILO when it comes to the use of wages as a means to promote productivity growth. Whereas Hausmann and Rodrik accepted that labour costs matter for employment and that labour policies should be tailored to suit local political and labour market conditions, and Porter recommended that governments should avoid intervening to lower labour costs (1990: 88), the ILO promoted policies to raise minimum wages *in order to* promote decent work and labour productivity growth.

This raises concerns about potential trade-offs between labour costs and employment. As Godfrey points out, there is a 'fundamental contradiction at the core of the decent work concept' because job creation (one of its four components) 'will usually trade-off against the other three components [worker's rights, social protection, and social dialogue] all of which generally mean an increase in labour costs' (2015: 500). Fields makes a stronger point in arguing that there is a 'decent work frontier' in which the quantity of work can be gauged as the volume of employment and the quality of work by the earnings level (2003: 244). For Fields, the negative relationship between the cost/quality of jobs and the number of jobs, means that countries have a choice, either to move in the direction of more, low-wage, jobs or fewer higher-wage, better-quality, 'decent' jobs. The decent work frontier shifts outwards as the economy grows, meaning that growth can accommodate rising wages and employment. Yet, when unemployment is high, generating more jobs by shifting along the decent work frontier would be more inclusive, even if the decent work frontier is moving out.

The ILO's 2014 *World of Work* report notes at the outset that a 'balance' needs to be found between creating more jobs and more productive/better/decent jobs (ILO, 2014: 5). This appears to accept Fields' warning that 'when conditions are such that 'more of both cannot be had... a choice must be made about where to locate oneself along the decent work frontier' (Fields, 2003: 252). Yet in practice and emphasis, the ILO underplayed this choice, describing the trade-off between wages and employment later in the report as a 'false dichotomy' that is 'either incorrect or significantly overstated' (ILO, 2014: 104).

There are two pillars to this ILO position. The first is that the trade-off between wages and employment is overstated because most empirical studies find the impact of minimum wages on employment to be broadly neutral (ibid., 2014: 88). We discuss this evidence in Chapter 5 and explain that it does not contradict the employment/wage trade-off. The second is that unemployment is generally not a problem (and hence not a priority area for policy) because the 'majority of the population in developing countries have low incomes and cannot afford not to work, given the limited availability of social protection or other forms of transfers' (ibid.: 33). This allows the ILO to conclude that it is thus 'the type of work performed and the income and working conditions attached to it [that] are of paramount importance in assessing employment performance' (ibid.) rather than the level of overall employment. Section 3.2 shows that this position is particularly problematic for surplus labour countries.

3.2 Trajectories of Labour Productivity and Employment Growth in Surplus Labour Countries

The extreme form of surplus labour—open unemployment—is evident in a number of mostly middle-income countries. Figure 3.1 draws on data from the

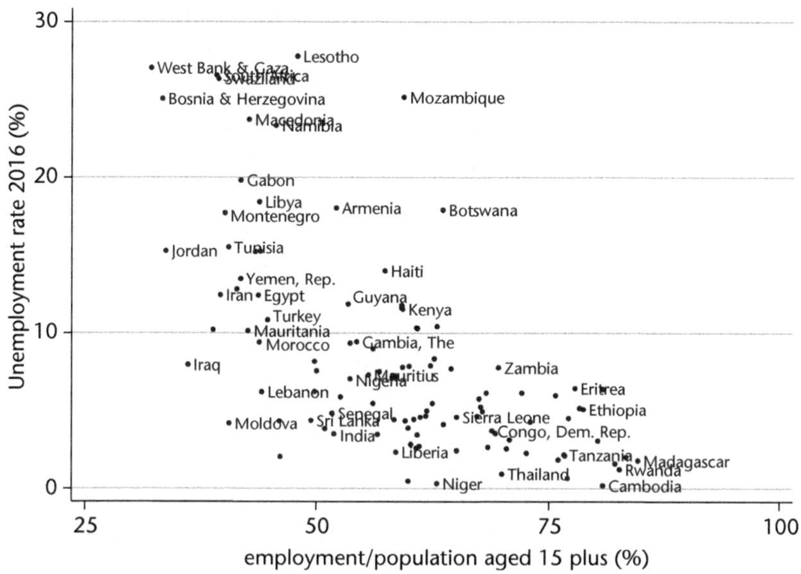

Figure 3.1 Employment and unemployment rates (110 low- and middle-income countries).

Source: ILO data (modelled estimates based on labour force surveys) reported in World Development Indicators. Available at: http://data.worldbank.org/data-catalog/world-development-indicators.

World Bank's World Development Indicators to report employment and unemployment rates for 110 low- and middle-income countries for which data existed for 2016. The employment rate is defined here as the percentage of adults aged 15 and above in employment (meaning in any income-earning activities whether formal or informal, full or part time).[2] The unemployment rate, estimated by the ILO based on labour force surveys, is the number of active jobseekers expressed as a percentage of the labour force (defined as the employed plus active jobseekers). Countries with low employment rates may have low unemployment rates for cultural reasons, for example religious beliefs discouraging women from entering the labour market—as is the case in the cluster of predominantly Muslim countries in the bottom left corner of Figure 3.1.

Unemployment rates are derived from labour force surveys and are subject to the vagaries of various decision rules. For example, the standard practice is to classify only active jobseekers as 'unemployed', which means that those without work who want it but regard it as pointless looking for work, will be counted as 'not economically active' (that is, they disappear from both the

[2] The World Bank defines the working-age population as anyone aged 15 or older and defines employment as 'any activity to produce goods or provide services for pay or profit, whether at work during the reference period (i.e. who worked in a job for at least one hour) or not at work due to temporary absence from a job, or to working-time arrangements'.

numerator and the denominator of the unemployment rate). Survey rules that classify underemployed people as 'employed' because they worked for more than a particular number of hours (five is a common rule) in the past week, overestimate employment. Both practices underestimate the potential additional labour supply that could become available if and when labour demand improves. Such fluidity between the non-economically active, the underemployed and the openly unemployed is why Lewis recommended that for countries with surplus labour 'if we wish to measure our achievements in development, we must measure them not by the fall of unemployment, but by the increase in employment' (Lewis, 1958: 45).

Countries in the top left quadrant of Figure 3.1 have high unemployment rates and low employment rates, meaning that a relatively high proportion of the working-age population is classified as being without employment and actively seeking it. These countries comprise a mix of mostly Southern African, post-communist and war-torn countries. Table 3.1 lists the thirteen countries whose unemployment rate in 2016 was exceptionally high, that is, over twice the mean of 8.2 per cent for low- and middle-income countries. We refer to these countries as 'surplus labour' countries. Their unemployment rates were persistently above the mean since internationally comparable labour force data were first made available (in 1991), indicating

Table 3.1 Surplus labour countries: key characteristics (2016)

Country	Real GDP per capita (purchasing power parity) in constant 2011 international dollars*	Gini coefficient (most recent)	Freedom House score
Post-communist			
Armenia	$8,190	32.5%	Partly free
Bosnia & Herzegovina	$11,328	32.7%	Partly free
Macedonia	$13,055	35.6%	Partly free
Montenegro	$15,725	31.9%	Partly free
Southern Africa			
Botswana	$15,723	60.5%	Free
Lesotho	$2,736	54.2%	Partly free
Namibia	$9,852	61.0%	Free
Mozambique	$1,123	54.0%	Partly free
South Africa	$12,260	63.0%	Free
Swaziland	$7,724	51.5%	Not free
Other			
Gabon	$16,786	42.2%	Not free
Libya	N/A	N/A	Not free
West Bank and Gaza	$4,389	33.8%	Not free

*An international dollar would buy in the cited country a comparable amount of goods and services that a US dollar would buy in the US.

Source: Calculated from World Development Indicators. Available at: http://data.worldbank.org/data-catalog/world-development-indicators; https://freedomhouse.org/report/freedom-world-2016/table-scores.

that their unemployment problem can be regarded as structural rather than temporary.[3]

Table 3.1 shows that the surplus labour countries fell into three distinct groups: four post-communist partially free European countries (Armenia, Bosnia and Herzegovina, Macedonia, Montenegro); six mostly free Southern African countries (Botswana, Lesotho, Mozambique, Namibia, South Africa, and Swaziland); and three not free countries: two oil/gas exporters, one in North Africa (Libya), the other in West Africa (Gabon); and occupied Palestine (West Bank and Gaza), a small conflict-ridden middle Eastern country intermittently at war with Israel and blockaded by it—clearly in a category of its own.

Apart from Montenegro (the country with the highest Gross Domestic Product (GDP) *per capita* in the group) where about a third of the unemployed have access to social security, these surplus labour countries have limited if any public or private funding mechanisms in place to protect the unemployed from loss of income. Figure 3.2 presents data from the ILO for the percentage of unemployed with access to social security. It also reports 'uncovered unemployment rates' (the number of unemployed without social security as a share of the labour force). Most of the unemployed in surplus labour countries do not have access to social security and are thus forced to rely on their own devices and kin for support.

The ILO defines people as being 'employed' whether they are engaged in income-earning activities on a full-time or part-time basis. Data on underemployment is limited, but the ILO does report the percentage of employed people who indicated to enumerators that they would prefer to work more hours. This measure would not capture those working full time at a very low marginal product (one of Lewis's notions of surplus labour), but it does provide a further indication of potential labour supply. Assuming that the average person saying they would like to work more hours is working half time (that is, 50 per cent of a working week), then we could estimate the available surplus labour amongst the underemployed as half the number of those saying they are underemployed. Figure 3.3 presents this indicative surplus labour rate calculated as the unemployed plus half the underemployed expressed as a percentage of the labour force for low- and middle-income countries for which data are available.

Figure 3.3 shows that as of 2016, the Southern African countries had relatively low levels of underemployment (indicated by the fact that their surplus labour rate was not much higher than the open unemployment rate) but continued to top the surplus labour chart by virtue of their high open unemployment rates. Relatively few data are available for countries on the African continent (only Ethiopia, Rwanda, Zimbabwe, The Gambia, Morocco,

[3] An earlier analysis conducted with 2013 unemployment rates included Serbia, Albania, and the Yemen, and excluded Mozambique (Nattrass and Seekings, 2018a).

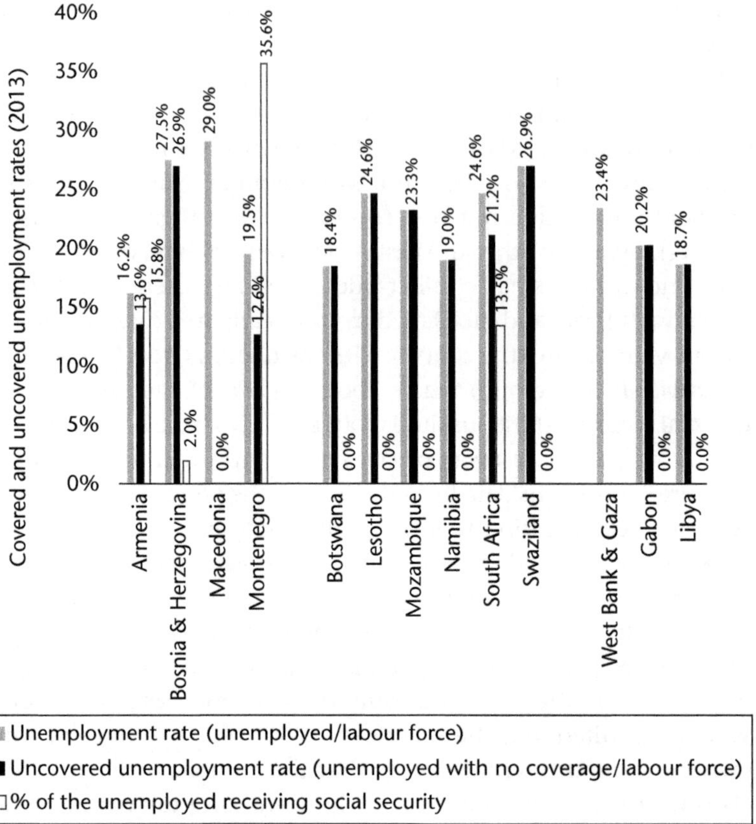

Figure 3.2 Unemployment rates (covered and uncovered) in 2013.

Source: ILOSTAT, World Development Indicators. Available at: http://data.worldbank.org/data-catalog/world-development-indicators; https://www.ilo.org/ilostat/

and Egypt). Rwanda and to a lesser extent Ethiopia have low unemployment rates, but relatively high underemployment—pushing them towards the higher end of surplus labour countries. The other African countries had surplus labour rates greater than the mean (12.3 per cent). Rwanda comes closest to Lewis's model of a 'country' with potential for development with surplus labour in that its unemployment rate was low and its employment rate high, but with employment characterized by a relatively high level of underemployment.

As noted in Chapter 1, creating new low-wage jobs when unemployment is high will raise *per capita* income (because more will be produced as employment is expanded) but it will have the arithmetic effect of lowering average labour productivity (total output divided by the employed). This is typically regarded as a source of concern by development strategists, given the link between labour productivity growth and living standards. As shown in the identity below, average *per capita* income (GDP/total population) can be

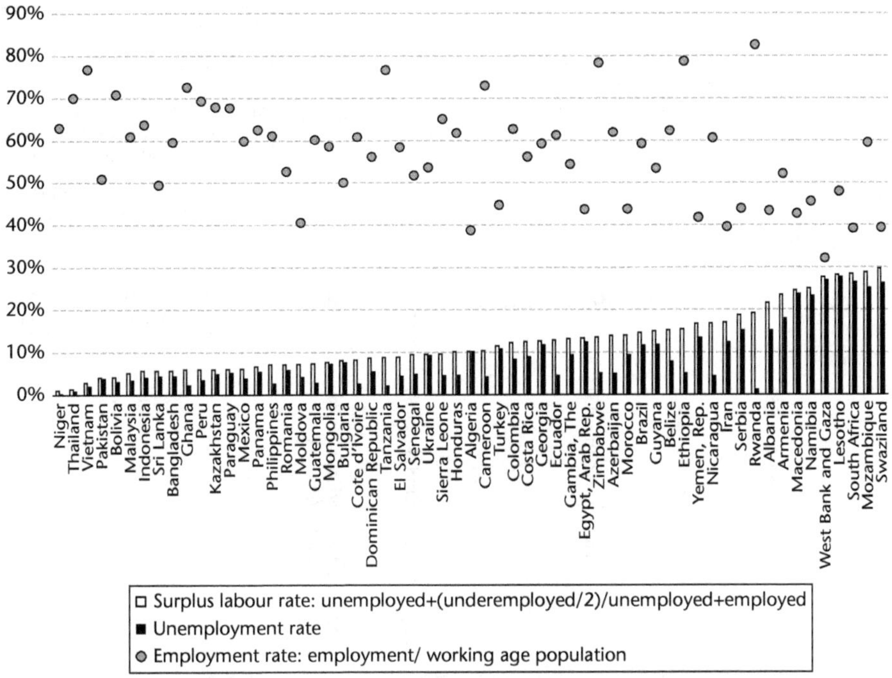

Figure 3.3 Unemployment and surplus labour rates (2016) in 59 low- and middle-income countries.

Source: ILO data (modelled estimates based on labour force surveys) reported in World Development Indicators. Available at: http://data.worldbank.org/data-catalog/world-development-indicators; and data on underemployment for ILOstat. Available at: http://ilo.org/ilostat/.

decomposed as the product of average labour productivity (GDP/employment), the employment rate (employment/working-age population) and the share of the population of working age (working-age population/total population). The decomposition thus highlights that rising output per worker is positively related to rising *per capita* income:

$$\frac{\text{GDP}}{\text{total population}} = \frac{\text{GDP}}{\text{employment}} \times \frac{\text{employment}}{\text{working} - \text{age population}} \times \frac{\text{working} - \text{age population}}{\text{total population}}$$

The ILO employs such a decomposition in its 2014 *World of Work* report (ILO, 2014: xix, 46) to emphasize the importance of labour productivity growth in accounting for rising GDP *per capita*. Figure 3.4 presents mean data for low-income, middle-income, and high-income countries as well as for the nine surplus labour countries identified earlier for which adequate data exist to do this decomposition. It shows that labour productivity growth was indeed a key

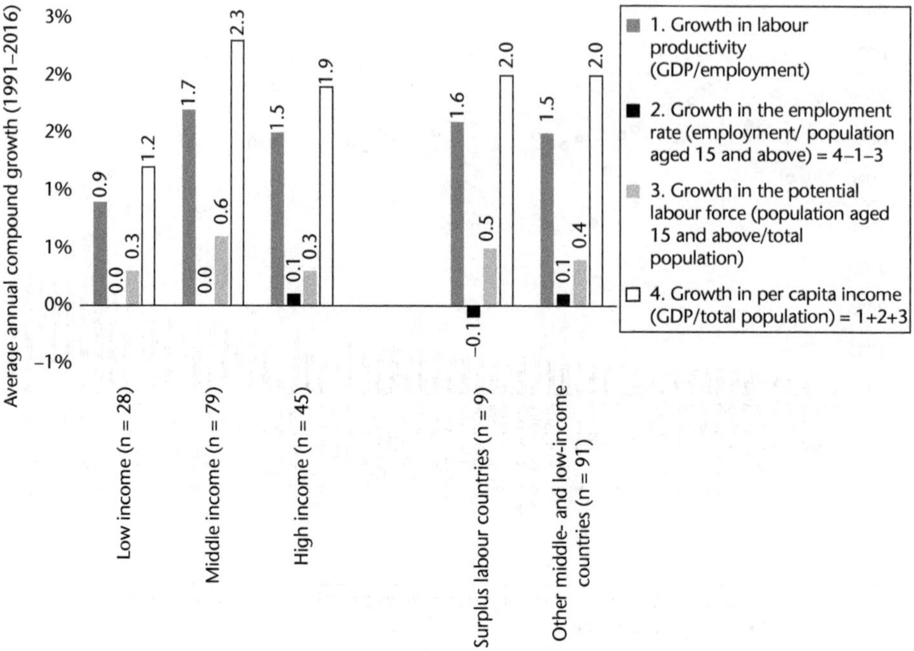

Figure 3.4 Decomposing growth in real GDP per capita (1991–2016).
Source: World Development Indicators. Available at: http://data.worldbank.org/data-catalog/world-development-indicators.

component of rising living standards between 1991 and 2016. Yet the consequence of rising aggregate labour productivity was falling labour-intensity and a declining capacity to generate new jobs out of growth. In the surplus labour countries, the employment rate actually fell. Rising labour productivity could not generate an increase in real GDP *per capita* fast enough to accommodate the growth in the share of the working-age population which meant that their 'high road' (as in rising labour productivity) to growth was one that could not provide employment fast enough to accommodate new entrants into the labour market. Their economies thus became less inclusive in the process.

Figure 3.5 decomposes *per capita* income growth into labour productivity growth, the growth in the employment rate, and growth in the share of the working-age population between 1991 and 2016 for the nine surplus labour countries for which data are available. It shows that only the two post-communist countries (Armenia and Macedonia) and Swaziland experienced rising employment rates over the period.

Economic growth in the post-communist countries came off a low base: in 1991 both economies were reeling from the collapse of the Soviet Union and related loss of investment and markets from Russia. Armenia was also

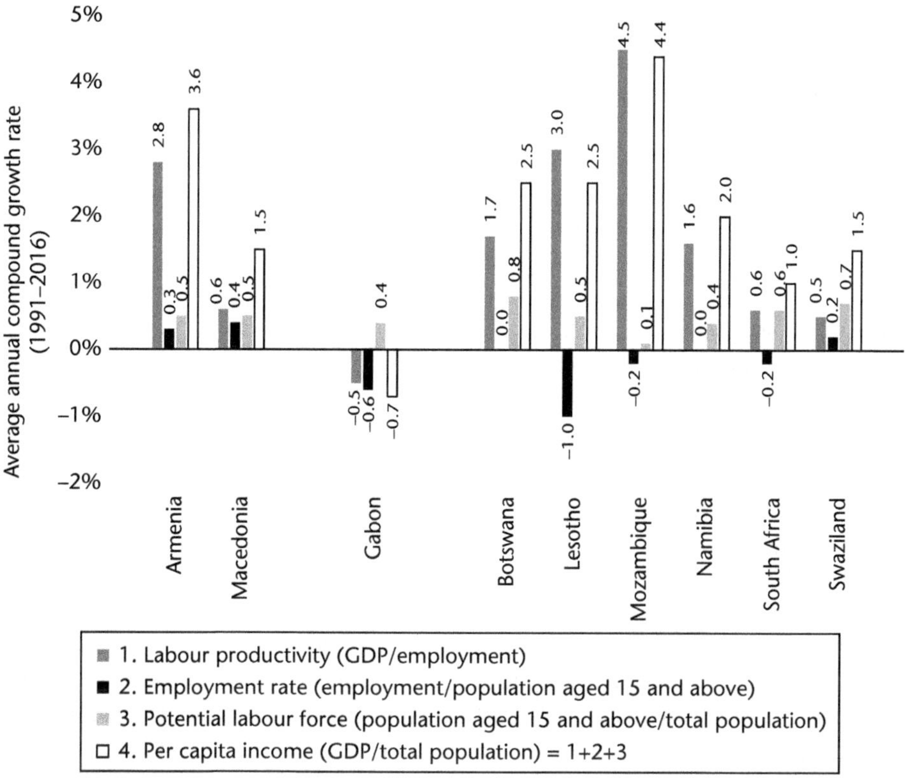

Figure 3.5 Employment, productivity, and per capita income growth in the surplus labour countries for which adequate data exist.

Source: World Development Indicators. Available at: http://data.worldbank.org/data-catalog/world-development-indicators.

negatively affected by regional conflict and experienced both deindustrialization and a contraction in agricultural employment (World Bank, 2017b). Growth in the service industry and in construction was the main driver of increased employment overall (ibid.: 4). Macedonia's employment growth was stronger, in large part due to growth in transport, the wholesale and retail trade, manufacturing (including the clothing industry) and government-supported infrastructure construction (World Bank, 2017c: 6, 16).

Gabon's economic growth between 1991 and 2016 was uneven, affected strongly by the rise and then a decline in oil prices. Average annual compound growth across the period was negative with regard to employment, productivity, and *per capita* income. The 2017 CIA Fact Book warned:

> Despite an abundance of natural wealth, poor fiscal management and over-reliance on oil has stifled the economy. Power cuts and water shortages are frequent. Gabon is reliant on imports and the government heavily subsidises commodities, including

food, but will be hard pressed to tamp down public frustration with unemployment and corruption.[4]

In Southern Africa, the growth in employment rates was typically negative or constant in the face of strongly growing labour productivity and in the share of the working-age population. The Southern African development trajectory delivered rising per capita income, but at the cost of a steadily widening gulf between the growth of employment and that of the labour force. Unlike the post-communist countries struggling to cope with the legacy of central planning, regional conflict, and the challenges of transitioning to a globally connected market economy, the Southern African countries are long-standing market economies and had, for the entire period, been pursuing development strategies under mostly democratic conditions (Swaziland and Lesotho being the exceptions). Their persistently high unemployment rates no doubt reflect structural features (discussed further below) but stagnant employment growth in the face of rising labour productivity also reflected policy choices—particularly within South Africa, the economic powerhouse of the region.

Figure 2.1 showed that agriculture provided an important source of employment in Mozambique and Namibia, but not in South Africa. Compared to countries at the same level of development (Peru, Colombia), the share of informal employment was very low in the Southern African middle-income countries of South Africa and Namibia. The drivers of informal employment are complex and context specific. Informal employment globally varies with macroeconomic conditions and is typically high in the presence of high labour costs in the formal sector (as in Latin America) and where taxation is high and governments perceived as corrupt (Johnson et al., 1998; Perry, 2007; Bernal, 2009; Charmes, 2012). Many of the ex-communist transitional economies had 'shadow' economies in the past, yet the informal economy (often in the face of continued bureaucratic restrictions) proved insufficiently dynamic to accommodate the many people rendered redundant through subsequent privatization and structural adjustment, especially after the 2008 global recession (Radovanović and Maksimović, 2010). In Southern Africa, dry climatic conditions and the legacy of colonialism constrained the growth of informal agricultural employment, and the policing of informal activities in urban areas probably limited the growth of informal manufacturing and services relative to that seen in Latin America. Whether informal employment is tolerated by government is important. We show in Chapter 6 how the strict enforcement of wages bargained between employers and unions in the formal clothing manufacturing industry lead to active job destruction in non-compliant, labour-intensive firms in South Africa.

[4] https://cia.gov/library/publications/the-world-factbook/geos/gb.html.

3.3 Unemployment and Lewis-like Growth in Southern Africa

The Lewis model described a developmental context in which land was relatively scarce and there was an abundant supply of labour available for industrialization (Chapters 1 and 2). Lewis believed this was not the case in Africa where in some countries, he observed, there was even an 'acute shortage' of labour, constraining industrial development (Lewis, 1954: 140). In Lewis's view, unless labour productivity could be improved in agriculture (thus potentially releasing a supply of labour for industry) or additional labour imported (for example, indentured Indian or Chinese workers), economic development in Africa would have to be capital-intensive. However, given the absence of an 'abundant reservoir of capital on which to draw', Lewis concluded that it was 'quite out of the question to do very much development of this type' (Lewis, 1951: 79).

Karshenas argued that as of the mid-1960s, agricultural labour productivity was similar in Africa and Asia, but supported Lewis's contention that lower labour-to-land ratios in Africa meant that the potential supply of labour to industry in Africa was limited compared to Asia and hence that wages were generally higher than in Asia (2001): 321–2. Karshenas showed that up until the mid-1980s, manufacturing wages were between 50 and 70 per cent higher in Africa than in Asia (ibid.: 323–4) and like Lewis (1951), argued that this accounted for relatively capital-intensive technologies in Africa and relatively slower growth.

Labour markets in Southern Africa were subject to massive intervention by colonial and settler states to free up supplies of labour. States resorted to a range of coercive policies (including taxation and land dispossession) in order to generate a supply of less skilled labour to mines, commercial agriculture and, later, secondary industry. In South Africa and Namibia (then a *de facto* colony of South Africa), apartheid policies further undermined the existing African peasantry. Apartheid South Africa notoriously forced African people into overcrowded reserves ('bantustans') in part to supply migrant labour to mines and farms (Legassick, 1974; Feinstein, 2005). This benefitted capitalists in these sectors, yet skilled labour shortages and apartheid-related racial restrictions on hiring African workers, together with labour market institutions designed to boost the earnings of white workers, kept manufacturing wages relatively high, acting as a persistent constraint on growth and maintaining the impetus for capital-intensive development (Seekings and Nattrass, 2005). Capital subsidies and high tariff barriers further encouraged mechanization, facilitating rising labour productivity but falling capital productivity and profitability over the apartheid period (Nattrass, 2014b).

South Africa was the engine of economic growth in Southern Africa and its mining industry sucked in migrant labour from across the region. For most of the twentieth century, development and poverty alleviation in Lesotho was almost entirely dependent on migrant remittances from South Africa (Gustafsson and Makonnen, 1993). The same was true in Botswana until its own mining sector took off in the 1970s (Colclough and McCarthy, 1980).

Rising population pressure in most of Africa resulted in falling agricultural productivity by the 1980s, increasing the supply of labour available for industry and reducing the gap between Asian and African wages (Karshenas, 2001: 324). Underemployment and open unemployment emerged in many African countries over the following decades (Baah-Boateng, 2015). In South Africa, open unemployment emerged from the mid-1970s as the result of a perfect storm of collapsed peasant agriculture, a growing population (and labour force), rising wages in mining and subsequently manufacturing (assisted also by the growing institutional power of organized labour as labour market institutions deracialized from the 1980s), and the slowdown in economic growth (Hofmeyr, 1994; Seekings and Nattrass, 2005). The economic effects reverberated through Southern Africa as migrant earnings fell, especially in Lesotho. By 1991 (the first year for which comparable international labour force data are available) between one-fifth and one-third of the labour force in Southern Africa was openly unemployed.

Figure 3.6 shows that about a quarter of the Southern African labour force was unemployed (actively looking for work). Lesotho was the only country to make a significant and sustained dent in the problem after 1991, helped by the

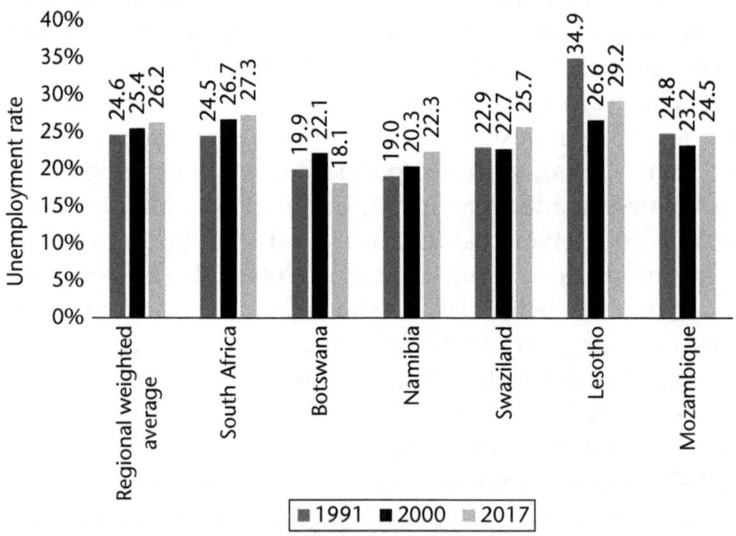

Figure 3.6 Unemployment in Southern Africa.

Source: World Development Indicators. Available at: http://data.worldbank.org/data-catalog/world-development-indicators.

development of a labour-intensive clothing manufacturing sector in the early 2000s (Chapter 4).

Colonial and post-colonial states in Southern Africa assumed that social networks and extended family structures would provide a social safety net of sorts where necessary. This social safety net, however, frayed over time as unemployment emerged as a persistent feature of the social and economic landscape, resulting in growing pressure on states to provide or expand social assistance. Social assistance programmes, focused on the elderly and disabled, and poor families with children, have proliferated across Southern Africa. Old-age pensions predated the 1990s in South Africa and its former colony Namibia, and were subsequently introduced in Botswana (1996), Lesotho (2004), and Swaziland (2005). Child grants of different kinds exist also in South Africa, Botswana, Lesotho, and Namibia. In Zambia and Zimbabwe, rising numbers of poor households, especially households comprising children and the elderly, are benefitting from cash transfer programmes. As has been widely documented, such programmes provide significant support for poor people in societies where the shortage of wage labour underpins much poverty (Garcia et al., 2012; Ferguson, 2015; World Bank, 2018). South Africa is an extreme case, spending over 3.5 per cent of GDP on social assistance to one in three South Africans (Seekings and Moore, 2014). In South Africa and Namibia, there have even been calls for the introduction of a Basic Income Grant for all citizens (Standing and Samson, 2003; Haarmann and Haarmann, 2012; Seekings and Matisonn, 2012).

The expansion of social assistance in Southern Africa is a response to the unemployment problem, but has also complicated it by affecting labour supply. Cash transfers can help finance job search, but there is also some evidence that they may be a disincentive to work, allowing people to wait for better-paying opportunities (Ranchhod, 2006; Seekings 2007; Woolard and Leibbrandt, 2013). Research from South Africa's relatively lush Eastern seaboard suggests that social grants might have helped facilitate a withdrawal from peasant agriculture as people aspired to better-paid employment in manufacturing and services (de la Hey and Beinart, 2017). The existence of a relatively high-wage formal sector clearly shapes the aspirations of unemployed people (see also Nattrass and Walker, 2005; Rankin and Roberts, 2011) and can affect labour supply decisions. Yet it is important to bear in mind that there is strong demand for low-wage work when it is available and that the unemployed have to rely primarily on indirect social assistance, notably living in a household with a pensioner, given the limited unemployment insurance available (Table 3.1). Generating a higher employment elasticity of growth by encouraging the expansion of labour-intensive jobs remains essential for inclusive development.

4

Trajectories of Development and the Global Clothing Industry

The clothing industry is the world's most labour-intensive manufacturing sector and was a key impetus for industrialization in many countries. It has been, and remains, an important focus of Lewis-like development, that is, rapid employment and output growth fuelled by a relatively low-wage labour-intensive manufacturing sector. Lewis's growth engine slows down when 'surplus' labour has been absorbed, prompting an increase in wages which in turn incentivizes firms to relocate to lower-wage regions or shift into capital- and skill-intensive activities. The national development 'trajectories' identified in Chapter 3 reflected to varying degrees such economy-wide processes of structural transformation as well as changes in productivity at the firm level.

This chapter uses UNIDO cross-country data to explore recent development trajectories for national clothing manufacturing industries (see also Nattrass and Seekings, 2018b). It begins with a brief history of the global clothing industry, touching on the transformation wrought by changing global regulation (notably the system of import quotas from 1974 followed by trade liberalization three decades later) and the rise of global value chains (GVCs).

It is often assumed that the dominance of low-wage Asian exporters in clothing GVCs mean that other countries need to move into economic niches higher up the value chain (for example into branded, high-end fashion production and retail) which are more capital- and skill-intensive and where barriers to entry facilitate higher profit margins. We draw on secondary sources to question any assumed necessary connection between upgrading and profitability, pointing out that firms can and do shift up and down the value chain when profitable opportunities arise. We also use UNIDO data to explore the assumed connection between economic upgrading (rising capital- and skill-intensity as reflected in rising labour productivity) and social upgrading (usually understood to mean higher wages). We show that trajectories of rising labour productivity growth ('upgrading') do indeed support wage increases, but this does not necessarily increase employment or profitability (in the sense of a rising share of income going to capital). We also question the negative connotations surrounding the term 'downgrading' (falling labour productivity) as this is associated with rising employment and can also drive higher wages and improved profitability.

4.1 Globalization and the Clothing Industry

As discussed in Chapter 2, the clothing manufacturing industry in the second half of the twentieth century came to play a key role in the early stages of industrialization, as a low-wage, labour-intensive sector producing for growing global markets. This had not been the case in the nineteenth or early twentieth centuries. Britain's industrial revolution had been capital-intensive, driven by the high costs of labour and low cost of energy, and involving primarily sectors where new technologies could rapidly raise labour productivity to compensate for high labour costs (Allen, 2009). Technological changes in clothing manufacture occurred relatively late, with the invention of power-driven sewing machines in the 1850s and electric sewing machines after 1889. Only at the very end of the nineteenth century were clothing factories able to outcompete independent producers. One consequence of this was that clothing production was almost all for domestic markets. In the early twentieth century, clothing production expanded in most industrialized countries, although the global clothing trade remained meagre.

This changed in the second half of the twentieth century. The technology (involving primarily electric sewing machines and, later, cloth-cutting machinery) was cheap and readily available and the modest skills required could generally be learned quickly. There was limited scope for major capital investments, with new technologies (such as computer-assisted design, marking, and cutting) being used mostly in the pre- and post-assembly stages of production. The only major change in the assembly stage—moving from production lines to 'modular' production in teams—did not involve any significant technological change. Rising incomes after the Second World War expanded rapidly the global market, whilst improved global communications and transport made it feasible for clothes to be produced and transported quickly, halfway across the world, to cater for consumers with fast-changing preferences. The result was, from the 1960s, an explosion of clothing exports from developing countries to the consumer markets of the industrialized economies of the global North.

Developing (i.e. low- and middle-income) countries accounted for a larger share of global clothing exports than in any other manufacturing sector. In 1963, 20 per cent of the clothing imported into the developed countries came from newly industrializing and developing countries. By 1976, their share had risen to 48 per cent. Moreover, the total value of these clothing exports from the global 'South' to the 'North' rose from US$0.3 billion p.a. to US$15 billion p.a. (in current prices) (De la Torre, 1984). In constant 2016 prices, the total value rose from $2.4 billion to $63 billion over just thirteen years.[1]

Rising exports from countries such as Hong Kong to the advanced industrial countries coincided with declining employment in the clothing industries in the latter countries. In the 1970s, these trends coincided also with growing unemployment across much of northwest Europe, fuelling demands for protection. From 1974 until 2005, global trade in clothing was structured by the Multi-Fibre Agreement/Arrangement (MFA) which introduced a quota regime (negotiated on a bilateral basis) affecting 73 developing countries, although most did not use their full quotas (Frederick and Staritz, 2012: 53). The hardest hit by the MFA were the large Asian exporters who found their access to European and North American markets severely curtailed. When country quotas were reached, Asian manufacturers searched for countries with under-utilized (or no) quotas and set up clothing manufacturing operations in Latin America, the Caribbean, and subsequently Africa (Lopez-Acevedo and Robertson, 2012). As Pickles et al. put it: these resulting 'geographies of quota-driven export production led to rapid expansion of low-wage employment in export platforms, border zones, special economic zones and green-field factories' (2015: 391), helping to kick-start processes of Lewis-like growth in developing countries. In Southern Africa, Chinese entrepreneurs from Taiwan and, subsequently, mainland China helped to develop clothing manufacturing industries in Mauritius, South Africa, and later Lesotho (Morris and Barnes, 2009; Morris et al., 2011; Godfrey, 2015; Morris and Staritz, 2017).

The 2000 US African Growth and Opportunities Act (AGOA) provided further impetus to the spread of labour-intensive clothing production in Africa. AGOA gave thirty-nine African countries duty- and quota-free access to the US. Kenya and more recently Ethiopia have benefitted the most from clothing exports to the US under AGOA (Wang et al., 2018). AGOA has strict rules of origin provisions but all African countries except South Africa qualify for its Third Country Fabric Provision which allows duty-free access to the US even if imported yarn and textiles were used in production. This provision was extended to 2025, giving African countries time to benefit from such preferential access to the US market and to build their own capacity in textile production (Wang et al., 2018). In 2001, the EU's 'Everything but Arms' initiative provided quota- and duty-free access to EU markets for producers in the least-developed countries (which further increased the attractiveness of

[1] Calculated using http://usinflationcalculator.com/.

low-income African countries for Asian clothing businesses seeking an entry into US and the EU).

In 1995, the Agreement on Clothing and Textiles brought the MFA under the rules of the World Trade Organization, with countries agreeing to the elimination of quotas by January 2005. The process was designed to be gradual, but most quotas were removed only at the end of 2004 (Kaplinsky and Morris, 2006). This sparked an abrupt reorganization of global clothing production in that the availability of suitable labour, wage and other costs, access to markets, domestic infrastructure, and industrial policy as well as participation in global production networks determined the global pattern of production and employment rather than quota restrictions. African countries struggled to maintain a foothold in the export market as clothing production shifted east.

China benefitted the most from the ending of the MFA, increasing its exports of clothing by 76 per cent between 2004 and 2006 (Cling et al., 2009: 242). This had a significant impact on employment (Figure 4.1). The top fifteen clothing-exporting countries (including Bangladesh, Cambodia, India, Indonesia, and Vietnam) increased their export share from 77.4 per cent to 84.6 per cent between 2004 and 2008 (Frederick and Staritz, 2012: 59). Relative labour costs were key in driving this outcome, but in a context shaped by a complex system of bilateral and regional trade agreements and preference schemes with specific textile and clothing clauses (Pickles et al., 2015: 391–8). Low-income countries like Bangladesh and Cambodia benefitted from such schemes and from participating in Asian production networks, especially after wages started to rise in China (Alam et al., 2017). They were helped after 2008 also by what Lopez-Acevedo and Robertson call the '*Walmart* effect' referring to the fact that whilst retail sales were generally repressed by the financial crisis, *Walmart* sales went up between 2008 and 2009 as consumers switched to purchasing cheaper clothes—benefitting low-cost producers in the process (2012: 221).

Sub-Saharan Africa was the biggest loser from the end of the MFA, as clothing employment and exports fell (Kaplinsky and Morris, 2009). Although Mauritius, Kenya, Madagascar, Egypt, and Ethiopia had lower labour costs per worker than China, productivity was lower and logistics costs significantly higher in these countries (Conway and Shah, 2011: 38). It was only once labour costs rose in China from the mid-2000s that African countries could (with the assistance of AGOA) gain a competitive foothold in clothing manufacturing (Wang et al., 2018). South Africa, where logistics performance was comparable to that of China, could not compete because labour costs were much higher than in China (ibid.) and because South African producers had less favourable access to US markets than firms elsewhere in Southern Africa, notably Lesotho.

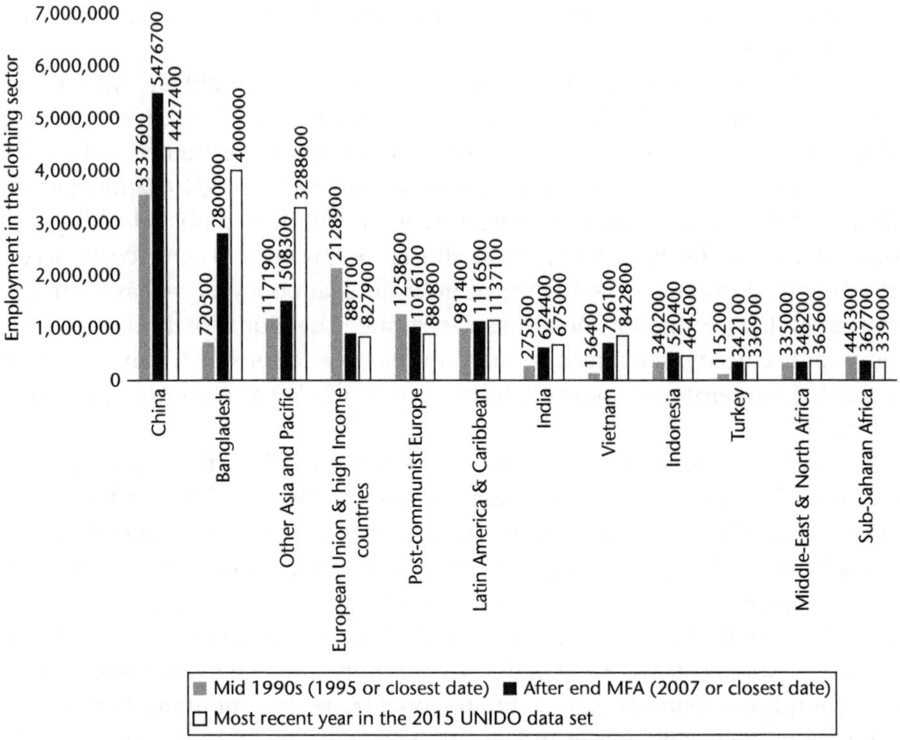

Figure 4.1 Global clothing employment before and after the MFA, major countries.

Note: These data are for formal employment only. European Union countries: Austria, Belgium, Denmark, Finland, France, Germany, Greece, Ireland, Italy, Luxembourg, Netherlands, Portugal, Spain, Sweden, United Kingdom; high-income countries: Australia, Canada, Cyprus, Israel, Japan, Malta, New Zealand, Norway, United States; post-communist countries: Azerbaijan, Bulgaria, Croatia, Czech Republic, Estonia, Georgia, Hungary, Kazakhstan, Kyrgyzstan, Latvia, Lithuania, Macedonia, Moldova, Poland, Romania, Russia, Slovakia, Slovenia, Tajikistan, Ukraine; Other Asia and the Pacific: Taiwan, Macau, Cambodia, Fiji, Korea, Malaysia, Mongolia, Nepal, Pakistan, Philippines, Singapore, Sri Lanka, Thailand; Latin America and Caribbean: Argentina, Brazil, Chile, Colombia, Dominican Republic, Ecuador, Honduras, Mexico, Panama, Peru, Trinidad and Tobago, Uruguay; Sub-Saharan Africa: Botswana, Cameroon, Gambia, Ghana, Ethiopia, Eritrea, Lesotho, Madagascar, Malawi, Mauritius, Nigeria, South Africa; Middle East and North Africa: Egypt, Iran, Iraq, Jordan, Kuwait, Lebanon, Morocco, Oman, Palestine, Qatar, Syria, Yemen.

Sources: INDSTAT4 (2015) available from UNIDO (https://stat.unido.org/) supplemented with industry sources for Bangladesh, Cambodia, Dominican Republic, and Pakistan.

Some high-wage countries were able to increase their exports of clothing after the end of the MFA, in particular Denmark, Switzerland, and the United Kingdom (Lopez-Acevedo and Robertson, 2012: 22) but they did so in the context of falling employment and accounted for a mere 2 per cent of global clothing employment. The only significant expansion of clothing employment in Europe after 2005 was in Turkey. We show later that Turkey's clothing industry was on a 'downgrading' trajectory in that it was accompanied by

Table 4.1 National profit shares in the clothing manufacturing industry by average wage and labour productivity

Average wage (in US dollars)	Labour productivity		
	Lowest third	Middle third	Upper third
Upper third		Malaysia (36.1%) Mauritius (30.6%) Romania (29.0%)	Ecuador (83.0%) Colombia (76.1%) Iran (64.5%) Lebanon (60.6%) Mexico (59.5%) Taiwan, China (58.8%) Russia (49.4%) South Africa (44.8%) Turkey (43.4%)
Middle third	Bulgaria (52.1%) Azerbaijan (42.9%) Georgia (38.0%)	China (68.6%) Thailand (58.1%) Palestine (53.4%) Moldova (47.0%) Macedonia (29.1%) Morocco (27.9%)	Yemen (80.7%) Jordan (78.5%) Pakistan (77.6%)
Lowest third	Eritrea (76.4%) Nepal (64.8%) Egypt (62.1%) India (55.4%) Madagascar (43.4%) Mongolia (37.8%) Vietnam (37.7%) Ethiopia (36.2%) Philippines (33.1%)	Indonesia (76.5%) Sri Lanka (74.9%) Peru (74.8%)	

Source: INDSTAT4 (2015). Profit share in parentheses.

falling labour productivity. It was nevertheless pro-labour in that the share of value-added going to labour (the total wage bill) rose as did average wages for an expanding workforce.

Table 4.1 uses data from UNIDO's INDSTAT4 (2015) database to classify developing country clothing industries (where data are available for wages, employment, and output) according to whether they were in the top, middle, or bottom third of countries with regard to average wages and labour productivity. Table 4.1 shows that countries cluster according to whether the industry in aggregate is competing on the basis of a relatively high-wage or low-wage trajectory. Countries in the bottom left corner (including India) have clothing industries that are in aggregate relatively labour-intensive (low wages and low labour productivity) and countries in the top right (including South Africa) have relatively skill- and capital-intensive industries (high wages and high labour productivity). Countries in the middle box (including China) compete primarily on the basis of having mid-level wages and mid-level labour productivity. No country falls simultaneously into the highest wage category and the lowest labour productivity category, or vice versa.

The ratio of wages to labour productivity is important for profitability. Dividing average wages (remuneration/employment) by labour productivity (value-added/employment) results in remuneration/value-added, otherwise known as the wage share of value-added or unit labour costs. If the wage share of value-added rises, this means that wages have been rising faster than labour productivity. As value-added comprises wages plus profits, subtracting the wage share from 1 results in the profit share of value-added.

$$\frac{\text{Profits}}{\text{Value-added}} = 1 - \frac{\text{Wages}}{\text{Value-added}} = 1 - \frac{\text{Average wage}}{\text{Labour Productivity}}$$
$$= 1 - \frac{\text{Wages/employment}}{\text{Value-added/employment}}$$

Table 4.1 reports the profit share in parentheses for the clothing manufacturing industry in each country. It shows that countries (including Pakistan) ranking in the top third of labour productivity and paying mid-level wages achieved relatively high profit shares. Countries (including Malaysia) paying relatively high wages and achieving mid-level labour productivity had relatively low profit shares.

China's continued dominance of the global apparel market was based on its ability to improve labour productivity as wages rose from the early 2000s, whilst keeping non-labour costs, including packing and shipping, very low. Table 4.1 shows that the ratio of wages to labour productivity was lower in China than India (as reflected in China's higher profit share). This reflected not only the capacity of Chinese entrepreneurs to improve labour productivity as wages rose from the early 2000s, but also the benefits of industrial policies that helped improve efficiency in other ways. Chinese investment in infrastructure resulted in shipping costs a third lower than India's. China's mega factory and single-product clusters facilitated enormous economies of scale, whereas Indian firms remained much smaller (Gereffi and Güler, 2010: 113–4).

India was able to expand clothing employment to become the world's third largest industry (after China and Bangladesh) by the mid-1990s, partly through expanding export-oriented contract manufacturing, but also by producing for the growing domestic market, thereby helping to support product development, design, and even branding (Abras, 2012). Indian 'upgrading' strategies benefitted from the presence of a large and diverse textile sector, government assistance, and the legacy of government policy towards the clothing industry. Up until the mid-1980s, clothing manufacturing was effectively restricted to small firms (through licensing regulations and restrictions on investment). Although this undermined the development of economies of scale, Tewari argues that it led to the creation and preservation of 'generalist skills—of the master tailor—at the heart of the Indian apparel industry'

(2005: 33). Small firms also learned 'to manage small batch production and variability in orders, efficiently' thereby placing India at an advantage later in terms of winning contracts from the higher-end retailers such as *Liz Claiborne*, *Ann Taylor* and *Abercombie & Fitch* (ibid.: 29). Some analysts conclude that this prevented the '*Walmart*ization' of the Indian clothing industry (Hirway, 2010: 171), thereby promoting differentiation within the industry and the retention of skills.

The Indian clothing manufacturing industry also has a large, lower-wage, lower-productivity informal sector accounting for the bulk of employment but less than a third of output (Abras, 2012: 109). This illustrates how the presence of a large, low-wage, labour-intensive clothing manufacturing segment does not necessarily stand in the way of upgrading elsewhere in the industry and can contribute significantly to job creation within the sector. Workers in the formal sector are unionized, have access to social security and earn higher wages than their informal sector counterparts (see e.g. Barrientos et al., 2010). According to Hirway, the clothing manufacturing industry is bifurcated between the production of 'low/medium value-added products' by contract workers and home-workers with 'relatively low skills and low productivity', and the production of higher value-added products by means of 'capital-intensive technology and a skilled and stable workforce' (Hirway, 2010: 173).

South Africa and Turkey fall into the relatively high wage, high labour productivity international cluster and have relatively low profit shares. Yet these countries had very different trajectories in the 2000s, with Turkey expanding employment (and labour-intensity) whereas in South Africa's case, the benefits of rising labour productivity were shared between capital and a shrinking pool of employed workers. We discuss their different trajectories further in section 4.3.

4.2 Value Chains and Firm Strategies

The post-MFA era presented producers in low- and middle-income countries with threats (notably competition from China) as well as opportunities to participate in GVCs and (over time) to move into market niches vacated by Chinese firms as Chinese wages increased. In the 1950s, when Lewis imagined a development path fuelled by low-wage labour-intensive industrialization, the image he probably had in mind was of an industrial sector producing a completed product for sale domestically and abroad. The rise of a global division of labour within the clothing industry, culminating in GVCs, opened up possibilities for firms in low-wage countries to compete in the production of components or intermediate products rather than finished products, and for industrial policies to focus on particular tasks and capabilities rather than entire industries (Cattaneo et al., 2013; OECD, 2013; Baldwin, 2014).

By the mid-2000s, over half of the world's manufactured imports were intermediate goods and more than half of export values were products traded through GVCs (Backer and Miroudot, 2013). As Gawande et al. put it evocatively, 'the iPhone's supply chain, which traverses more than ten countries for eventual assembly in China is the new "new"' (2014: 3). Even simple products, like the t-shirt, were caught up in GVCs, with cotton grown in the US, exported to China for the manufacturing of clothing and then shipped back to the US for imprinting with logos and marketing, and then shipped to developing countries as used garments or scrap textiles to be used as furniture padding (OECD, 2013: 10). The developing country share in global trade increased from 20 per cent in 1990 to over 40 per cent by 2015, with participation in GVCs contributing an estimated 28 per cent of their GDP on average and providing millions of jobs (Barrientos et al., 2016: 1214–15).

The clothing GVC emerged as a 'buyer-driven' value chain where powerful retailers in the US and the EU adopted global sourcing strategies (Gereffi, 1994). Some brand manufacturers have their own factories and retail stores (e.g. *Levis*) whereas others such as *Polo* and *Liz Claiborne* control the branding and marketing of their products but outsource the production entirely. Retailers deal directly with apparel manufacturers or with a sourcing agent who might even coordinate the entire supply chain. Giant contract manufacturers and traders such as *Foxconn* in electronics and *Li & Fung* in clothing have become increasingly important as supply chain coordinators and hence are powerful players in GVCs (Gereffi, 2014: 16).

The literature on GVCs emphasizes the unequal power relations within global supply chains and production networks. A central pioneering idea was that 'lead firms' (those in a position to set terms to other participating in the GVC) effectively 'govern' the value chain, allowing them to extract economic 'rents' (profits attained through market power) in the process (Gereffi, 1994). Clothing GVCs are 'buyer-driven' when dominated by mass marketers such as *Walmart* and *Target* as well as the more upmarket branded retailers (such as *Gap Inc.*) that were able to 'extract substantial profits from bringing together their design, sales, marketing and financial expertise with strong brand names and access to large consumer markets in developed countries' (Coe and Yeung, 2015: 10). Profit margins (sometimes referred to as 'rents' to emphasise a privileged position in the market) are typically assumed in the GVC literature to be greater higher up the value chain in the design and retail stages than in the manufacturing stage as these activities are supposedly 'protected by higher entry barriers and are the core competencies of lead firms, typically large global retailers and brand owners' (Frederick and Staritz, 2012: 47–8). As GVC analysis evolved, more attention was paid to the ownership structure of firms, characteristics of end markets (whether it is the US, or the EU, or more recently emerging and regional markets), and associated trade agreements and preference schemes, in shaping the sourcing strategies of retailers and the emergence of new, regional value chains (Pickles et al., 2015; Morris et al., 2016).

Depicting the clothing GVC as buyer-driven or buyer-governed highlights the power of those higher up the value chain to extract profits/rents and the dangers for firms (and country industries) of being located only within the ultra-competitive, labour-intensive, contract manufacturing sector, where barriers to entry are low. For example, the United Nations Conference on Trade and Development (UNCTAD) warned that:

> developing countries at an early stage of industrialization may become locked into low-value-added activities due to stiff competition from other suppliers to keep labor costs low, and because the tight control over intellectual property and expensive branding strategies of the lead firm block them from moving up the value chain. Even relatively successful middle-income countries do not face a level playing field in many of these networks.
>
> (OECD, 2013: 14; UNCTAD, 2014: x; see also 104–5)

The notion that countries may get 'locked into' low-margin segments of GVCs suggests that, rather than providing a first step on the development ladder, attempting Lewis-like development through the expansion of low-wage labour-intensive clothing employment (for example, in cut-make-and-trim contract manufacturing) could potentially condemn the country industry to a 'race to the bottom'. As discussed earlier, such analysis justifies and frames a particular vision for industrial policy (especially for middle-income countries) to help firms position themselves more favourably within GVCs by shifting 'up the value chain' into more capital- and skill-intensive activities, such as into own equipment manufacturing and even own-brand manufacturing where competition is assumed to be less intense (and profits accordingly higher). This includes, inter alia, moving into more sophisticated product lines ('product upgrading'), using superior technologies such as lean manufacturing to minimize inventories and reduce lead times ('process upgrading') and increasing the skills content of operations ('functional upgrading') (Humphrey and Schmitz, 2002). There is significant policy-relevant literature on the clothing industry based on this approach (see e.g. Kaplinsky et al., 2003; Gereffi and Fernandez-Stark, 2011; Frederick and Staritz, 2012: 50; Cattaneo et al., 2013; Gereffi, 2014: 18–19). In the strong 'upgrade or die' version 'upgrading is argued to be imperative, not only to capture increasing value within these global industries, but ultimately to survive within the industry' (Psilos and Gereffi, 2011: 3).

Some policy analysts distinguish between 'economic upgrading', that is, encouraging firms to improve productivity and enter into higher value-added niches within GVCs, and 'social upgrading', that is, improved working conditions, skills development and higher wages which in addition to improving productivity are socially desirable (e.g. Staritz, 2010; Barrientos et al., 2011a, 2011b; Fernandez-Stark et al., 2011; Gereffi and Fernandez-Stark, 2011; Gereffi, 2014). Social and economic upgrading is often portrayed as synergistic components of a 'high road' to growth: social upgrading incentivizes firms to upgrade their processes and products (to earn higher rents and achieve higher labour productivity to protect their profits from being eroded by higher wages); and higher valued-added production is more skill-intensive, thereby increasing the demand for skilled and better-paid workers. The ILO's argument for promoting decent work as a development strategy, discussed in Chapter 2, falls within this genre.

We have argued in preceding chapters that labour productivity growth (as an essential component of economic upgrading) supports higher wages but that growth trajectories characterized by rising average labour productivity are problematic in surplus labour countries, especially when premised on the destruction of lower-wage, labour-intensive jobs. Social upgrading, in such contexts, requires the expansion of labour-intensive jobs, an outcome which would be reflected in falling aggregate labour productivity (and even in falling average wages as new relatively low-wage employment expands). In Chapter 1 we argued for an approach of inclusive dualism in which industrial policies to improve labour productivity, skills, technological advancement etc. formed part of a differentiated strategy to promote competitiveness across a range of technologies whilst prioritizing the expansion of labour-intensive activities. The clothing industry is one of the few manufacturing industries that can offer entry-level jobs to unskilled men and (especially) women. Upgrading reduces the capacity of the industry to generate additional jobs out of growth and there is evidence that industrial upgrading is biased against the employment of women (Tejani and Milberg, 2016). As illustrated by the Turkish case (discussed further below), falling labour productivity (associated with rising labour-intensity) is not necessarily a 'low' (in the negative normative sense of the word) road in that it can be associated with both rising employment and wages as well as new employment opportunities for women with few, if any, other alternatives.

Whilst it is obviously the case that contract cut-make-and-trim clothing manufacturing is highly competitive and there is potentially greater space for profit higher up the value chain, this does not mean that upgrading necessarily supports higher profits (as often assumed in the GVC literature). More than a decade ago Pickles et al. pointed out that 'it remains an empirical issue as to whether... relative changes in position in international value chains reflect significantly on the financial position and regional impacts of specific firms' (2006: 2319). There is no systematic cross-country analysis of profitability within GVCs, yet there is a growing number of case studies suggesting that opportunities for profitable production emerge at various points along GVCs and that upgrading is not necessarily always economically optimal. For example, Gibbon showed that Mauritian clothing firms that adopted classic GVC 'upgrading' strategies in the 1990s by upgrading functionally into own-design and own-brand manufacturing discovered that this was a costly and unsuccessful strategy because Mauritius was 'simply too far from end markets to set, or even closely follow, fashion trends' (2008: 45). By contrast, firms that retained capacity in Mauritius for higher-value-added production with short lead times whilst opening satellite operations in lower-cost Madagascar—that is, followed a 'downgrading' strategy—were more successful. They were able to 'offer a broader mix of products with a wider range of price points and lead times to a wider range of customers, including some who, on this basis, offered them better contractual conditions (i.e. greater stability of demand) than they had enjoyed previously' (ibid.: 45; see also Gibbon, 2004: 155–6). Recent research indicates that firm strategy with regard to choice of end market and positioning within regional or international value chains is influenced in complex and dynamic ways by firm ownership and national strategy (e.g. Morris and Staritz, 2014; Morris et al., 2016).

The GVC approach evolved to focus increasingly on dynamic coordination within value chains (e.g. Gereffi et al., 2005) but remained vulnerable to criticisms that it still paid insufficient attention to broader business objectives and profitability (e.g. Gibbon, 2008), was overly determinist and failed to appreciate the role of agency (specially the way that firms engaged in flexible, dynamic strategic coupling with other firms), history, geography (especially proximity to export markets), and place-specific cultural and institutional conditions (see e.g. Henderson et al., 2002; Pickles et al., 2006; Coe et al., 2008; Gibbon, 2008: 37–47; Coe and Yeung, 2015). The extent of local ownership (or embeddedness) of a developing country's clothing industry and implications of this for social and economic upgrading is a growing field of research (Barrientos et al., 2016). Staritz and Whitfield (2017) emphasize the diversity of ownership in the Ethiopian clothing industry and the developmental benefits of locally owned firms participating in export production. Godfrey (2015) and Morris and Staritz (2017) found that Taiwanese exporters in Lesotho were linked into international value chains in ways that incentivized them to focus on extracting AGOA-related rents through the production of relatively low-wage products rather than moving up the value chain. They argue that greater potential existed for upgrading strategies in firms located within regional value chains, many of whom had moved to Lesotho to avoid higher wage costs in South Africa.

Precisely where, and how, opportunities for profitable engagement function within value chains remains a relatively underdeveloped but important area for research. As Gibbon concluded, 'to play a useful ongoing role in GVC theory, our understanding of upgrading trajectories should be clearly tied to empirical findings regarding the conditions that allow supplier profitability, while at the same time recognizing that these are subject to continuous transformation' (2008: 46).

Whilst it is likely that rents are easier to extract through branding and retail than they are in the contract clothing manufacturing sector (where there are fewer barriers to entry and hence competition is fiercer), profits potentially exist at all points along the value chain, and flexible dynamic firms are always alert to these possibilities. Pickles et al. (2006) showed that manufacturers in Eastern and Central Europe produced for lead firms, developed their own brands, and included low-value products and high-value products in their portfolios. Tokatli (2013) showed a similar flexibility amongst Turkish producers. For example, *Erak* produced and retailed its own branded products (*Mavi Jeans*) whilst continuing to offer full package manufacturing services to many international retailers including *Esprit, Calvin Klein, Armani, Timberland* and *Tommy Hilfiger* (Tokatli, 2013: 998–9). Clothing firms in Turkey, China, and India adopted different strategies for different markets, notably contract manufacturing (sometimes owning their own equipment, sometimes not) with regard to apparel exports, but including also own-brand manufacturing capabilities in their home markets (Frederick and Staritz, 2012: 51). *Mithat,* which also produced its own brands for the Turkish market, continued to provide full package services for fast fashion outlets *H&M* and *Zara* as it expanded into cut-make-and-trim operations in Morocco for *Gap Inc.* (Tokatli, 2013: 999).

Fast fashion retailers develop products inspired by the most promising trends in fashion shows and magazines. They work with manufacturers (some of them in-house factories, others outsourced) to produce clothes quickly for the mass market. They use increasingly sophisticated electronic monitoring systems to adjust volumes, colour etc., continually restock and alter product lines throughout the year, and sell at affordable prices (Caro and Martinez-de-Albéniz, 2015). The pioneer of fast fashion was *Zara*, part of the Spanish group *Industria de Diseno Textil* (*Inditex*). *Zara* illustrates the dynamism and flexibility that is increasingly evident in GVCs. As of the early 2000s, *Zara* was able to design, produce, and deliver a new garment and put it on display in its stores worldwide in a mere fifteen days (Ferdows et al., 2004: 1). Rapid restocking and changing products encouraged customers to pay the full price for clothes they liked rather than wait for seasonal sales. This allowed *Zara* to collect 85 per cent of the full ticket price on its retail clothing, when the industry average was 60 to 70 per cent (ibid.: 2), thereby achieving a net margin on sales of 10.5 per cent as opposed to 7 per cent for *H&M* and near zero for *Gap Inc.* (ibid.: 1–2). Another element of the *Zara* model was careful monitoring of consumer responses and feedback at the store level, and using this information to determine orders and to guide new designs (Tokatli, 2008: 29).

In the early 2000s, *Zara* maintained strong control over its factories, many of which were in Spain, prompting industry commentators to hope that the fast fashion model might keep clothing producers in the higher-wage, European countries—the idea (common in the upgrading policy literature) being that higher labour costs there would be more than compensated for by faster turnaround times, lower inventory costs, higher quality etc. (discussed in Tokatli, 2008). By the late 2000s, however, *Zara*'s supply line extended across a larger range of countries including Turkey, China, India, Pakistan, Bangladesh, Sri Lanka, Indonesia, Morocco, Vietnam, and Lithuania—a development Tokatli attributed to the growth of new competencies in low-wage countries to manufacture intricately worked, high-quality garments (ibid.: 25). Tokatli noted that the capacity of low-wage producers to move into the luxury end of the market had become 'painfully obvious with the proliferation of counterfeit versions of luxury goods, manufactured by Chinese and other partially industrialized country firms, that were, at least to an untrained eye, indistinguishable from the originals' (ibid.). Retailers in the advanced capitalist countries increasingly noticed that countries such as India and Turkey were 'exactly where quality is to be found, because of the availability of a large supply of highly skilled tailors' who had moved out of small businesses and into the larger companies. In the case of *Zara*, 'instead of *Zara* changing the geography of jobs, the geography of competencies and jobs... changed *Zara*' (ibid.: 22).

The *Zara* case illustrates how new models and competencies can emerge quickly in clothing GVCs and that niche markets higher up GVCs are never entirely safe. This provides additional support for a diversified industrial strategy that is alert to changing economic conditions and provides support across a range of business strategies and technologies, whether this be upgrading or downgrading.

In South Africa, prior to the 1990s, large clothing producers, such as *Kingsgate* in Durban and *Rex Truform* in Cape Town, essentially decided what to produce and sold their output through a large network of small High Street retailers. As Graham Choice (*Prestige Clothing*) put it, the large producers 'dictated terms to the retailers'.[2] It was a good example of a domestic 'producer-driven' value chain. This changed with the global development of fast fashion models and the opening up of the South African clothing manufacturing industry to competition from imports. The large clothing producers

[2] Discussion, 21 January 2013.

did not survive the abrupt reduction in tariffs and large retailers emerged with the market power to source designs and supplies from around the world, shifting the power dynamics within the industry from producers to retailers. By the early 2000s, the South African domestic retail sector was highly concentrated, with a handful of national retail chains accounting for between 60 and 70 per cent of domestic sales (Robbins et al., 2004: 15). The subsequent entry of large supermarkets like *Pick n Pay* into the clothing retail sector, speciality stores, branded franchises, and informal markets subsequently challenged this dominance. Yet, as of 2012, the top six retail companies (*Edcon, Truworths, Mr Price, Pepkor, Woolworths,* and *Foschini*) still accounted for almost half (44 per cent) of domestic retail value (Euromonitor International, 2013: 7).

South Africa's largest value retailer, *Mr Price,* opened its first shop in 1985 and then rapidly expanded during the 1990s. By 1995 there were 237 stores throughout the country[3] and as of the mid-2010s it had retail outlets all over Southern Africa. *Mr Price* targets the sixteen to twenty-four-year-old mostly middle-class market, or in the language of the South African Advertising Research Foundation, Living Standards Measure (LSM) 6 to 10. The ten LSM categories are widely used by retailers and the advertising industry regularly provides information by LSM category about education, household assets, and consumer preferences. LSM 6–10 comprises 56 per cent of the adult population, two-thirds of whom are in LSM 6 and 7.[4] *Mr Price* draws on local, regional, and international value chains for its products. *Edcon,* another South African clothing retail giant, owns a range of branded outlets targeted at different parts of the South African consumer market. For example, *Jet* aims at the lower- and middle-segments of the market (LSM 4–7), whereas *Edgars,* like *Mr Price,* targets LSM 6–10.[5] They all adopt eclectic sourcing strategies, balancing price and quality depending on the product.

Some South African retailers (like *Foschini* and *Fashion World*) have some in-house design and production capacity as well as long-standing relationships with a range of cut-make-and-trim operations in different regions. According to industry sources, relatively small, metro-based firms are typically given contracts for the manufacture of quality products for the top end of the market, especially fashionable items requiring a quick turnaround from order to delivery. For other orders, South African retailers typically make use of

[3] 'The *Mr Price* story', available at: http://mrpricegroup.com/getmedia/ae33d50f-f34f-4cec-a2e1-ef10ee34101c/Mr-Price-history.pdf.aspx.

[4] See information about LSMs at: http://saarf.co.za/lsm-presentations/2012/LSM%20Presentation%20-%20February%202012.pdf.

[5] Factsheet September to December 2014. Available at: http://www.edcon.co.za/pdf/fact_sheet/factsheet_september_december_2014.pdf?1;

See information about LSMs in: http://saarf.co.za/lsm-presentations/2012/LSM%20Presentation%20-%20February%202012.pdf.

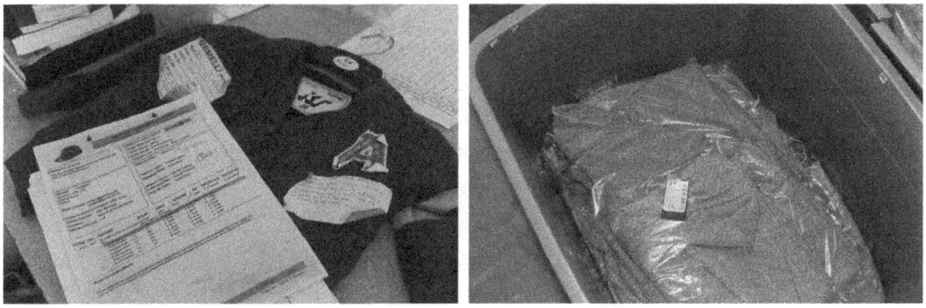

Figure 4.2 A cut-make-and-trim sample for an order for *Mr Price* via the design house (*Gemelli*) and a completed order for *Jet* ready for shipment from Newcastle to the retailers.

'design houses' which function as middlemen between low-cost, high-volume producers and the retailers.

Design houses obtain designs from the retailers or obtain designs from overseas and market them to the retailers. When an order is secured, they purchase materials, produce patterns and request cut-make-and-trim clothing manufacturers to tender for the business. Design houses evolved in part to provide supply chain coordination for the large retailers, and in part to enable the retailers to have an arm's-length relationship with low-wage producers (giving them some fig leaf of deniability when challenged about sourcing products from firms paying below the legal minimum wage). Figure 4.2 depicts an order for a cut-make-and-trim firm in Newcastle from the Durban-based design house *Gemelli* for delivery to *Mr Price*. It also shows a completed order, awaiting final packaging and shipment to the value retailer *Jet*. The firm, once it gets the order, is responsible for making the garment, attaching the retailer's tags, wrapping each garment in plastic, placing them in boxes and loading them onto trucks. Any delays risk the imposition of stiff fines and even cancellation of the order (leaving the firm in debt to the design house for the material used).

There is some evidence that clothing producers accept contracts from design houses and then sub-contract parts of the production process to smaller cut-make-and-trim operations, though the extent of this practice is unclear (see e.g. Altman, 1996: 394; Todes, 2002: 386; Rogerson, 2010). According to interviews with industry sources in 2011 and 2012, some firms, who are paying the legal minimum wages, sub-contract aspects of clothing manufacturing production (and sometimes even complete garments) to non-compliant firms, and they do this both directly and indirectly via the design houses.

The design house typically takes a mark-up of 40 per cent over the price paid to the producer to cover costs of material inputs, design plus a profit margin

(Mauda, 2014: 6). Judging from the orders and final prices of products produced in Newcastle, the mark-up between the design house and the retailer varies from 100 per cent for the value retailers targeting low- and middle-income consumers, to over 300 per cent for stores like *Edgars*, which offer strongly branded items to the upper-middle and top end of the clothing market. High mark-ups, however, do not necessarily translate into high profits for retailers. In December 2018, *Edcon*, the group that owns *Edgars* and *Jet*, asked the big shopping malls for a large discount on the rent it paid for its retail space to prevent large-scale closures and job losses (Child, 2018). High mark-ups are necessary to cover the cost of retail space, shop assistants and corporate overheads, and if these costs rise and/or retail sales slump, retail profits can quickly turn to losses. It is unwise to assume that retailers are the most profitable part of the value chain.

4.3 'Upgrading' and National Development Trajectories in the Clothing Manufacturing Industry

Robertson (2012) was the first to identify various national development trajectories for the clothing manufacturing industry in the period since the end of the MFA. In his analysis, some countries 'downgraded', meaning that they expanded the very labour-intensive end of the clothing manufacturing industry and/or expanded into the lower-value-added products, whereas others 'upgraded' by becoming more capital- and skill-intensive, and producing a greater share of higher-valued products. He also distinguished between trajectories in which employment expanded and those where it contracted (see Table 4.2). Thus, for example, both Pakistan and the Caribbean were classified as having adopted a downgrading trajectory but employment expanded in the former and fell in the latter. India and Mauritius followed an upgrading trajectory but with rising employment in the former and falling employment in the latter.

Table 4.2 National trajectories in the clothing manufacturing sector

	Rising employment	Falling employment
UPGRADING (more capital-intensive, higher-valued products)	Bangladesh, China, India, Vietnam	Hong Kong, South Korea, Malaysia, Mauritius, Singapore, Sri Lanka, Taiwan, Thailand, Morocco, Turkey
DOWNGRADING (more labour-intensive, lower-valued products) or no change	Cambodia, Indonesia, Pakistan	Caribbean, Honduras, Sub-Saharan Africa, Mexico, Romania

Source: Robertson (2012: 29–30).

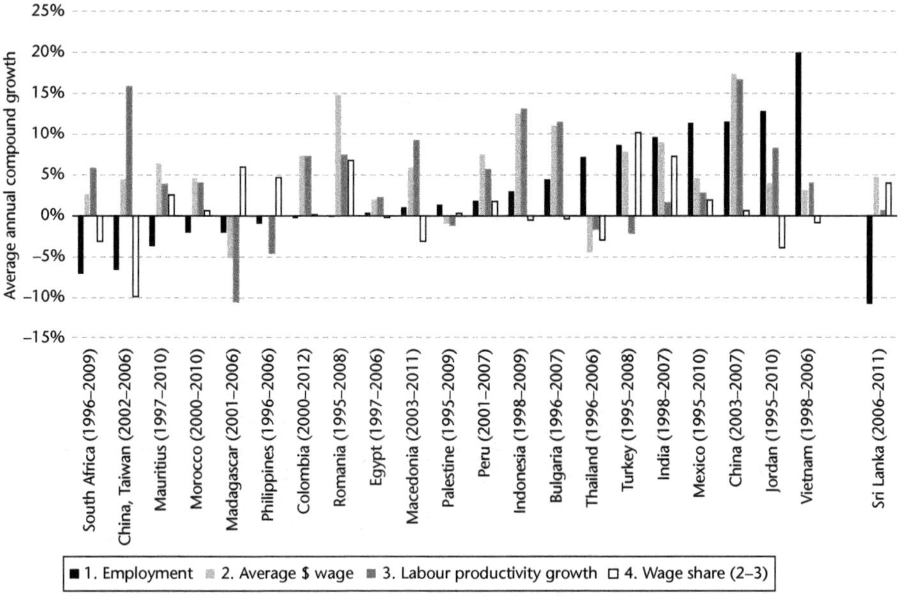

Figure 4.3 National clothing manufacturing industry trajectories in middle-income countries.

Note: Average annual compound growth in employment, average wages, labour productivity, and the wage share (from the mid-1990s to the most recent year post-2005 that data were available).

Source: INDSTAT4 (2015), available from UNIDO (https://stat.unido.org/).

Robertson's typology is innovative in that it attempts to link the experience of employment creation to different development trajectories. Yet his analysis is not based on systematic analysis of cross-country data and does not speak to the implications for average wages and the distribution of value-added between labour and capital. We use UNIDO's INSTAT4 (2015) database in an attempt to remedy this.

To keep the analysis of national clothing industry trajectories manageable, Figure 4.3 reports trends in middle-income countries that have a sizeable clothing manufacturing sector (at least 10,000 employees).[6] It reports average annual compound growth rates from 1995 (or the closest available year during the MFA period) to the most recent year that data are available for employment, labour productivity (value-added/employment), and the wage share

[6] A sizeable clothing sector does not necessarily mean a high proportion of clothing employment in total manufacturing. The share of clothing in manufacturing employment (for the end period listed for each country) varied from less than 10 percent (China, China (Taiwan), Egypt, India, Mexico, South Africa) to between 10 and 20 percent (Colombia, Indonesia, Jordan, Palestine, Peru, Philippines, Romania, Turkey, Vietnam) to over 20 percent (Bulgaria, Macedonia, Madagascar, Mauritius, Morocco, and Sri Lanka).

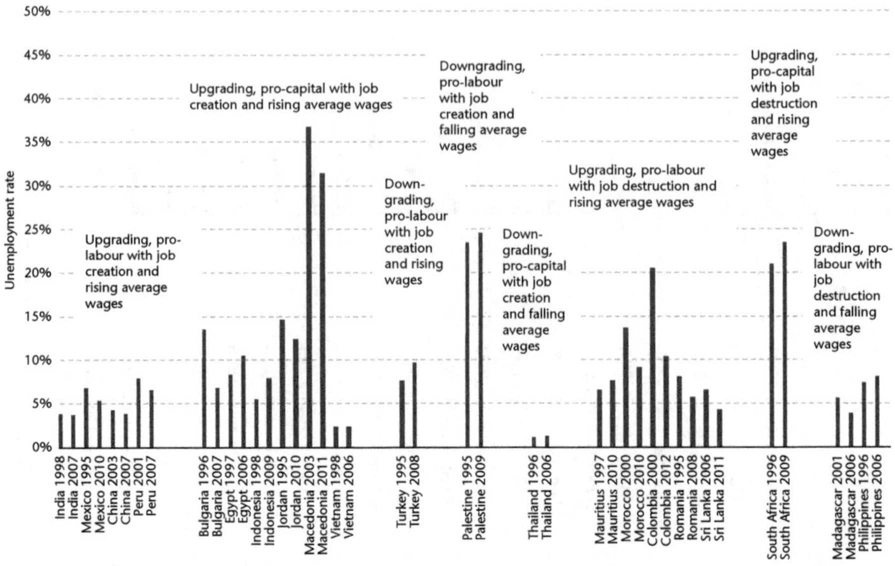

Figure 4.4 Development trajectories for the clothing manufacturing industry in middle-income countries in the context of national unemployment rates.

Note: Taiwan (upgrading, pro-capital with job destruction and rising wages) does not appear as no World Bank data are available on the unemployment rate.

Source: INDSTAT4 (2015), available from UNIDO (https://stat.unido.org/) and World Development Indicators (http://data-worldbank.org/data-catalog/world-development-indicators).

(wages and salaries/value-added) post-2005. Figure 4.4 arranges country results in order of smallest to largest employment growth. It includes trends for Sri Lanka (separately) as the only available data are from 2006 (after the end of the MFA) to 2011. Figure 4.4 shows that there were multiple trajectories (combinations of wage and productivity growth) shaping the employment outcomes in the clothing sector.

South Africa experienced the greatest percentage loss in employment of all countries for which data are available both before and after the end of the MFA. Table 4.3 provides data from the 2008 and 2014 South African manufacturing survey, illustrating that this trend continued.

Table 4.3 shows that firms in South Africa's composite 'Textiles, Clothing, Leather and Footwear' (SIC 31) sector were substantially more labour-intensive than the average manufacturing firm in South Africa (see also Tregenna, 2010). The textile sector produces fabric and yarn and is much more capital-intensive than clothing production. Whereas it took R150,000 of capital equipment to provide a job in manufacturing as a whole, in 2008, the corresponding amount was R28,000 in textiles, clothing, leather, and footwear, and a mere R10,000 in clothing manufacturing. Clothing accounted for less than half a per cent

Table 4.3 Key indicators: South African clothing and manufacturing industries

	2008			2014		
	Clothing (SIC 314)*	Textiles, clothing, leather, and footwear (SIC 31)	Total Manu-facturing	Clothing (SIC 314)*	Textiles, clothing, leather, and footwear (SIC 31)	Total Manu-facturing
Salaries & wages (R billion) (% of total expenditure)	R2.7 billion (19.2%)	R8.1 billion (18.7%)	R146.7 billion (10.4%)	R3.3 billion (17.7%)	R7.9 billion (17.4%)	R218.3 billion (10.8%)
Employment (% manufacturing)	73,642 (5.5%)	168,912 (12.5%)	1,344,170 (100%)	63,646 (5.2%)	113,186 (9.5%)	1,190,436 (100%)
Average weekly wage (2008 data in 2014 prices)	R696 (R968)	R918 (R1,276)	R2,098 (R2,917)	R1,007	R1,336	R3,527
Turnover/employment (2008 data in 2014 prices)	R183,224 (R254,719)	R250,586 (R348,366)	R1,063,049 (R1,477,856)	R297,238	R408,399	R1,775,947
Net profit after tax (2008 data in 2014 prices) (R million)	R67 (R93)	R406 (R564)	R114,952 (R159,807)	R777	R1,619	R93,984
Net profit margin (net profit after tax/ turnover)	0.5%	1.0%	8.0%	4.1%	3.5%	4.4%
Value of plant, machinery and equipment (R million)	R701 mil	R4,652 mil	R201,367 mil	N/A	N/A	N/A
Capital: labour	R9,519	R27,541	R149,808	N/A	N/A	N/A

*SIC 314 is the 'apparel' (clothing) industry. It is a sub-sector of 'textiles, clothing, and footwear' (SIC 31).

Sources: StatsSA, Manufacturing Industry: Financial Report No. 30-20-30 (2008, published 2010). Available at: http://statssa.gov.za/publications/Report-30-02-03/Report-30-02-032008.pdf; StatsSA, Manufacturing Industry: Financial, 2014, Report number 30-02003 (2014) 26 September 2016. Available at: http://statssa.gov.za/publications/Report-30-02-03/Report-30-02-032014.pdf.

of total capital stock in manufacturing, yet was responsible for about 5 per cent of total employment and 2 per cent of salaries and wages.

Average wages are lower in clothing production than for the manufacturing sector as a whole, reflecting the lower labour productivity characteristic of labour-intensive production. Turnover divided by employment is a rough indicator of labour productivity. Table 4.3 shows that the clothing manufacturing sector is about three-quarters the level in the textiles, clothing, leather, and footwear sector. Clothing manufacturing is a highly competitive sector and profit margins are typically low (and often seasonally fluctuating). Whereas the average profit margin (net profit after tax/total income) was 8 per cent in 2008 for manufacturing as a whole, it was only 1 per cent for the textile, clothing, and footwear sector, and a mere 0.5 per cent for clothing.

Not only is employment relatively inexpensive to generate (in terms of the necessary capital investment) in the clothing manufacturing industry, but the sector also has strong employment and growth multipliers—that is, the industry stimulates employment and output elsewhere (DTI, 2011: 22). This is because it has backward linkages into textiles, forward linkages into retail, and displaces imports that would otherwise exercise a drain on foreign exchange reserves. The clothing manufacturing industry is thus a valuable industry for a small, open, high-unemployment country like South Africa. Yet (and consistent with UNIDO data in Figure 4.4) Table 4.3 shows that employment has been falling in this sector as real wages and profitability rose along with labour productivity.

Our analysis allows us to revisit Robertson's notion of country trajectories for the clothing manufacturing sector, this time including information about wages and labour productivity. We identify development trajectories for national clothing manufacturing industries in terms of performance in employment, labour productivity, average wages, and the wage (and profit) share. These are summarized in Table 4.4 and Figure 4.4 (which also presents data on national unemployment rates). Robertson found that clothing manufacturing in China, India, and Vietnam became more capital-intensive (experienced economic upgrading) as employment rose. Our analysis is consistent with this as it shows rising labour productivity (a trend to be expected when the industry becomes more capital-intensive on aggregate) in these countries. We also show that clothing manufacturing in these countries (as was characteristic of clothing manufacturing in all countries experiencing rising labour productivity, i.e. upgrading) also delivered rising average wages.

When average wages rise faster than labour productivity, the share of value-added going to labour (the wage share) will rise and the share going to capital (the profit share) will fall. We classify such trajectories as 'pro-labour'. Pro-capital trajectories are those where labour productivity rises faster than

Table 4.4 Labour productivity and wages in the clothing manufacturing industry: different trajectories revisited*

	JOB CREATION Rising employment	JOB DESTRUCTION Falling employment
UPGRADING: PRO-LABOUR Rising labour productivity and rising wage share (falling profit share)	*With rising average wages* India, Mexico, China, Peru	*With rising average wages* Mauritius, Morocco, Colombia, Romania, Sri Lanka
UPGRADING: PRO-CAPITAL Rising labour productivity and falling wage share (rising profit share)	*With rising average wages* Bulgaria, Egypt, Indonesia, Jordan, Macedonia, Vietnam	*With rising average wages* South Africa, Taiwan
DOWNGRADING: PRO-LABOUR Falling labour productivity, rising wage share (falling profit share)	*With rising average wages* Turkey *With falling average wages* Palestine	*With falling average wages* Madagascar, Philippines
DOWNGRADING: PRO-CAPITAL Falling labour productivity, falling wage share (rising profit share)	*With falling average wages* Thailand	

* This analysis is based on data from mid-1990s to most recent year post-2005 for which data are available—see Figure 4.4.

average wages, resulting in a rise in the profit share (and a fall in the wage share). Table 4.4 follows Robertson in distinguishing further between trajectories in national clothing manufacturing industries that deliver rising or falling employment.

India, Mexico, China, and Peru experienced pro-labour upgrading development trajectories that delivered rising average wages to an expanding workforce. But pro-labour outcomes were also consistent with job destruction, that is, higher wages for fewer workers (Mauritius, Morocco, Colombia, Romania, and Sri Lanka). Upgrading trajectories were characterized by rising average wages, but in some cases delivered employment growth (Bulgaria, Egypt, Indonesia, Jordan, Macedonia, Vietnam) and in other cases job destruction (South Africa and Taiwan). Downgrading trajectories were also diverse, sometimes delivering falling wages and employment and sometimes rising wages and employment (as in Turkey).

The developmental relevance of these different trajectories in the clothing manufacturing depends on the broader economic context. Notably, where labour market conditions are relatively tight, meaning unemployment is low and falling, the potential economic costs of a pro-labour upgrading trajectory for the industry (slower capital accumulation resulting from a falling profit share and a lower employment elasticity of growth) are of little importance. Figure 4.4 shows that the countries with upgrading pro-labour trajectories in clothing manufacturing that delivered both rising average wages and employment (India, Mexico, China, and Peru) did so against a backdrop of generally low and falling unemployment. With the exception of Egypt and Indonesia, countries pursuing upgrading pro-capital trajectories also delivered rising average wages and employment in the context of falling unemployment. Only in the case of Macedonia (one of the high-unemployment (surplus labour) countries identified in Chapter 3), was this upgrading outcome possibly questionable from a developmental point of view, given that a more labour-intensive (downgrading) trajectory could have delivered more jobs per unit of output. Even so, the fact that clothing manufacturing was delivering rising average wages and employment—as well as placing more value-added in the hands of capital (rising profit share)—suggests that the prospects for sustained capital accumulation (funded out of profits) and continued job creation were good.

The other three countries reported in Figure 4.4 with unemployment over 10 per cent were Colombia, Morocco, and South Africa, all of whom had upgrading trajectories. Clothing manufacturing in all three countries experienced rising average wages and job destruction, though in Colombia and Morocco, the trajectory was pro-labour (associated with a rising wage share) and in South Africa it was pro-capital (associated with a rising profit share). The shift away from labour-intensive clothing production in these countries was developmentally questionable given high background levels of unemployment, although at least in the case of Colombia and Morocco, unemployment was on a downward trend. In South Africa, by contrast, the development trajectory for the clothing manufacturing industry delivered a higher share of value-added to capital—and rising average wages for significantly fewer workers—against a backdrop of high and rising unemployment. We argue in Chapter 6 that this was a function of rising minimum wages, especially for the relatively low-cost non-metropolitan producers, in the face of growing international competition. In some cases, large firms split up their production units to take advantage of regional wage differentials, keeping orders requiring skilled workers and where quality was more of an issue than price in South Africa, and opening production units in lower-cost Lesotho (Skinner and Valodia, 2002: 61; Staritz and Morris, 2011: 9). Between 2006 and 2010, clothing exports from Lesotho to South Africa increased twenty-fold (from R17 million to R335 million) (Staritz and Morris, 2011: 9), facilitated by direct relationships between South African-owned and South African market-directed firms in Lesotho and South African retailers (Morris et al., 2011: 105). South Africa's upgrading trajectory thus assisted and reflected Lewis-like growth in Lesotho.

Robertson classifies the Indonesian clothing manufacturing industry as having expanded employment through a downgrading strategy, that is, becoming more labour-intensive (see Table 4.2). We find, however, that labour productivity increased along with average real wages and employment, hence we classify this as an upgrading trajectory. The overall share of value-added going to wages declined (and the profit share rose) because labour productivity rose faster than wages.

Robertson classified Turkey's clothing manufacturing industry as having experienced economic upgrading and falling employment, but the data available for our analysis suggests that Turkey managed to recover and expand the number of clothing manufacturing jobs (in relatively labour-intensive activities) in the post-MFA context, resulting in an overall downgrading trajectory. This trajectory delivered rising average wages and a rising wage share (hence we classify it as pro-labour). Employment expanded for women, some of them working at home, others in workers' co-operatives, performing relatively labour-intensive embroidery and embellishments for fast fashion items (Tokatli et al., 2011). Such labour-intensive sub-contracting is associated with 'low-road' labour practices, yet as Tokatli et al. observe, it facilitated income earning (and empowerment) for women living in a context where working outside of the home or their neighbourhoods was socially unacceptable (ibid.: 1212). The Turkish clothing industry is deeply embedded in GVCs supplying the US and the EU, but also, increasingly its own domestic market (Pickles et al., 2015).

Figure 4.4 shows that the clothing manufacturing industry in Sri Lanka suffered a large decrease in employment between 2006 and 2011. Sri Lanka is an interesting case because the government embarked on a major policy initiative to assist the clothing manufacturing industry to move up the value chain in order to remain competitive in the post-MFA world (Savchenko, 2012). Clothing manufacturing in Sri Lanka originally expanded in the 1970s when 'quota hopping' and government incentives (such as duty-free imports of inputs and capital goods and freedom to expatriate profits) brought East Asian clothing exporters (mostly from Hong Kong) and European investors to the country (Lopez-Acevedo and Robertson, 2012: 442–3). In 2002, the Sri Lankan government sought to reposition the industry through a five-year upgrading strategy. The central objective was to shift away from contract clothing manufacturing to the provision of fully integrated services, to focus on 'high value-added apparel instead of low-cost apparel' and to establish 'an international reputation as a superior manufacturer in four product areas: sportswear, casual wear, children's wear and intimate apparel' (Savchenko, 2012: 172). Upgrading took place along every dimension and significant resources were channelled into enhancing firm and worker capabilities.

Many Sri Lankan clothing firms established their own design centres 'with in-house designers that work closely with the design teams of brand owners, interpreting their designs, making suggestions, sometimes giving them ideas' (Lopez-Acevedo and Robertson, 2012: 449). Employment fell as the industry 'consolidated' around large firms, upgraded its technology, implemented lean manufacturing and shifted into niche markets like lingerie and swimwear (Savchenko, 2012: 170, 178). The large manufacturer *MAS* established its own-brand (*Amante*) and opened design studios in the United Kingdom, the US, and Hong Kong to offer design solutions to its main customers *Victoria's Secret, Gap Inc.* and *Speedo* (Lopez-Acevedo and Robertson, 2012: 449). Sri Lankan clothing manufacturers subsequently opened factories in Jordan, Kenya, Madagascar, Mauritius, Bangladesh, India, and elsewhere in South Asia (ibid.: 182).

Sri Lanka's 'proactive' industrial strategy has been hailed as a success, often contrasted with that of Cambodia (which is regarded as continuing with a 'low-road' to growth) or Sub-Saharan Africa, where policymakers are depicted as largely inert (e.g. Savchenko, 2012). Yet Sri Lanka's clothing manufacturing industry continued to shed jobs post-2006. This suggests that despite being on a pro-labour trajectory (rising wage share) the benefits going to labour went to a shrinking pool of workers, thereby limiting the 'social upgrading' to fewer workers. Yet given the context of low and falling unemployment, this outcome was less socially problematic than was the case in South Africa. Sri Lankan workers who lost their jobs because of upgrading were better placed to find alternative employment.

In sum, the data above suggest that the global clothing manufacturing industry has, in the post-MFA period, displayed different national development trajectories with differing implications for labour and capital. Real average wages rose in all cases of upgrading, that is, when the sector as a whole experienced rising labour productivity (falling labour-intensity), but it is important to distinguish further between pro-labour upgrading trajectories that facilitated job growth, and those associated with job destruction. Where upgrading trajectories deliver rising average wages but fewer jobs, this poses policy dilemmas in countries where job creation is a priority. Upgrading strategies can be 'pro-capital' (associated with a rising profit share, which can be important when accumulation is a key objective) whilst delivering benefits to workers in terms of higher average wages and employment. Yet upgrading strategies may also deliver higher average wages to fewer workers—which, in high-unemployment contexts, indicates a trade-off between increasing wages and employment. So-called 'downgrading' trajectories (falling labour productivity and rising labour-intensity) were less common, but these too could be pro-labour or pro-capital, and with differing implications for average wages and employment. Turkey's downgrading trajectory delivered both rising average wages and employment.

There is an implicit normative hierarchy within the GVC policy literature in which upgrading is presented as economically and socially preferable to downgrading. Our analysis shows that this simple dichotomy can be misleading, given the diversity of outcomes with regard to average wages, employment, and in the distribution of value-added between capital and labour within upgrading and downgrading trajectories.

The normatively laden notions of upgrading as a high road to growth (and downgrading as a low road) are especially problematic in the context of high and rising unemployment. South Africa is a case in point. We showed that the South African development trajectory in the clothing manufacturing industry was one of industrial upgrading that delivered relatively high and rising average wages for workers. Yet this supposedly high road occurred in the context of significant job losses. In other words, rather than expanding labour-intensive activities (as in Turkey), the upgrading trajectory was increasingly skill- and capital-intensive, delivering higher wages for declining numbers of workers. The growth path in this industry thus undermined rather than facilitated inclusive development in the country.

5

The Moral Economy of Low-Wage Work

Labour-intensive industry, by its very nature, employs relatively large numbers of workers whilst requiring little capital. It is thus of potentially great benefit for regions with scarce capital and surplus labour. Yet labour-intensive manufacturing—and clothing production in particular—is also ripe with the distasteful odour of the 'sweatshop'. Precisely because little capital is required (sewing machines in the case of clothing manufacturing), it is easy for new competitors to enter the industry. Profit margins are thus usually tight and depend on maximizing labour effort at the lowest possible cost.

Clothing manufacturing, relying as it does on relatively simple machinery and mostly relatively unskilled female labour, is the archetypal sweatshop industry, raising concerns about egregious exploitation and posing social and ethical challenges almost as old as the industrial revolution itself. Wages are amongst the lowest in manufacturing, coercive labour practices are common and piecework payment systems (linking wages to output) have long generated concerns about 'sweating' (Hart, 1994: 16).

The clothing industry was once an important manufacturing sector in all industrialized countries and remains a central component of Lewis-like growth in developing countries today. For more than a century, social reformers and policymakers (starting in England) grappled with the distasteful juxtaposition of impoverished, powerless, and unorganized clothing workers producing relatively cheap items for better-off consumers. The tension between providing much needed employment for poor people and the relatively low pay and poor quality of these jobs, is at the centre of rival conceptions of the moral economy of labour-intensive development. Concerns about exploitation, beginning in nineteenth-century Britain, continue today with implications for development strategy and minimum wages.

This chapter shows that the moral economy of rival positions entails different understandings of how the economy functions, especially the relationship between wages and employment. Many contemporary arguments in South Africa and elsewhere reflect those made over a century earlier in Britain.

There is one important difference, however: in the late early twentieth century, British Fabian socialists sought (and achieved) the simultaneous expansion of labour protection (minimum wages and safety regulations) *and* welfare support for the unemployed (Hart, 1994: 15). By the early twentieth century in Britain, those who lost their jobs because of higher minimum wages could expect support from the welfare system. By contrast, the contemporary international anti-sweatshop movement focuses on improving wages and working conditions, applying pressure on retailers and manufacturers to do so. Workers who lose their jobs fall out of the movement's sphere of interest and off their proverbial radar screens. Unfortunately, given porous and inadequate social insurance and social protection in most developing countries, those who lose their jobs also fall straight through whatever meagre social safety nets exist.

The ILO collects labour and welfare data from countries all over the world through household surveys. As of 2018, the ILO's 'ILOSTAT' database reported only eighteen out of 113 low- and middle-income countries as having *any* unemployed people receiving social security payments, and of these countries, coverage was low (averaging 13 per cent in these eighteen countries for the year 2013, the most recent year for which most countries had data). By contrast, the unemployed accessed social security in 36 out of 48 high-income countries, with coverage ranging from 11 to 91 per cent. Given limited access to social security for the unemployed in developing countries, losing a job, even a low-wage job, can have crippling economic consequences for workers involved. This is why the ILO added its voice to calls for international retailers not to abandon Bangladesh after the collapse of the Rana Plaza, but rather to improve workplace safety (ILO, 2017: 02). The subsequent 'better work' campaign sought also to improve the worker's voice (such as by improving factory-level representation) but did not confront the issue of wages directly. The contrast between this and the ILO's more assertive 'decent work' agenda (Chapter 3) of the 2000s is quite marked, presumably because the need for labour-intensive development is clear for a low-income country like Bangladesh where there is no social security, and a poorly paid job (by international standards) is still better than no job.

Figure 3.2 reported that social security coverage for the unemployed was low and mostly non-existent for the thirteen surplus labour countries identified in Chapter 3. Under these conditions, job creation even at low wages will help alleviate poverty. Indeed, encouraging economic development to become more employment elastic (i.e. better able to generate new jobs out of growth) is essential for reducing social and economic marginalization in countries with surplus labour. This, however, requires that minimum wage-setting is sufficiently accommodating—a difficult challenge in some contexts given pressure for higher minimum wages, including at national level.

Contemporary calls for higher minimum wages in the global clothing industry and elsewhere are, in part, a reaction against the rise of inequality, nationally and globally. Especially since the 2008 global financial crisis, which put the spotlight on the excessive incomes of the very rich (and their role in driving the financial crisis) there has been mounting concern about inequality and associated social exclusion (Chapter 2). We discuss this further in the closing section of the chapter, arguing that raising minimum wages can potentially help address the problem, but only where employment losses are unlikely and where there is adequate welfare support for the unemployed.

5.1 Minimum Wages, Welfare, and Employment

It is clear from our preceding discussions that the clothing manufacturing industry is important for Lewis-like growth and can be a 'channel for social upgrading' (Lopez-Acevedo and Robertson, 2012: 12–14) especially for women with few, if any, better income-earning alternatives. For example, Cambodian garment workers, despite being in a low-paying industry in global terms were, as of the mid-2000s, earning 67 per cent above the mean wage and 80 per cent more than women with similar skill levels in other occupations (Neak and Robertson, 2009). In Bangladesh, Cambodia, Honduras, India, Pakistan, Sri Lanka, and Vietnam, average wages in clothing manufacturing were higher than in agriculture, and the percentage of working poor lower (Lopez-Acevedo and Robertson, 2012: 13; see also Keane and te Velde, 2008). Yet a large part of the moral conundrum over sweatshops is that these relatively good jobs by developing country standards are poorly paid by advanced capitalist country standards. As of 2018, the minimum wage in Cambodia for clothing workers was only $170 a month—yet this amounted to a significant increase over the previous year, sparking concerns that Cambodia's clothing export industry might suffer (Whelan, 2018).

When the anti-sweatshop movement gained traction on US university campuses in the late 1990s, mainstream development economists were sceptical of its economic and moral underpinnings. Jeffrey Sachs observed, somewhat facetiously, that his concern was 'not that there are too many sweatshops but that there are too few' (in Myerson, 1997). Speaking specifically about contemporary Africa, he argued that 'those are the jobs that have to come to Africa to get them out of their back-breaking rural poverty' (ibid.). Sachs was being characteristically pugnacious, but his statement embodied the essential moral economy of narratives favouring labour-intensive industrialization. Paul Krugman was more specific about the ethical problems facing the anti-sweatshop movement. After being challenged by critics for arguing that low-wage jobs were better than rural poverty, he penned the following irritated response, accusing his detractors of not thinking the issue through:

> as long as you have no realistic alternative to industrialization based on low wages, to oppose it means that you are willing to deny desperately poor people the best chance they have of progress for the sake of what amounts to an aesthetic standard—that is, the fact that you don't like the idea of workers being paid a pittance to supply rich Westerners with fashion items. In short, my correspondents are not entitled to their self-righteousness. They have not thought the matter through. And when the hopes of hundreds of millions are at stake, thinking things through is not just good intellectual practice. It is a moral duty. (Krugman, 1997)

There have been two broad responses to such defences of labour-intensive industrialization. The first is to assert that sweatshops are simply morally/socially unacceptable and that co-ordinated action must be taken to rid the world of this 'low road' to growth. A linked claim is that clothing producers are caught in a race to the bottom as they compete for orders from the fast fashion retailers—the implication being that setting a global wage floor will prevent this. International non-governmental organizations like *Fair Trade* and the *Fair Labor Organisation* draw up international standards and encourage major retailers to source items only from producers who adhere to them. Movements like the *Clean Clothes Campaign* mobilize for a cross-country 'Asian wage floor' and encourage consumers to purchase clothes certified as 'sweatshop free'. The main idea is that wages and working conditions in developing countries can be improved dramatically, for limited additional cost to rich country consumers, through such co-ordinated action.

This is a position that is at once utopian (the collective action challenges are immense) but hypothetically achievable if the movement for international standards keeps gaining momentum and as long as better-off consumers are prepared to pay a premium for 'clean clothes'. Research from the early 2000s showed that significantly higher clothing wages in developing countries were possible at the cost of a relatively small increase in the sale price of the final product in developed countries. Citing survey data from the US, Pollin et al. (2004) argued that a 100 per cent wage increase for Mexican clothing workers would require only a 2 to 6 per cent increase in the US retail price of imported clothing, and that this was in line with what consumers were prepared to pay for ethically produced products. Even so, poorer consumers in developing and advanced capitalist countries are likely to remain price-sensitive, thereby limiting the potential market for higher-priced 'clean' clothes. The fact that US consumers switched to low-price retailers like *Walmart* in the aftermath of the 2008 financial crisis in such great numbers that *Walmart*'s revenues increased as retail sales sagged across the economy (Lopez-Acevedo and Robertson, 2012: 221) is a cautionary tale.

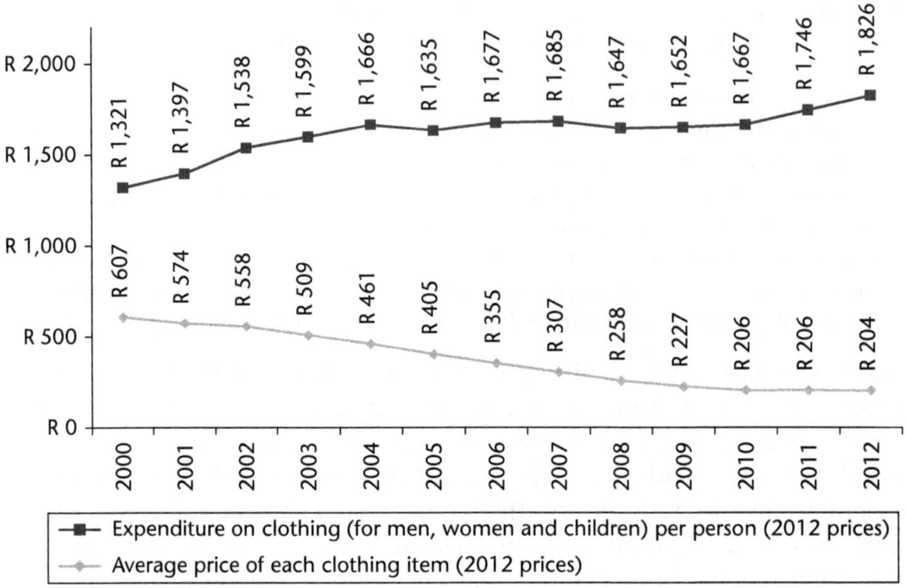

Figure 5.1 Real annual expenditure on clothing per person and average real price per clothing item in South Africa: 2000–2012
Source: Euromonitor 2013, population from ASSA2008 model.

It is important to bear in mind that whilst clothes can be a luxury good for Northern consumers of fast fashion, they are also necessities—especially for poorer people. Clothes in this sense are wage goods and when the price of wage goods falls, real incomes rise. Hence cheaper clothes, forged by rising global competition, have important welfare effects too. This is the case not only for poorer consumers in advanced capitalist countries, but also for consumers in developing countries. For example, in South Africa the real price per unit of clothing sold fell by over two-thirds in the 2000s, largely driven by competition from China (see Figure 5.1 and Morris and Einhorn, 2008), with significant implications for consumer welfare. As shown in Figure 5.2, the average South African spent 3 per cent of average *per capita* income on clothing in 2000 and in 2012 yet could purchase nine items in 2012, compared to only two items in 2000. This suggests that raising the price of clothing will reduce the number of clothing items purchased, and this, in turn, has ramifications for employment in clothing manufacturing. Whether clean clothes premiums can be absorbed by consumers in the form of higher prices is likely to vary by type of product and category of consumer—and thus is ultimately an empirical issue with results likely to vary across countries. The relationship between wage increase and ultimate price paid also depends on whether any additional mark-up is taken by middle-men and retailers, and this too is likely to vary across countries.

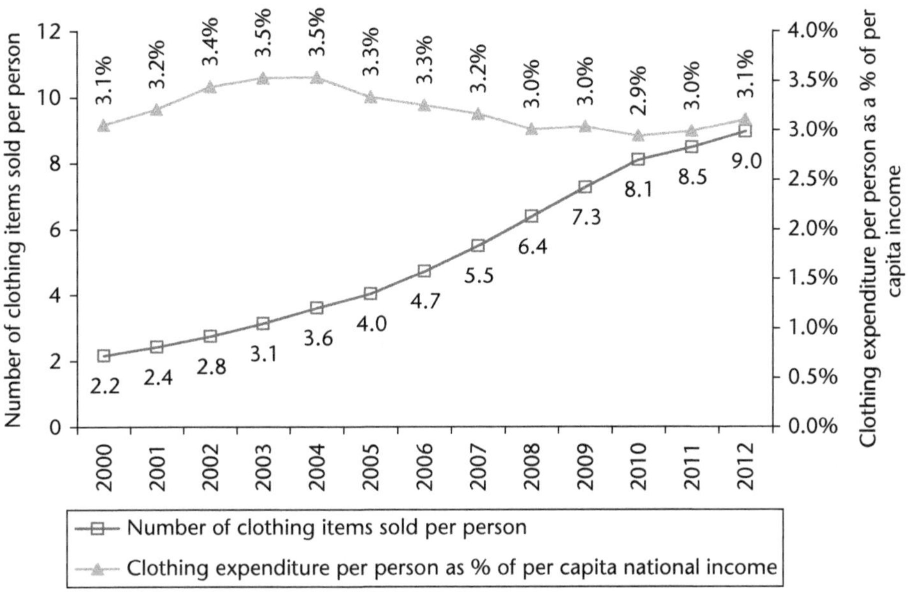

Figure 5.2 Annual income share spent on clothing and clothing items sold per person per year in South Africa: 2000–2012

Source: Euromonitor 2013, population from ASSA2008 model.

Another distributional consequence of imposing an international wage floor on producers in poor countries is that it disregards the fact that it is likely to be the very poorest countries that run the greatest risk of losing jobs. Policymakers in these countries might reasonably fear that clothing firms that had opted to locate in very poor areas because of low labour costs might decide to move elsewhere where infrastructure is more developed, markets are closer, and hence lower logistics costs could make up for the higher wage imposed by the international floor. Under such conditions, workers in the higher-wage areas would benefit, but at the cost of job losses in poorer areas.

The second argument in favour of higher minimum wages is to claim, in effect, that the trade-off between higher minimum wages and jobs is exaggerated, if it exists at all (which, as discussed in Chapter 3, is one of the claims made by the ILO in support of its decent work agenda). The implicit assumption here is that firms can tolerate lower profits and/or find ways other than shedding labour to improve efficiency. A related macroeconomic argument suggests that higher minimum wages will actually increase overall employment by putting additional income into the hands of poor workers, thereby fuelling consumer demand and hence boosting growth. Such 'wage-led' growth is theoretically possible on a sustained basis if the increase in demand is significant and if this has a greater positive impact on investment than any negative effect caused by higher wage costs (Marglin and Bhaduri, 1990). Such positive macroeconomic effects, however, are less likely in an open economy where consumer demand sucks in imports and where higher wages can undermine international competitiveness (Bowles and Boyer, 1995). An undervalued nominal exchange rate can provide some space for rising wages (causing the real exchange rate to appreciate) as was arguably the case in China during the 2000s (Fisher, 2010). Even so, there are limits to this strategy as an appreciating real exchange rate eventually places pressure on competitiveness.

The microeconomic argument that there may be space for wage increases without sparking employment losses is on stronger grounds than macroeconomic claims. The idea that firms will be able to absorb increases in minimum wages by improving efficiency and tolerating lower profits is rooted in an institutionalist analysis that is over a century old (discussed more below). It reasonably rejects the neoclassical assumptions that competition ensures that firms are as efficient as possible and that wages reflect the marginal product of labour, arguing instead that wages are the outcome of a bargaining process where workers are in a much weaker position than that of employers. The working assumption of this economic perspective is that wages are likely to be low in sweatshops not only because workers are relatively unskilled (and hence less productive) but also because they have limited bargaining power. The implication is thus that employers are earning rents or 'super'/'surplus' profits (i.e. in excess of what they would be getting if wages were truly in line with productivity) and that workers are consequently being exploited. Under such conditions, higher minimum wages in support of a fairer distribution of value-added between wages and profits could generate rising wages without loss of jobs. Whether these conditions hold (and whether exploitative employers have options to relocate elsewhere) is, of course, an empirical question. Clothing firms in Indonesia were able to absorb a significant increase in the minimum wage during the 1990s without sparking job losses (Harrison and Scorse, 2003) whereas this was not the case in South Africa in the 2000s (Chapter 6).

Most empirical studies of the impact of minimum wage hikes on employment find weak or indiscernible effects (see reviews of the literature in Freeman, 2009; Betcherman, 2015; ILO, 2015a: 59; Broecke et al., 2017) although there is evidence that job losses following minimum wage hikes are greater when measured over the longer term (Meer and West 2013; Aaronson et al., 2018; Sorkin, 2015). Labour force survey data suggest that the impact of minimum wages on employment in Africa is typically neutral or negative, but that effects can vary widely depending on the sector and the level of compliance (Bhorat et al., 2017).

As Freeman observes, most legislated minimum wage increases are modest and the fact that employment effects are so small suggests that 'governments set minimum wages with due consideration to the risk that minima can cause more harm than good' (2009: 13). In South Africa, government bodies involved in minimum wage-setting have taken into account possible employment effects. The Wage Board (and from 2000, the Employment Conditions Commission), which sets minimum wages in sectors where trade unions and employers were not organized into bargaining councils, generally increased minimum wages cautiously, with some exceptions, notably the politically driven sharp increase in agricultural minimum wages in 2013 (Seekings, 2016a). This contrasts sharply with minimum wage-setting through bargaining councils (and their extension to all firms by the Minister of Labour), notably in the clothing manufacturing sector (Chapter 6).

For advocates of minimum wages, the paucity of international evidence showing large immediate job losses following minimum wage increases indicates that concerns about the wage–employment trade-off are misplaced. However, this ignores the fact that the extent of job losses will depend on the extent of the minimum wage hike, and that job losses when they occur are born by the most vulnerable. A key finding from the international literature on the impact of rising minimum wages on employment is that the primary losers are lower-skilled workers at and below the level that the minimum wage 'bites' (Betcherman, 2015: 8). A study of the effect of increased minimum wages in China during the 2000s showed that young, female and unskilled workers lost jobs in disproportionately high numbers (Fang and Lin, 2015). A more recent review of the impact of minimum wages in developing countries found that overall employment effects were limited (due to lack of enforcement/tolerance for informality) but that more vulnerable groups were more adversely affected (Broecke et al., 2017).

There is some evidence that greater labour market flexibility (allowing a wider dispersion of wages and/or making it easier to hire and fire workers) can help reduce unemployment, although as such labour market reforms tend to be instigated during periods of weak economic performance and high unemployment, ordinary least squares estimates of the effect of labour market institutions on unemployment are likely to be biased downwards (Bernal-Verdugo et al., 2012: 3). Using a panel of 97 countries from 1985 to 2008, Bernal-Verdugo et al. (2012) nevertheless found that policy-related improvements in labour market flexibility had a statistically significant effect on unemployment: controlling for demographic and macroeconomic factors (urbanization, population density, openness to trade, size of government, state of the business cycle, a crisis dummy, and lagged unemployment), a one standard deviation increase in the Fraser Institute's composite labour market flexibility indicator reduced the unemployment rate by 0.3 to 1.3 percentage points depending on the specification. This suggests that broad-ranging labour market reforms, ideally supported by macroeconomic policy, could potentially help address unemployment, albeit marginally (see also Feldmann, 2009; Crivelli et al., 2012). Avdagic and

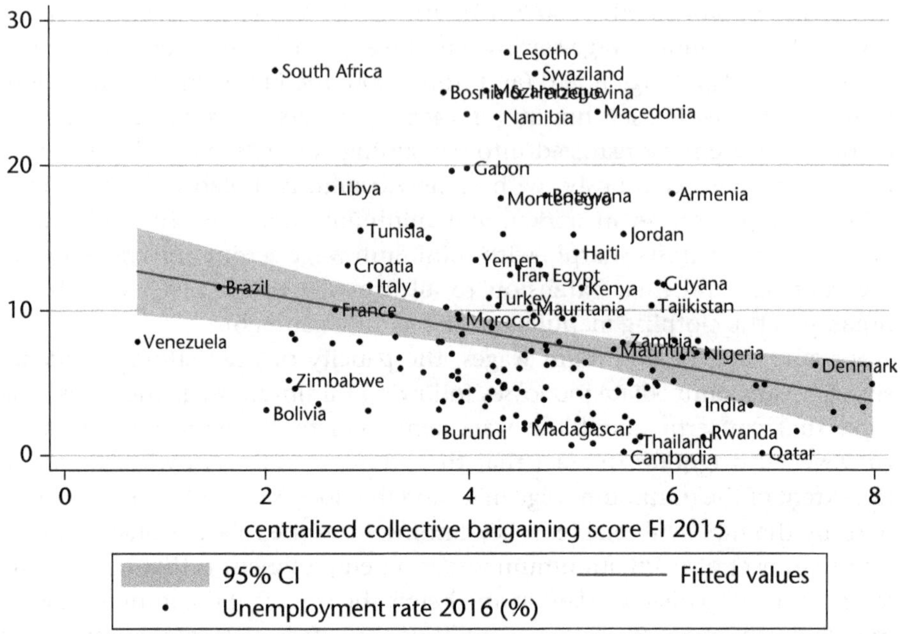

Figure 5.3 Unemployment rate and centralization of collective bargaining (150 countries).
Source: Fraser Institute data, World Development Indicators.

Salardi (2013), however, warn that conclusions about labour market reforms and unemployment are subject to country selection, indicator, and model specification.

The Fraser Institute provides a range of measures of labour market flexibility. Figure 5.3 shows the negative, but weak, relationship between the unemployment rate and the centralized bargaining indicator (which draws on data from the World Economic Forum's *World Competitiveness Report* to provide an indicator that is higher for countries with more decentralized systems of collective bargaining). The simple regression line indicates that for a unit increase in the measure (that is, towards more decentralized wage-setting), unemployment declines by 1.2 percentage points ($t = -3.31^{***}$, prob $> F = 0.001$). The high unemployment countries of Southern Africa are in the top left-hand quadrant, that is, they fall above the mean for global unemployment and on or below the mean for the centralization of wage-bargaining (meaning they are on the centralized part of the global distribution of collective bargaining systems). South Africa's relatively centralized score reflects the predominance of wage-setting through collective bargaining and its extension across industries to non-parties.

Irrespective of the precise relationship between minimum wages and employment, an inclusive growth path would ensure that workers who lose their jobs as a result of rising minimum wages would either get quickly absorbed into new jobs elsewhere as the economy expands (perhaps assisted to do so by training and job-placement programmes) or would receive social security and other welfare-related assistance. As discussed below, the argument for a minimum wage floor, initially made for the clothing industry in late nineteenth-century Britain, presented minimum wages as potentially beneficial at both microeconomic and macroeconomic levels. Importantly, however, the argument was made in the context of parallel reform efforts to broaden the welfare system to protect people against poverty.

5.2 Wages and Welfare: Debating Minimum Wages and Sweated Labour in Late Nineteenth-Century Britain

The argument that higher minimum wages would be good for workers and for economic development first rose to prominence in late nineteenth-century England. Such arguments continue to resonate today within the anti-sweatshop movement. They also resonate in the 'upgrading' literature (Chapters 3 and 4) where a common assumption is that higher minimum wages will not only facilitate social upgrading, but will promote economic upgrading by encouraging/forcing firms to improve efficiency.

During the late nineteenth century in Britain, key thinkers such as John Hobson and Sidney and Beatrice Webb helped pioneer the 'institutional' approach to industrial relations (Rutherford, 2007). Although marginalized by mainstream economists, they were highly influential in shaping the British liberal economic and welfare reforms of the early twentieth century. The Webbs were founder members of the Fabian Society and helped set up the London School of Economics and Political Science in 1895 to circumvent the Marshallian neoclassical hegemony of Oxford and Cambridge. They emphasized the existence of 'rents' in economic life, that is, economic returns in excess of real economic contribution, and argued that the limited bargaining power of relatively unskilled workers drove wages down to poverty levels, generating a 'low' road to growth (Kaufman, 2013: 778). The implication of this argument was that setting higher minimum wages would rid society of 'parasitic' industries in which workers earned below-subsistence wages, thereby placing the burden on family, friends, and charities. Raising wages would also, in their view, boost consumer demand and encourage further economic innovation. Hobson's arguments that capitalism was an inherently unstable system, prone to disruptive under-consumption and over accumulation (e.g. Hobson and Durbin, 1933), gave additional weight to these claims—and support to calls for higher minimum wages and a more egalitarian society.

Hobson and the Webbs were writing at a time when the issue of 'sweated labour', especially in the clothing industry, was already a major social issue. As Hart observes:

> By the 1890s, sweating was widespread. Manufacturers capitalized on an oversupply of unskilled labor to meet the demands of a mass market for ready-made products. Production was disaggregated into multiple simple operations and piecework, and more tasks were farmed out in more industries to more people, often women, sometimes immigrants, working in small shops and their own homes. The kinds of people involved and the scattered workplaces made regulation and organization difficult. (1994: 17)

Up until 1814, the Statute of Artificers (passed in 1562) had regulated various crafts, stipulating inter alia certain wage rates and training requirements, notably serving a seven-year apprenticeship. Having protected the tailoring trade for over two and a half centuries, its repeal totally transformed clothing manufacturing. The craft of tailoring was 'debased' by relatively unskilled workers hired to sew simple garments, or simple parts of garments, without requiring much specialized training. Thus the sweatshop was born:

> The ease of setting up in business within the sweated sector led to a proliferation of workshops. All that was needed to begin was a small workroom or a room in the worker's own home and the minimum of capital. Most sweated outwork was carried out by hand, but if simple apparatus such as a sewing machine was required, it was easily obtainable on a cheap hire-purchase basis. Forced to accept lower and lower rates, however, the small master had no surplus to spare for decent rooms or for keeping them in a clean and healthy state.
>
> (Blackburn, 1991: 46)

The misery and poverty associated with such downward pressure on earnings in this labour-intensive sector became a public issue and eventually a source of moral outrage. In 1843, Thomas Hood published a poem in *Punch* called 'The Song of the Shirt' to highlight the plight of a seamstress who had ended up in the poorhouse after becoming indebted to her employer. The poem exposed the misery of many clothing workers, causing something of a sensation amongst the Victorian intelligentsia. Here is one of the verses:

> Oh, Men, with Sisters dear!
> Oh, men, with Mothers and Wives!
> It is not linen you're wearing out,
> But human creatures' lives!
> Stitch—stitch—stitch,
> In poverty, hunger and dirt,
> Sewing at once, with a double thread,
> A Shroud as well as a Shirt
>
> (Hood, 1843)

Various newspaper exposés (by Henry Mayhew, the co-founder of *Punch*) were published, followed in 1850 by an influential pamphlet titled 'Cheap Clothes and Nasty'. The author, Charles Kingsley, a novelist, historian, and priest of the Church of England, fulminated against the 'sweaters' in London's poorer East End who were out-competing the 'honourable' West End tailors. Drawing on evidence from a local inquiry, he described how the sweaters were able to supply retail shops with cheap clothes by employing women at starvation wages either as home workers or in small production units crammed into unhygienic tenements. He recommended that affected workers 'combine' to cut out the sweater and create their own workshops, and that consumers stop buying cheap clothes from the 'temples of Moloch' (retail stores) whose 'thresholds are rife with human blood'. In his view, the sweatshops and the economic dynamics that encouraged their emergence were nothing short of the devil's work:

> But it is so hard to deprive the public of the luxury of cheap clothes! Then let the public look out for some other means of procuring that priceless blessing. If that, on experiment, be found impossible—if the comfort of the few be for ever to be bought by the misery of the many—if civilization is to benefit everyone except the producing class—then this world is truly the devil's world, and the sooner so ill-constructed and infernal a machine is destroyed by that personage, the better.
>
> (Kingsley, 1850, no page number)

Blackburn argues that such mid-nineteenth-century revelations amounted to little more than a 'short-lived moment in the consciousness of the rich' and that it was only with the advent of working-class militancy and economic depression a quarter of a century later that the issue achieved renewed and sustained attention (1991: 47–8). However, women's organizations also contributed significantly to a broader social mobilization (Hart, 1994) including amongst intellectuals and politicians.

In 1890, a select committee of the British House of Lords highlighted the problem of sweated labour, defining it as 'a rate of wages inadequate to the necessities of the workers or disproportionate to the work done' (cited in Hansard, 1909: 343). A raft of factory legislation subsequently sought to improve the working conditions of factory workers but the problem of low pay persisted in the face of what Blackburn describes as 'the Victorians' extreme reluctance to intervene in the wage bargain', something she attributes in large part to the laissez-fair economic ideology of the day (1991: 49). Yet, as discussed below, the debate was more complex than this. Rival moral economies of capitalism, and especially the role of low-wage employment, were at play.

In 1906, the sweatshop issue gained further social traction with a widely attended 'Exhibition of Sweated Industries' organized by the *Daily News* in

London. Workers, quite literally exhibited to the public in stalls and on stages, showed curious visitors what they did for a living, and discussed their wages and working conditions. This prompted the formation of the National Anti-Sweating League (NASL), and the organization of a conference in London bringing together trade unions, anti-Sweating activists, socialists, women's organizations, politicians etc. (NASL, 1907: 3). John Hobson, introducing the arguments that remain powerfully evident today, argued that minimum wages would not necessarily lead to employment losses because higher wages would help improve productivity, that many employers could afford higher wages, and that there were economy-wide benefits of putting a greater share of income in the hands of workers.

On the productivity issue, Hobson articulated what became known as the efficiency-wage argument, notably that wage increases 'will have some effect in raising the standard of efficiency of labour; better nourished, more energetic and more cheerful workers give out a larger amount and better quality of labour power' (in NASL, 1907: 54). Referring specifically to the impact of the various factories acts, all of which raised the cost of production, he argued that this did not result in falling employment because:

> the fear of reduced profits acted as a stimulus to improved economy in the control of their business. A rise in the wage-bill or in other expenses led to the invention or adoption of improved machinery, the utilisation of hitherto wasted products, or other improvements either in the technique or in the administration of the business. A trade dependent for its economy upon abundance of cheap, low-grade labour is notoriously an unprogressive trade; an enforced rise of wages will commonly be a spur to progress. (Ibid.: 55)

Hobson also maintained that 'a far larger proportion of the total number [of employers] than is commonly supposed, are able to afford a rise in wages' because they are earning 'surplus profits', that is, profits that are 'higher than is necessary to maintain the capital and business enterprise' (ibid.: 55). These employers might choose to accept lower profits rather than raise their prices and risk lower sales (and subsequent job losses). Even so, Hobson emphasized, 'we are not justified, I think, in assuming that the economic effects of the legal minimum can always be confined to the stimulation of efficiency of production or the reduction of surplus profits' and that in some sweating trades the impact will be to raise prices and lower employment (ibid: 56). He argued that this was the likely outcome in those cases where sweating was 'a genuinely economical method of production', that is, when labour-intensive methods were the most efficient. He predicted that the worst paid workers would lose their jobs 'and be reduced to worse straits than before' and that any expansion of factory employment would not fully compensate for these job losses.

In other words, he accepted that there might thus be some trade-off between higher minimum wages and employment and that the lowest paid workers were likely to be the ones losing their jobs. His view was that this was a necessary price to pay for a healthier economy:

> From the standpoint of the national economy our answer is: let the sweated trade go abroad, mere quantity of employment is not our first concern, it is not the true interest of Great Britain to seek to retain within her borders a degraded parasitic trade, whose presence generates physical and moral disease in our industrial society. (NASL, 1907: 56)

Even so, he distinguished between the standpoint of the benefits to the national economy, and the circumstances of the individual worker, arguing that it was the role of the state to compensate workers harmed in the process:

> if a result of a legal minimum wage or of any other measure operating in the public interest is to throw out of employment any body of workers previously employed, it is manifestly the duty of the State to take care of these displaced workers as a part of the public provision for the unemployed now recognised as devolving on the State. To make proper provision for the unemployed persons at the public expense is a better, and, in the long run, a cheaper social policy than to allow them to continue to work for sweating wages in unsanitary workrooms, breeding and bringing up a new generation of physical, industrial and moral inefficients.
> (Ibid.: 57)

Then, in a macroeconomic narrative foreshadowing that of Keynes, Hobson linked overall employment to the level of demand, observing that even if employment in sweated industries falls, the net impact of higher minimum wages on aggregated employment might be positive because the effect of transferring 'profits to wages will be to raise and to regularise the demand for commodities' (ibid.: 57). He argued that concentrating income in the hands of the rich caused economic instability because the rich spent their money on 'capricious luxuries, whose fluctuating demand stamped irregularity upon the trades producing them' and because surplus profits were partly accumulated in 'excessive capital not required for the maintenance of the ordinary current of production', thereby 'breeding congestion and commercial depressions' (ibid.: 57). Redistributing income to workers would exchange 'the demand for necessities or conveniences on the part of workers for the luxurious expenditure of the rich' thereby boosting the 'sound stable industries of furnishing the necessaries and conveniences of life' (ibid: 58). Hobson was the first person to articulate the core ideas associated with Keynes, but whereas Keynes saw the solution to insufficient demand in additional government spending, Hobson favoured redistribution from capital to labour.

In response to pressure from groups like the Fabian Society and the NASL, the newly elected liberal government subsequently enacted the Trade

Boards Act in 1909 that established procedures for minimum wage-setting in 'sweated industries' including tailoring and machine lace-making (Bean and Boyer, 2009: 240–1). In introducing the Bill, the Parliamentary Secretary Mr H. J. Tennant explained that minimum wages were not designed to supplant market wage-setting but rather to cure those 'industrial diphtheritic spots' and 'exceptionally unhealthy patches of the body politic where the development has been arrested in spite of the growth of the rest of the organism' (Hansard, 1909: 344). He argued that below-subsistence wages threatened to catapult entire families into the poorhouse (and onto the government budget) whereas higher wages would increase efficiency and stimulate 'the inventive genius of the people who give their minds to mechanics' (ibid.: 346). Tennant was thus relying on productivity growth to accommodate higher wages without loss of employment, noting that Britain's relatively capital-intensive cotton industry was already competing successfully with lower-wage producers in India and Japan (ibid.: 347). This argument resonates today, more than a hundred years later, for those proposing higher-wage, higher-productivity development as an alternative to labour-intensive development.

Some members of the House of Commons objected to the proposed minimum wages arguing that they would simply 'increase the amount of goods produced by sweated labour abroad' (ibid.: 361) and that Ireland in particular would become the 'very home of sweated industries' unless minimum laws were extended there as well (ibid.: 364). John Hayden, an Irish representative, took exception to the notion that minimum wages should be imposed on Ireland, arguing that it would amount to yet another English law designed with the 'sole purpose of destroying [Irish] industries for the benefit of English manufacturers' (ibid.: 377). Foreshadowing the arguments made half a century later by development economists such as Lewis (and more recently by Krugman and Sachs), he argued that Ireland should be exempt from the minimum wage because it was a poorer, more rural country than Britain and because low-wage jobs were important sources of employment.

As is the case today, not everyone agreed with Hayden's representation of the interests of less developed regions. In a reflection of the current contestation between those who represent the interests of (typically better-off and relatively skilled) urban workers and those making the case for low-wage labour-intensive development, his fellow countryman, Mr Nannetti, describing himself as a representative of the 'working men of Dublin', objected to Hayden's argument:

> It is all very well for Members to stand up and say that by the passing of this Bill you will be killing Irish industries. I am as anxious as any man to see the

> resuscitation of Irish industries, but if they are to be resuscitated at the expense of the flesh and blood of the people of the country, then I say, with all the responsibility of my position, that I would be prepared to see Irish industries languish rather than that the people engaged in them should be exploited, as I understand they are at present in certain trades. (Ibid.: 397)

Nannetti was effectively channelling Kingsley's preference, expressed more than half a century earlier, that it was (presumably on moral grounds) better to have no economy than one based on exploitation. Hayden, of course, saw things differently, envisaging labour-intensive industry as a means of poverty alleviation even at low wages. Their dispute rehearsed the disagreements that continue to this day over the moral economy of labour-intensive growth in developing countries. Yet there are important differences of context. Minimum wages were introduced to combat sweated labour in Britain the year after the 1908 Old Age Pension Act was passed and a mere two years before the 1911 National Insurance Act established compulsory systems of health and unemployment insurance. In contrast, most developing countries do not provide comprehensive social insurance and assistance programmes. The implicit social bargain forged in Edwardian England was that if minimum wages undermined jobs, the state would protect the unemployed from destitution. No such bargain exists in developing countries, and hence the moral economy of using the wage to drive out socially unacceptable forms of low-wage labour is crucially different.

5.3 Debating the Ethics of Sweatshops and Minimum Wages in the Twenty-first Century

In the contemporary debate over sweated labour, the 'moral imagination' of rival positions boils down to the economic plausibility of contesting narratives (Powell and Zwolinski, 2012). The anti-sweatshop movement draws on two narratives in particular. The first is that there is no necessary reason why a rise in minimum wage should result in employment losses because there is likely to be an efficiency-wage effect—that is, workers become more productive because they are better nourished and morale is higher (e.g. Arnold and Hartman, 2005, 2006). This is the argument first made by John Hobson and the Fabian socialists in England during the anti-sweating movement at the end of the nineteenth century. The second is that some of the wage increase can be passed on to higher-income consumers in the form of a price increase. This, as noted earlier, is the essence of the argument for Asian wage floors and wage increases financed by clean clothes premiums.

Critics are sceptical of these claims. For example, Powell and Zwolinski see 'no reason to believe that pushing for higher wages will result in higher productivity in most sweatshop jobs' (2012: 454) or that consumer tolerance for higher prices is likely to be universal. In their view, 'the standard economic model that predicts higher wages will lead to lower employment still holds' (ibid.). Their case is plausible, but they provide no empirical evidence to support their contention. Their stance is simply to accept the 'standard model' (the neoclassical model of the downward-sloping demand for labour curve) as true, whilst challenging others to provide (what they judge to be) compelling evidence against it. This is not an especially helpful approach given that arguments about minimum wages and sweatshops are embedded in different microeconomic and macroeconomic narratives, all of which (including 'the standard model') should be open to scrutiny and empirical investigation.

Another argument employed by the anti-sweatshop movement is to make the macroeconomic claim that the expected harm (employment contraction) needs to be calculated and then set against the expected benefits (higher wages for workers who keep their job and increased employment resulting from wage-led growth) in order to get an estimate of the overall 'harm' to workers. Coakley and Kates, for example, employ such claims to conclude that 'even if Powell and Zwolinski are correct about the sweatshop employment effects, it nevertheless still does not follow that there are negative employment effects overall' (2013: 555). Rather:

> there is a strong *prima facie* reason for believing that increasing worker wages will lead to an overall increase in employment in the developing world since both the share of the product price from wages is small and the local employment multiplier from increased worker spending is likely to be large (due to significant underutilization in the local economy). Sweatshop regulation that dramatically boosts worker wages is thus likely to increase employment in the developing world overall even if it decreases sweatshop employment at the margin. (Ibid.: 557)

The argument between Powell and Zwolinski on the one hand, and Coakley and Kates on the other is broadly representative of the firm-level and economy-wide economic arguments about minimum wages and employment. Yet such debates are ultimately unsatisfactory because, in the absence of systematic assessments of particular economic contexts, they end up in a stalemate of counter claims based on assumptions. Coakley and Kates (2013) are correct to say that macroeconomic dynamics matter and that it is hypothetically possible for higher wages to generate greater demand and hence higher employment. Yet this outcome is dependent on a range of conditions, including the size of the wage increase, the extent of the domestic market, the openness of the economy, availability of spare capacity, determinants of investment etc. The range of context-specific considerations is clear from the following discussion of the South African debate over the macroeconomics of minimum wage increases and employment.

5.3.1 *The Macroeconomics of Minimum Wages and Employment in South Africa*

Supporters of increased minimum wages in South Africa argue in Keynesian fashion that it would be good for job creation because it puts additional income into the hands of relatively poor people, thereby boosting demand and hence local output and employment (see e.g. Adelzedeh, 2016; Strauss and Isaacs, 2016). As discussed above, this demand-driven logic has long been a staple argument of anti-sweating activists. It initially appeared in South Africa in the early 1990s in the run-up to South Africa's first democratic elections when the ANC argued for 'growth through redistribution' (ANC, 1990). The core idea was that higher incomes in the hands of the poor (from wages and social grants) as well as pro-poor government spending, such as low-income housing programmes, would act as a 'spur' to growth by boosting demand. This understanding of what was required to transform the economy rested on a characterization of the apartheid economy as being constrained by South Africa's high level of inequality, notably the concentration of income in white hands (e.g. Saul and Gelb, 1986: 71, 80–1). By redistributing income to the (predominantly black African) poor and allocating government expenditure to social infrastructure (schools, low-income houses), it was hoped that the size of the domestic market would expand and the balance of payments would improve as luxury consumer imports declined (see e.g. Bond, 1991; Lewis, 1991; and an overview of this argument in Moll, 1991).

The issue of whether demand-led growth was a sustainable growth strategy for South Africa dominated the economic debate in the early 1990s. Economists pointed out that there was limited spare capacity in the South African economy and that structural constraints inherited from the past (notably shortages of skilled labour and an import-dependent, inefficient manufacturing sector) would quickly emerge to choke growth—as had happened with every post-war economic upswing (Moll, 1991). Such concerns, together with anxiety over the possibility of macroeconomic collapse following over-rapid increases in government spending (widely recognized to have undermined left-wing governments in Chile and Nicaragua) contributed to ANC policymaking in the early 1990s emphasizing the need for macroeconomic balance rather than boosting demand (Nattrass, 1994; Hirsch, 2005: 52–3; Gelb, 2010: 37). Essentially, the structural problem policy-makers recognized was that whenever economic growth picked up, so too did imports, thereby driving the current account of the balance of payments (exports minus imports) into deficit and rendering the country more dependent on capital inflows.

Soon after the transition to democracy, the ANC had to confront problems of inherited unsustainable levels of government debt as well as investor uncertainty. The new government's 1996 Growth, Employment and Redistribution framework (DOF, 1996) was an attempt to encourage domestic and international investment by providing a vision of growth consistent with 'fiscal discipline', openness to international trade, privatization, and macroeconomic stability (Gelb, 2010: 39–40; Nattrass, 2014a). Capital accumulation in South Africa has long relied on corporate savings and capital inflows because the government and household sectors are typically net borrowers. Subsequent national development plans have all accepted that the South African economy's binding constraints are on the supply side (notably skilled labour shortages, infrastructural bottlenecks and investment finance), not the demand side. The argument was made especially forcefully by the international expert panel on South African growth chaired by Harvard professor Ricardo Hausmann in 2006–2007.[1]

Yet the notion that the South African economy could be kick-started by a major injection of demand continued to smoulder. For example, in the national debate that emerged in 2014/15 over the level of the proposed national minimum wage, COSATU favoured its introduction at a relatively high level (over twice the weighted average of sectoral determinations set by the Employment Conditions Commission). Pro-labour advocates (e.g. Coleman, 2012) justified this by referring to the Brazilian case, the so-called 'Lula moment' when economic growth, driven primarily by the commodities boom, benefitted also from increases to the Brazilian national minimum wage and linked social security payments during President Ignacio Lula da Silva's second term of office (2006–2010). There is evidence that rising minimum wages and social security payments in Brazil helped cushion the effect of the global economic crisis, create jobs, and lower inequality and poverty (ILO, 2011; Serrano and Summa, 2011). But in sharp contrast to South Africa, this occurred in the context of a tight labour market (very low unemployment) and where Brazil financed its investment largely from domestic sources. South African households, by contrast, borrow to finance consumption—and this trend worsened in the post-apartheid period.

Two published macroeconomic analyses of the South Africa economy (using macroeconomic simulations and data from the 1990s and 2000s respectively) concluded that wage-led growth was not feasible in South Africa, and that increasing the wage share would undermine investment, growth,

[1] The synthesis report and background papers are available at: http://www.treasury.gov.za/publications/other/growth/01-Overall%20Summary%20and%20Final%20Recommendations/default.aspx.

and employment and generate balance of payments problems (Gibson and Van Seventer, 2000; Onaran and Galanis, 2013). A subsequent simulation by the South African National Treasury came to the same conclusion, notably that the South African economy 'is profit/investment driven' rather than 'wage/consumption driven' because profits are the main source of funding for investment and wages, and because a significant amount of consumption (following from wage increases) gets spent on imports (MacLeod, 2015). The model predicted that if a national minimum wage was set at 60 per cent of the median wage and was rigorously enforced, it would result in a 2.1 per cent fall in employment and a 2.5 per cent fall in output. The National Treasury estimated that such a national minimum wage would affect 45 per cent of unskilled workers, 43 per cent of workers in agriculture and 52 per cent of workers in private households. Workers who retained their jobs would benefit from the higher wage. But if the national minimum wage were to be enforced rigorously, the economy would become less labour-intensive and the burden of adjustment would fall mainly on the poor. This finding was consistent with an earlier macroeconomic simulation by Pauw and Leibbrandt (2012) which concluded that higher minimum wages hurt the poor and hence were inappropriate instruments for addressing household poverty.

Two COSATU-aligned macroeconomic modelling projects, however, continued to present an alternative narrative, that higher minimum wages would be good for growth in South Africa. The models assumed that higher minimum wages would result in higher productivity (whilst leaving employment largely unchanged) and that the impact of higher demand on the balance of payments and investment would be insufficient to derail wage-led growth (Adelzedeh, 2016; Strauss and Isaacs, 2016). Unemployment remained stubbornly high even in these optimistic projections, but because the models assumed limited job losses and a narrowing of the wage distribution, they projected an overall decrease in inequality.

Such wage-led modelling narratives depend on bold and creative assumptions and are inconsistent with historical trends in the South African economy. They paint a rosy picture/fantasy that this time, things will be different: that higher wages will somehow translate automatically and instantaneously into higher productivity, meaning that savings and investment would not be undermined. Such narratives emphasize the benefits of reduced wage inequality but never confront the fact that unemployment remains high and that the chances of less skilled workers ever getting jobs decreases. Wage-led growth in other (advanced capitalist) countries typically benefits skilled workers because it encourages mechanization: skilled labour is a complement to capital-intensification, whereas less skilled workers lose their jobs (Bentolila and Saint-Paul, 2003; Checchi and García-Peñalosa, 2010; Young and Lawson, 2014). This dynamic is already strongly evident in the post-apartheid economy; the modelling by the National

Treasury predicted that a dramatically increased national minimum wage would exacerbate that trend, making growth ever more non-inclusive.

COSATU demanded a minimum of R4,500 per month (about 65 per cent of GDP per capita) but parliament eventually agreed, in 2018, to set the national minimum wage at R20 per hour, that is R3,500 per month (about 50 per cent of GDP per capita) for implementation in 2019. Probably in response to the National Treasury's warnings about the potentially negative impact on low-wage workers in agriculture and domestic service, provision was made (at least for a year) for lower wages in agriculture (R18 per hour) and domestic work (R15 per hour). The government exempted its own public works programmes (setting the minimum at R11 per hour) but made no exemptions for unskilled workers in the private sector—or for labour-intensive industries like clothing manufacturing. Firms could also apply for (time-bound) exemptions and the national minimum wage was to be enforced through the mechanism of complaints by workers to the Commission for Conciliation, Mediation and Arbitration rather than via inspections and external enforcement. This suggests that government accepted the moral logic of a minimum wage floor set at a politically acceptable standard of living for wage earners—but was concerned also to limit potential job losses. Even so, the fact that the national minimum wage was higher than the bargained minimum wage for sewing-machinists in rural areas suggests that the national minimum wage could constrain future labour-intensive industrialization if it maintains its real level. As discussed further in Chapters 6 and 7, the growth of workers' co-operatives in clothing manufacturing offers some hope in terms of saving (and perhaps even expanding) jobs as members share profits, rather than earn wages, and hence neither the NBC minimum wage nor the national minimum wage applies to them. It is doubtful, however, that such enterprises can spearhead the scale of labour-intensive growth required to address unemployment in the wider economy.

Labour-intensive manufacturing has generally been tainted with sweating, whether in Britain in the early 1900s or the global South in the early 2000s. The arguments for regulating working conditions—especially ensuring workers' safety—are compelling in all circumstances. The arguments for regulating wages are also compelling, but the extent to which they should be regulated varies according to the circumstances. Where the labour market is tight (such that retrenched workers are likely to find new employment elsewhere) or the state protects the unemployed against poverty through the welfare state, the moral case for setting high minimum wages is strong. In the presence of surplus labour and the absence of social protection for the unemployed, the moral case is weak.

6

Decent Work Fundamentalism and Job Destruction in the South African Clothing Manufacturing Industry

Minimum wage-setting has long shaped the nature and location of the South African clothing manufacturing industry. Collective bargaining in regional industrial councils initially served to protect white workers under apartheid but evolved to protect mostly higher-paid workers on a non-racial basis in the metropolitan areas. Minimum wages in rural areas were less regulated, allowing some low-wage, labour-intensive development. Yet regional minimum wage differentials in clothing manufacturing industry narrowed quickly in the post-apartheid period, altering the development trajectory of the industry. This chapter tells this story, showing how rising minimum wages, enforced as an instrument of economic upgrading (what we termed 'decent work fundamentalism' in Chapter 1) contributed to job destruction and deindustrialization in poorer parts of the country.

6.1 Minimum Wage-setting in the Clothing Manufacturing Industry

The South African clothing manufacturing industry originated in Cape Town, expanding into the Witwatersrand (the economy's mining and industrial heartland in the interior Transvaal province) in the 1920s and 1930s and across the country after the Second World War (Barker, 1962). Helped by higher tariffs (which protected domestic producers against imports), clothing manufacturing employment grew to an estimated 50,000 workers in the late 1950s. The workforce comprised primarily white women (on the Witwatersrand, protected by racially discriminatory job reservation policies) and 'coloured'[1] women (in Cape Town). Collective bargaining in clothing manufacturing originated in the Transvaal where a regional industrial council set wages at a level deemed socially appropriate for white workers. This relatively high level was affordable because of tariff protection and because Johannesburg clothing manufacturing firms produced primarily for the higher-income (mostly white) consumer market.

When the Wage Board proposed that similarly high minimum wages be set for clothing manufacturing firms in the rest of the country to protect white workers everywhere, Western Cape employers pushed to create their own regional industrial council and helped a regional trade union to organize their (mostly coloured) employees. Separate, regional industrial councils were established in the Western Cape, Natal and Eastern Cape (Barker, 1962: 373; Nicol, 1984). This resulted in a patchwork of regionally differentiated minimum wages.

In the 1940s and 1950s, many lower-wage producers in Johannesburg relocated to smaller towns just outside the regional scope of the Transvaal industrial council. These included Parys and Kroonstad (across the provincial border, in the northern Orange Free State), Charlestown and Ladysmith (across the provincial border, in northern Natal), and Stanger, Port Shepstone, and George along the Natal and Cape coasts. In these newer industrial areas, most workers were black African and were paid significantly lower wages than white workers covered by industrial councils. Labour productivity in the newer industrial areas was lower than on the Witwatersrand or in Cape Town where production was more capital-and skill-intensive, but lower-wage costs compensated for this difference and for the greater distance from both the sources of textiles and clothing markets (Barker, 1962: 373–4).

Firms shifting to the non-metro locations tended to produce the basic commodity products such as workwear, school uniforms, simple cotton shirts and skirts, jeans, and chinos. The first factory to move away from an industrial council area to Umtata in the Eastern Cape (in 1949) was a factory 'producing cheap men's and boy's outerwear, and shirts, of cotton, rayon or fiocco', and the first factory to move to Charlestown in rural Natal from Johannesburg (in 1950) produced 'lower-grade men's and boy's outerwear and shirts' (ibid.: 109). Such products targeted the mass market, including the growing numbers of urban black African workers (Nattrass, 1993). Firms that remained in Johannesburg produced 'high-grade fashion wear' for relatively high-income

[1] Coloured is a peculiarly South African term referring to people who are neither 'white' (understood broadly as being of European ancestry) nor 'black' or African (indigenous to Southern Africa) nor of South Asian descent (so-called 'Indian'). This category includes primarily people of Malay descent, people born of mixed parentage and some minority indigenous people such as the San and Khoi.

people where the higher wage costs could be 'passed on to the consumer' (Barker, 1962: 410).

Such dualism within the industry was recognized by the Wage Board. An investigation by the Wage Board found that, in 1955, the average weekly wage on the Witwatersrand was between two and three times the wages in the new industrial areas and that because of the differentiated nature of the industry, the imposition of nationally uniform wages was not practicable, economically justified, nor in the public interest (in ibid.: 375).

Tariff protection was crucial in the development of South Africa's clothing manufacturing industry, then an important vanguard of South African import-substitution industrialization (Nicol, 1984; Gibbon, 2004: 158; Rogerson, 2004). Beginning in the 1960s, the apartheid state sought to promote industrialization and employment in the bantustans and used lower wages as an incentive for labour-intensive firms to set up operations in industrial areas within the bantustans (such as Isithebe, on the Natal North Coast). In addition to exempting employers in these areas from even the Wage Board's wage determinations, the state provided a range of subsidies. Bell (1983, 1986) and Hart and Todes (1997) showed how clothing manufacturing employment grew rapidly in decentralized industrial areas within and adjacent to the bantustans, aided by government incentives (1954–1996) and by the fact that firms in such areas were not covered by collective agreements over minimum wages. Total wage employment in clothing manufacturing rose to 170,000 in the early 1980s and remained closed to this level into the early 1990s. The proportion of wage employment in the Transvaal declined from about 50 per cent in the 1940s to 10 per cent by 1985. Cape Town became the centre of higher-wage production. Meanwhile, the proportion of employment in areas outside of industrial councils' jurisdictions rose to about 30 per cent by 1991 (Altman, 1994: 8, 38, 41, 200). Decentralization was encouraged further by apartheid legislation that imposed constraints on the employment of black African workers in Johannesburg. Yet, even after racially discriminatory job reservation was scrapped and decentralization incentives were reduced from 1991 (ending in 1996), firms continued to locate in non-metro areas for wage-related reasons (Robbins et al., 2004: 25–6).

By 1991, between 15,000 and 25,000 workers were employed in the four so-called 'independent' apartheid-era bantustans in industrial areas such as Dimbaza (in the Ciskei), Butterworth (in the Transkei), and Babalegi (in Bophuthatswana). Perhaps as many as 20,000 were employed in the 'self-governing' bantustans, mostly in KwaZulu (in Isithebe, near Durban, as well as in Newcastle and Ladysmith) and Qwa-Qwa (in Phuthaditjaba). About 15,000 were employed in other small towns and about 100,000 were employed in the major metropolitan areas (Altman, 1994: 41; RSA (Swart Commission), 1994: 38).

Dualism remained strongly evident in that the higher-wage firms typically employed more skilled workers and specialized in higher-quality, custom-made clothing items using finer and more expensive fabrics whereas the lower-waged firms typically produced cheaper, lower-quality commodity garments and utility wear, for which labour costs were by far the most important cost item (Coughlin et al., 2004). Many firms in the metropolitan areas remained competitive into the 1990s by producing for the higher end of the clothing market (Kesper, 1998)—although intensified competition had increased across the industry and there was no evidence that any clothing firms (whether high or low wage) earned super-profits (Burns, 1998).

As of the mid-1990s, the South African clothing manufacturing industry accounted for about 10 per cent of manufacturing jobs and varied significantly across regions. Wages in Cape Town and Johannesburg were approximately three times higher than in towns such as Newcastle (in Northern KwaZulu-Natal) and wages in Phutaditjaba (in the southern Free State) were even lower than in Newcastle. Wages lay between these poles in the Eastern Cape, the northern Free State, Northern Cape and other parts of KwaZulu-Natal. The industry was thus differentiated, with higher-wage clothing firms in the metropolitan areas typically producing for the fashionable top end of the domestic market, whereas producers in lower-wage areas mostly targeted the mass market (Chapters 2 and 4).

When South Africa made the transition to democracy in 1994 there were five regional industrial councils (subsequently renamed bargaining councils) in the clothing manufacturing industry covering 70 per cent of workers, mostly in the metro areas (Altman, 1994: 41). In March 1996, the first post-apartheid Minister of Labour, Tito Mboweni, instructed the Wage Board to advise him on Wage Determination (WD) 471. During apartheid, WD 471 had applied to clothing workers outside the scope of the regional industrial/bargaining councils excepting workers in the (supposedly independent) 'bantustan' territories. As noted in Chapter 1, one of Minister Mboweni's first tasks was to consider how best to extend WD 471 to workers across the country whilst taking account of 'the problems being experienced in this industry'.[2] The Wage Board recommended expanding coverage to all workers outside the scope of bargaining councils but keeping the minima low, especially in Phuthaditjhaba, located in a particularly poverty-stricken former bantustan.

In 2000, the Minister of Labour instructed the new Employment Conditions Commission, which replaced the old Wage Board, to recommend new minimum wages for the approximately one in three clothing workers covered by the old WD 471. Under strong pressure from the SACTWU, the Employment

[2] 'Partial Wage Board Investigation: Amendment of Wage Determination 471: Clothing and Knitting Industry, RSA', *Government Notice* R.1733 (25 October 1996).

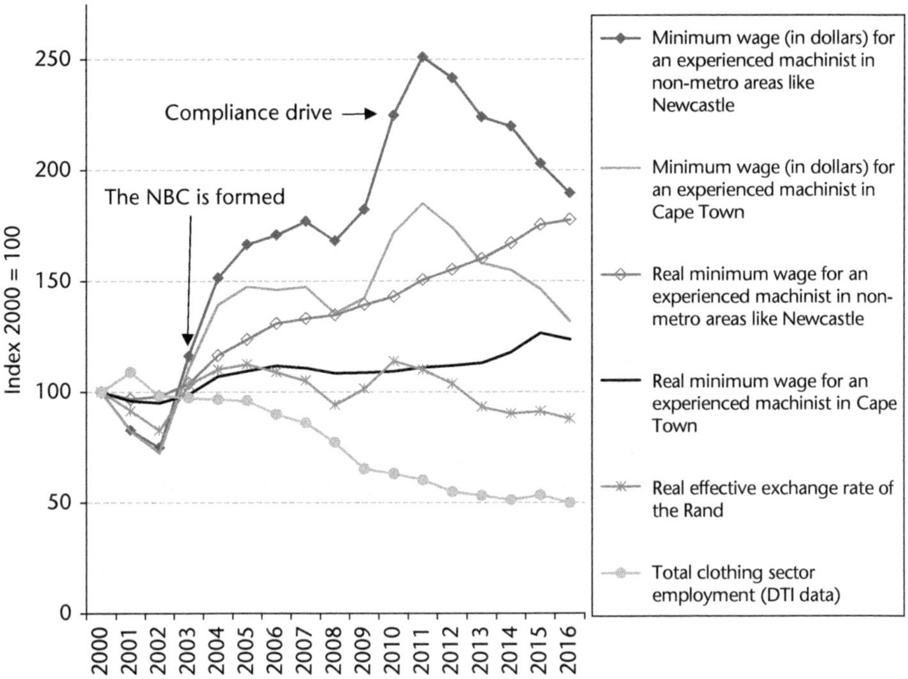

Figure 6.1 Trends in employment and minimum wages in the South African clothing manufacturing industry: 2000–2016.

Sources: NBC collective agreements, DTI data as reported in Barnes (2018), South African Reserve Bank (https://www.resbank.co.za) for price data.

Conditions Commission recommended raising the real minimum wage by 50 per cent. Fortunately for the affected firms, this increase occurred just as the Rand weakened from R6.94 to the US dollar in 2000 to R10.52 in 2002, giving them some protection against imports (which become more expensive as the domestic currency depreciates) and making exports more competitive on international markets. As can be seen in Figure 6.1, the real effective exchange rate, that takes into account the value of imported inputs such as textiles as well as the dollar cost of wages, fell sharply in 2001 and 2002,[3] giving clothing producers space to absorb the costs of higher minimum wages. Despite rising real wages in Rand terms, wages fell by about one-quarter in dollar terms from 2000 to 2002. This boosted the competitiveness of South African clothing producers and many reneged on their domestic orders to enter the lucrative export market (Morris and Einhorn, 2008). The value of South African exports of manufactured apparel (clothing) to the US, UK, France, Italy, and Germany

[3] The depreciation of the Rand increased the cost of imported textiles, but tariff reduction on textiles over the preceding years had helped decrease clothing producers' costs in this regard.

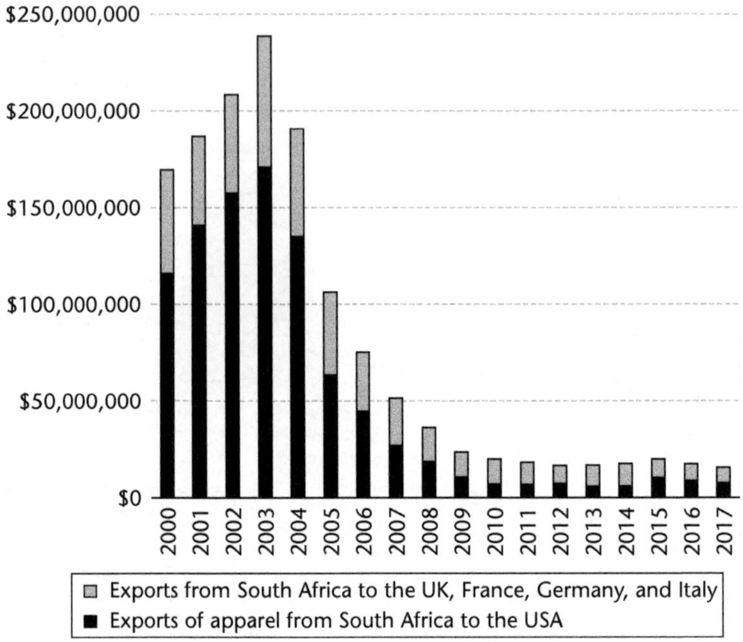

Figure 6.2 Exports of South African apparel to the US, UK, France, Italy, and Germany.
Sources: Comtrade (https://comtrade.un.org/data), data for HS 61 and HS 62.

rose sharply (Figure 6.2). An assessment of the strengths and weaknesses of South Africa's clothing manufacturing industry in 2000 concluded that despite production costs being higher than Asia, South Africa was internationally competitive in cut-make-and trim because of faster response times from local firms compared to firms in East Asia (Engelbrecht, discussed in Anstey, 2004: 1843).

This favourable situation was, however, reversed by the appreciation of the Rand from 2003 to 2005, which drove up dollar wages sharply (Figure 6.1). Exports collapsed and never recovered (Figure 6.2). South African clothing producers, finding themselves no longer competitive on international markets, sought to reconnect with domestic retailers, only to find that South African retailers had 'discovered' China (Morris and Einhorn, 2008) and were even engaging the services of *Li & Fung*, the large contract manufacturer and supply chain coordinator at the heart of the international clothing global value chain. Despite the 45 per cent tariff, imports of apparel rose sharply, especially from China, but also other low-cost countries (Figure 6.3).

Imports from Lesotho and Swaziland also increased steeply in the 2000s. South African firms and investors from other countries (including Mauritius) opened production plants in Lesotho and Swaziland to take advantage of

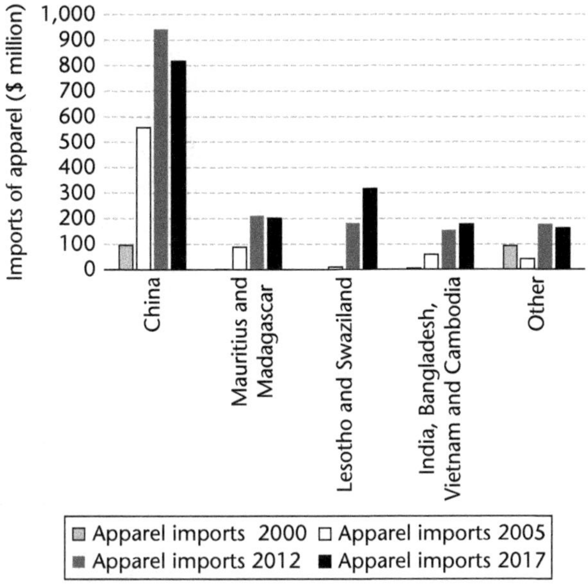

Figure 6.3 Imports of apparel into South Africa.
Sources: Comtrade (https://comtrade.un.org/data), data for HS 61 and HS 62.

relatively low labour costs as well as to escape 'the rigid and inflexible labour market conditions governing South African labour relations' (notably that piecework payment systems were accommodated in these countries but not in South Africa) and to enjoy a 'more compliant union environment' (Morris et al., 2011: 98, 102, 106; Shakya, 2011). South African-owned operations in Lesotho are easily able to continue to supply South African retailers as Lesotho and Swaziland are members of the Southern African Customs Union, giving them duty-free access to the South African market. Geographical proximity with South Africa allows South African clothing manufacturers to retain their head offices in South Africa and to send managers to Lesotho and Swaziland when necessary (Morris et al., 2011: 106; Morris and Staritz, 2017). Lesotho also benefits from duty-free access to US and European markets (via AGOA and the Cotonou Agreement).[4]

By the mid-2000s, there were almost fifty major firms in Lesotho employing a total of 47,000 workers. Lesotho had become the largest exporter of clothing to the US in Sub-Saharan Africa (Morris et al., 2011: 97; Morris and Staritz, 2017: 307). Whilst the majority of this workforce was employed in factories producing for export to the US, more than 5,000 workers were working

[4] The Lesotho Ministry of Trade and Industry, Cooperatives and Marketing published a glossy Practical Guide to Doing Business in Lesotho, setting out the benefits of relocation to Lesotho (Lesotho, 2008).

for eight companies producing primarily for the South African market,[5] including (for example) *Tern Sportswear*, which moved from Isithebe on the KwaZulu-Natal North Coast. The Lesotho industry contracted in 2008 due to a combination of factors (including the global financial crisis and currency appreciation) but recovered subsequently to stabilize at about 39,000 workers by 2012 (Morris and Staritz, 2017: 307). Employment in clothing manufacturing in Swaziland stabilized at around 12,000 by the late 2000s (Morris et al., 2011: 102).

By contrast, the South African clothing manufacturing industry contracted sharply in the 2000s. As Godfrey puts it:

> Apparel manufacturers were now caught between a rock and a hard place. On the one hand, the retail sector was importing increasing volumes of apparel and driving down prices, exports were not an option with a stronger Rand, and manufacturers were getting little help from government to assist them to respond to this challenge. On the other hand, labour costs were rising and the strength of SACTWU had closed off the option of a low-wage competitive strategy to counter foreign competition, although relocation to lower wage regions provided some respite. The result was that the formal (regulated) industry began to shrink.
>
> (2015: 496)

According to data from the NBC, the number of clothing employers fell from 1178 in 2005 to 947 by 2012 and total employees fell from 94,851 to 54,620 over the same period. Estimates from the Department of Trade and Industry (DTI) covering both formal and informal[6] enterprises suggest that clothing manufacturing employment was higher, but similarly on a strong trend decline (from 147,000 in 2005 to 84,000 in 2012).[7] Domestic production of clothing as a share of total domestic demand fell from 75 per cent in 2005 to

[5] *BA Tex* (1997), *Jonsson* (2002), *Humin Jeanswear* (2002), *Ace Apparel* (2005), *Corporate Clothing* (2006), *Chelsea West* (2006), *Peter Blond* (2006) and *Tern Sportswear* (2007).

[6] SACTWU suspected that there were significant numbers of clothing workers employed informally as homeworkers. However, after going on a recruitment drive in 1999, by mid-2001 SACTWU had only 172 members who could be classified as industrial homeworkers (of whom 72 were paid-up). The Self-employed Workers Union had 1,200 self-employed members in the clothing industry, mostly in Durban, and it was unclear how many were previously employed formal clothing workers (Bennett, 2003: 14, 34).

[7] The industrial/bargaining councils collated data on employees in registered firms, but these did not cover the entire country until 2003/4 and always omitted employees in unregistered firms (i.e. firms that failed to register with the NBC). The DTI provides data from 1993, but it is unclear precisely what the data cover. The DTI data approximately track data from the NBC from 2003. The first data (from 1993) are higher than data for employment in areas covered by the old regional industrial councils (as reported in Altman, 1994: 41 and 200), but a lot lower than data on total clothing employment including employees *outside* of the industrial council areas (ibid.; see also Godfrey, 1997: 48). The data for 1998–2003 are substantially higher than the aggregate data from the old regional councils. The data for the 2000s are substantially lower than estimates derived from the Labour Force Surveys.

60 per cent in 2011 as the import share rose from 25 per cent to 40 per cent (Morris and Barnes, 2014: 10).

Godfrey argues that retrenched workers 'flowed' into informal and unregistered firms (2015: 496). There is some evidence that retrenched workers in 1990s and early 2000s purchased machinery from liquidated factories and went into business on their own (Godfrey, 1997: 126, fn 67; Skinner and Voladia, 2002: 82; Rogerson, 2010: 693). Many of these firms would have been operating 'under the radar', attempting to avoid detection by the regional bargaining councils and hence might not have been recorded as being in the industry. Even so, there is no evidence from the Labour Force Surveys that declining formal employment was compensated for by rising informal employment in South African clothing manufacturing. Indeed, Godfrey et al. show that the number and proportion of jobs in clothing manufacturing enterprises that were not compliant with labour legislation shrunk, perhaps because some enterprises had become formal businesses or workers' co-operatives, but more likely because they had gone out of business (Godfrey et al., 2010: 162).

In early 2005, Cape Town's iconic *Rex Trueform* closed. The mothers of both SACTWU's General Secretary (Ebrahim Patel) and the Minister of Finance (Trevor Manuel) had worked at *Rex Trueform* and its closure was emblematic of a wider collapse in competitiveness in the industry. Competition from low-wage countries was crucial, but rising minimum wages—an entirely home-grown shock—formed the other arm of the vice. From 2004, rising minimum wages were the responsibility of the new NBC (discussed further below), which deliberately sought to reduce wage differentials across regions and to promote higher-wage, higher-productivity 'decent work'.

6.1.1 *Decent Work Fundamentalism and the NBC*

SACTWU was formed in 1989 through the amalgamation of various independent trade unions in the South African clothing and textile industries. It originally had few members in lower-wage areas and was more concerned with countrywide wage parity than with protecting low-wage employment in rural areas. It sought, and eventually succeeded in 2003 in creating, the NBC 'as a vehicle to reduce the regional wage differentials in the sector' (Godfrey et al., 2010: 155). The regional employer associations outside the Western Cape (representing 45 per cent of employers) initially resisted the formation of the NBC, although some higher-wage employers recognized the benefits in terms of regulating wage-based competition. Employer's associations from the lower-wage areas were concerned about the agenda of narrowing wage differentials and wanted to retain a more flexible wage structure, including provision for piecework payments. The different employers' associations eventually agreed to abolish the regional councils and establish the NBC when SACTWU (and the Department of Labour) increased the pressure, and an agreement was brokered in terms of which the statutory wage differentials between regions were to be narrowed in return for the promise of a new national wage structure or model providing for variations in wages and payment systems on some basis other than region alone (Anstey, 2004: 1846–52; Seardel, 2004: 19–20).

This agreement implied broad acceptance of differentiation (dualism) within the industry. Commenting soon after the agreement, the facilitator of the NBC creation process observed that:

> the days of a 'one size fits all' approach to wage bargaining are clearly past.... [I]n the context of a global economy in which employers find themselves in very diverse situations of competitiveness and in which it is critical to preserve and create jobs it is inevitable that one or even a few sizes will not fit all. (Anstey, 2004: 1862)

Despite some discussions, however, no new national wage structure or model was ever agreed. In practice, the NBC became the vehicle for a coalition of well-organized, high-wage employers and the trade union, to restructure the clothing manufacturing industry by pushing it towards uniform minimum wages without any substitute 'wage model'. NBC minimum wages continued to vary across regions, but differentials narrowed over time and collective agreements limited the space for productivity-linked pay. This harmed the most labour-intensive firms where the preferred wage model is to pay low basic wages (below the current minimum wage) combined with production-linked pay (piece-work) for particular categories of worker, notably machinists. In this system, average wages are lower than in NBC-compliant firms, but some workers (the most productive machinists) are able to earn substantially more than others and hence there is substantial variation in actual wage income within a factory. This is typical of piecework systems in general that have been shown to result in greater productivity, greater variation in earnings and higher average earnings than in systems without piecework (Seiler, 1984; Lazear, 2000).

In 1996, *Time Clothing*, a factory outside of East London, experimented with a wage model in which workers were hired as 'individual contractors' and organized into production lines. At the end of each week, production was assessed and workers were paid proportionately. The factory found that it no longer had to hire supervisory monitors because the workers 'policed themselves'. However, the legal basis for his model was undermined by a change in the law (requiring that individual contractors had to own their own machinery or be counted as employees) and, after being threatened by the NBC, the factory went back to its old model. According to the production manager, productivity plummeted and they were forced to rehire monitors.[8]

[8] Interview with John Goldhill, 19 August 2015.

After the creation of the NBC, wages for labour-intensive firms in the non-metro areas rose faster than metro wages. SACTWU set the target of raising minimum wages in low-wage areas (which in 2004 were about 40 per cent of Cape Town wages) to 80 per cent of the metropolitan minima (Harrison, 1997: 95). As can be seen in Figure 6.1, real wage growth was faster in places like Newcastle than in Cape Town until 2010. This was a strategy of decent work fundamentalism. The union seems to have imagined that jobs would not be destroyed (because firms in low-wage areas were supposedly earning super-profits through the exploitation of workers, and could therefore pay for higher wages) or, if 'sweatshop' jobs were destroyed, that the industry was better off without them. The union's objective was to work with government's industrial policymakers to push the industry onto an 'upgrading' (more skill- and capital-intensive) trajectory and to obtain capital assets within the industry itself (and later also in the casino business), as we discuss further in Chapter 7.

On the union side, SACTWU did organize a majority of workers (although its membership was inflated by closed-shop agreements, and the union remained dominated by its mostly male Cape Town-based officials and members).[9] But the employers' associations in the NBC never represented a majority of firms in the industry. The larger, higher-wage firms in Cape Town dominated the NBC, whilst smaller, lower-wage firms in KwaZulu-Natal and the Free State were largely unrepresented. As the only union, SACTWU controlled 50 per cent of the votes on the NBC and needed to recruit only one of the various regional employers' associations to conclude national collective agreements, which would then be extended across the industry by the Minister of Labour. Whereas the technocrats in the Wage Board and Employment Conditions Commission had an obligation to worry about job destruction, and the regional bargaining councils in lower-wage areas would not agree to wage increases that threatened the local industry, the formation of the NBC allowed higher-wage employers to join with the union to shut down lower-wage firms.

In July 2003, the Minister of Labour extended countrywide for the first time the minimum wages agreed in the NBC. This occurred in the context of a strongly appreciating Rand between 2003 and 2005, resulting in a sharp increase in dollar wages and an abrupt decline in competitiveness (Figure 6.1). Exports contracted sharply (Figure 6.2) and the large knitwear exporters in Newcastle shut down. The remaining clothing firms in the non-metro areas either shed jobs or simply refused to comply with the new wage rates. The

[9] In 2003, 53 per cent of SACTWU's 59,574 members were in the Western Cape. By January 2011, membership had dropped to 47,815 (of which 32 per cent were in the Western Cape). SACTWU's membership in KwaZulu-Natal rose from 25 per cent to 42 per cent over the same period—in part because the compliance drive increased registration of firms and as SACTWU mobilized workers on the issue.

NBC responded by issuing non-compliance notices—the first step in taking legal action—against almost 1,000 employers during this period (Anstey, 2004: 1859).

Feeling steam-rolled by SACTWU and the Cape Clothing Association, employers' organizations in most non-metro areas (including Newcastle) withdrew from the NBC. Three non-participating employer associations initiated in 2005 a legal challenge against the extension of minimum wages to them, but dropped the case after receiving legal opinion that they would lose.[10] By 2010, only 10 per cent of registered KwaZulu-Natal clothing firms and 25 per cent of all registered clothing firms countrywide were represented by the employers' associations still in the NBC. These 'party' firms were, on average, almost three times larger than 'non-party' firms[11] but they employed only one-third of all clothing workers in registered KwaZulu-Natal firms and less than half of all clothing workers in registered firms across South Africa as a whole. They were even less representative of the broader clothing industry if one also takes into account the fact that some (perhaps many) firms opted not to register with the NBC despite being legally obliged to do so.[12]

Between 2002 and 2010, the NBC and the Minister of Labour (through extensions) raised minimum wages in the low-wage areas by a further 50 per cent. The relatively labour-intensive employers in non-metropolitan areas like Newcastle and elsewhere were squeezed hard by the combination of fast-rising minimum wages and currency appreciation, which together doubled their labour costs in dollar terms (Figure 6.1). This contributed to the collapse in employment and rising average labour productivity, as only the relatively capital- and skill-intensive enterprises survived.

6.2 Trade and Industrial Policy

By the end of the 2000s, South Africa had the fourth highest dollar wages in clothing manufacturing out of the thirty-six low- and middle-income countries presented in Table 4.1, but only the tenth highest labour productivity,

[10] Interview with John Lingenfelder on 26 February 2014.

[11] In 2011, party firms employed on average 114 workers, whilst non-party firms employed only forty-one (NBC, 'Employment strengths as of 28th February 2011', data provided by the NBC).

[12] The March 2011 Labour Force Survey estimated that total wage employment in clothing manufacturing was about 60 per cent higher than that recorded by the NBC, suggesting that there are large numbers of workers in unregistered firms. A 2011 list of non-compliant firms from the NBC's Durban office recorded 89 known but unregistered firms in KwaZulu-Natal, employing 4,680 workers. If one includes these 'known and unregistered' firms in the calculation of representivity, then only 8 per cent of firms in KwaZulu-Natal, collectively employing only one quarter of the province's clothing workers, were party to the NBC. Whilst we do not have comparable information for other provinces, it is clear that, by late 2010, substantially less than half of clothing workers countrywide were employed in firms that were represented in the NBC.

making it one of the least competitive in terms of unit labour costs. Between 1996 and 2009, South Africa's clothing manufacturing industry trajectory was one of rising average labour productivity, achieved in large part by the destruction of lower-wage and productivity jobs in more labour-intensive firms (Figure 4.4). Labour productivity rose faster than average wages (making this a pro-capital growth path) but not fast enough to improve international competitiveness to a level required to prevent further import penetration and a precipitous collapse in exports and employment. The South African government responded by focusing on industrial policy to boost labour productivity further, yet such industrial policy efforts proved belated and inadequate to stem job losses.

Back in 1992, as South Africa was beginning the negotiated transition to democracy, employers joined with SACTWU and government officials in a tripartite 'panel' and 'task team'—which together became known as the Swart Commission—to draft a long-term strategic plan for the clothing and textile industries. The Commission reported that protection and isolation had left most parts of the textile and clothing industries uncompetitive internationally and the combination of expensive inputs (notably high tariffs on important fabric to protect the textile industry) and relatively high wages meant that South Africa's clothing manufacturing industry was 'completely uncompetitive with countries such as Malaysia, Indonesia, China and Vietnam' (RSA, 1994: iv, 42, 89). In an early articulation of the 'upgrading' strategy that came to dominate post-apartheid South African industrial policy, the Commission recommended that the textile industry should become more 'outward-looking, more focused, high-technology driven, market-oriented and flexible' and that the clothing manufacturing industry should focus primarily on 'higher priced garment sectors and niches' (ibid.: iii). Employers and the union concurred on the necessity of export-driven growth, sharp tariff reduction (to put pressure on firms to upgrade) and state subsidies for new technology (to assist firms in meeting the challenges of a competitive global order). Overall, these were the kinds of measures intended to raise labour productivity and allow higher wages that were recommended at the same time by the separate, COSATU-linked Industrial Strategy Project, including the Project's study for the clothing sector specifically (Altman, 1994).

Most of this analysis was endorsed within both COSATU and the ANC, both of which supported trade liberalization as a measure to promote industrial efficiency. In the mid- and late 1990s both the ANC-led government and COSATU seem to have imagined that the combination of the sticks of trade liberalization and wage increases, and the carrots of skills training and subsidies, would suffice to shift the economy towards higher-wage, higher-productivity forms of production. The first two Ministers of Trade and

Industry in the newly elected ANC governments—Trevor Manuel (1994–6) and then Alec Erwin (1996–2004)—reduced tariffs and introduced export incentives but opted not to implement the state subsidies recommended by the Swart Commission and the COSATU-linked Industrial Strategy Project (Hirschsohn et al., 2000: 71–4).

Tariffs were reduced sharply, faster even than required by the then international General Agreement on Tariffs and Trade (GATT) (Edwards, 2005). According to GATT, South Africa was committed to reducing its most favoured nation tariffs on imported textiles and clothing from 100 per cent in 1995 to 80 per cent by 2001, 59 per cent by 2004 and 45 per cent by 2006. Instead, South Africa started lowering tariffs in 1994 (to 90 per cent) dropping them sharply to 40 per cent by 2002 (tariffs were subsequently raised again to 45 per cent in 2009). This was justified by a development ideology depicting tariff reduction as an instrument of efficiency promotion. As Trevor Manuel, who became Minister of Finance after serving as Minister of Trade and Industry, was fond of saying: Tariff protection made firms 'lazy' (Pressly, 2007). For the ruling ANC, lowering tariffs was a way of disciplining business. The negative effects on clothing producers of falling tariffs on clothing imports were only partially offset by falling tariffs on textiles (which reduced the cost of importing material), from 100 per cent in the early 1990s to 28 per cent in 2001.

Collapsing employment refocused attention on the failure of industrial policy to compensate for rising wages and international competition. Under pressure from employers, the DTI initiated a consultative process to formulate a 'Customized Sector Plan' for the clothing industry. The plan focused inter alia on trying to improve coordination between producers and retailers (that is, encourage retailers to form supportive and more stable relationships with domestic producers and hopefully reduce their reliance on imported clothing). SACTWU initially remained aloof from this process but, when the draft sector plan was released in 2005, used its political influence to make changes to the document, thereby undermining the consultative process that had produced it, and alienating the retailers in particular (Morris, 2011; Morris and Levy, 2016). As discussed in more detail in Chapter 7, SACTWU preferred to work directly with the state (to obtain subsidies and restrictions on Chinese imports) rather than engage in bargaining with employers or retailers. Most of the sector plan's priority areas were defensive, for example dealing with under-invoiced imports, obtaining 'policy consistency' between members of the Southern African Customs Union and preventing illegal imports. The sector plan contained also a set of objectives from promoting black economic empowerment, to capital upgrading programmes and supporting regional 'clusters' (see Barnes, 2005: 11–14). No changes were proposed to the wage model. The result, according to Morris and Levy (2016), was a policy endorsed by SACTWU and the government but without the commitment or enthusiastic support of the other industry players. Under pressure from SACTWU, the government temporarily restricted Chinese clothing imports, and referred applications for exemptions to SACTWU—which empowered the union to compel employers to make further concessions (Morris and Levy, 2016). In the meantime, retailers sourced products from low-wage Southern African countries instead (Reed, 2012). As can be seen in Figure 6.2, imports rose from low-wage countries including Mauritius, Madagascar, Lesotho, and Swaziland.

Large capital subsidies were paid out under a Clothing and Textile Competitiveness Improvement Programme[13] in order to assist the large clothing producers to upgrade skills and production capacity. This included moving from 'bundle' systems (notably the manual passing of bundled, partially completed clothing items down a production line) to automated 'modular' systems focusing on teamwork including self-directed teams of workers responsible for quality, in which workers sit in a U-shaped arrangement rather than in production lines. Implemented well, this system had the potential to improve morale and productivity but was not particularly well suited to the production of basic garments in large quantities. Furthermore, a key requirement for industrial policy subsidies was that all parties complied with NBC agreements, thereby automatically rendering ineligible the most labour-intensive firms in the industry.

The DTI also offered production 'incentives' (then worth 10 per cent of value-added, later reduced to 7.5 per cent) to help fund capital investment. These, too, were available only to producers that were compliant with NBC collective agreements. By increasing their capital-intensity and enforcing higher wage costs, assisted firms were reoriented towards the higher-income consumer market. As the DTI put it, capital subsidies were 'expected to move the industry up the value chain to activities that are far more sustainable than competing against "sweatshop" labour practices and pervasive government subsidization in other developing countries' (DTI, 2010). Over the following three years, the DTI made 175 awards, totalling R470 million, to compliant clothing producers.[14] Given employment in compliant firms, and the fact that most but not all compliant companies received awards, this amounted to approximately R20,000 per worker, that is, double the 2008 manufacturing survey estimate of the capital costs associated with each job in the industry (Table 4.3)! *Seardel*—part-owned by SACTWU—received at least R67 million for its apparel division (*Seardel*, 2012) (see further

[13] http://www.thedti.gov.za/financial_assistance/financial_incentive.jsp?id=35&subthemeid=25
[14] Minister of Trade and Industry, written reply (April 2013) to written question 610 tabled in the National Assembly by Mr G. Hill-Lewis.

Chapter 7). This expenditure was designed to ensure that *only* those jobs at the top end of the clothing industry would survive. In the 2009 'Rescue package: Clothing and Textiles' that was adopted by the DTI and the NBC stated explicitly that a 'policy that seeks to base competitiveness on low wages would not be consistent with South Africa's human rights culture' and that 'sustainable human resource policies will allow the industry to compete in the market for high fashion and technical garments and textiles and to deliver innovative, quality products that require well-trained and productive workers' (DTI, 2009).

Substantial government funding has been directed towards the formation of 'clusters' of firms and retailers in the clothing industry, to consultants who conduct the benchmarking studies, and to firms to upgrade their technologies through production incentives and the like (Morris and Barnes, 2014: 16–17). The most successful cluster was the Cape Clothing and Textile Cluster facilitated by consultants. The Cape Cluster collected data on a range of performance indicators (such as absenteeism, production down-time and quality) to 'benchmark' firms against so-called international standards. A persistent theme of such analyses was that South African labour costs absorbed too high a share of total costs and that performance and quality tended to lag (e.g. CCTC, 2012). The proposed solutions were always to practice leaner manufacturing and generally improve labour productivity through the adoption of 'international best practice'.

Prestige Clothing was assisted to form closer relations with *The Foschini Group* and to transform the Cape-based business into a quick-response fashion producer with a strong working relationship with retailers. The success of *Prestige Clothing* indicates that it is certainly possible to use quick response approaches and to target the higher ends of the clothing market (Thomas, 2015). Other industrial policy-supported activities included the development of a design centre for firms owned by SACTWU (see Chapter 7).

The fact that industrial policy support was oriented towards the compliant firms (paying the legal minimum wages), and the higher-income end of the product market, was not regarded as a problem by the DTI or SACTWU. They saw the future of South African clothing manufacturing as dependent on firms being able to 'compete in the market for high fashion and technical garments and textiles and to deliver innovative and quality products that require well trained and productive workers' (DTI, 2009; Kriel, 2012: para 57). Indeed, pushing up minimum wages faster for the labour-intensive non-metro firms than for metro firms is part and parcel of this desired structural adjustment of South African clothing manufacturing towards higher-value-added products using 'upgraded' processes and machinery. The flip side of this decent work fundamentalism was the active destruction of lower-wage jobs in more labour-intensive firms.

6.3 Enforcing Minimum Wages and Job Destruction: The 2009–11 'Compliance Drive'

The 2009–11 'compliance drive' by NBC enforcement officials demonstrates the power of national bargaining councils to influence development trajectories. In this section we discuss the compliance drive in more detail. We focus, in particular, on the conflict this sparked between the NBC and labour-intensive clothing manufacturers in Newcastle.

By the end of 2009, the NBC had writs against over 400 non-compliant clothing factories, mostly in the lower-wage areas of Newcastle, Botshabelo, and Phutaditjaba. At the time, the NBC had 1,039 employers registered as falling under its scope. Some of the non-compliant factories had not registered with the NBC (despite being legally obliged to do so) but were known to inspectors and the NBC (and recorded as 'non-compliant, non-registered firms'). In 2010, the NBC launched a 'compliance drive' against what it termed the 'worst offenders', that is, clothing manufacturing firms that were neither paying fully their levies to the NBC nor the minimum wage that had been extended to them.

At the end of 2010, the NBC raised minimum wages again—and once again these minimum wages were automatically extended to all firms by the Minister of Labour. Faced with rising labour costs, and the increasingly aggressive enforcement of NBC collective agreements, a group of non-compliant firms formed a new employers' organization, the United Clothing and Textile Association. Five firms from Newcastle together with the new Association challenged the new minimum wages in court. At stake were somewhere between 20,000 and 28,000 jobs, most in non-metropolitan areas such as Newcastle where unemployment and poverty were pervasive. The issue generated considerable national and even international media attention.

The NBC had substantial capacity to enforce its regulations. Leon Deetlefs, the NBC's 'compliance manager' from 2003 until 2011 (Figure 6.4), was informed, on being hired, that he had '*carte blanche*' and that 'cost was no object' in the quest to enforce minimum wages throughout the clothing manufacturing industry (interview with Deetlefs, 21 August, 2014). He opened offices across the country, hired inspectors, purchased vehicles, and 'got his teeth into' the job. His *modus operandi* was to start with internal NBC hearings, followed by obtaining arbitration awards against recalcitrant firms (which were subsequently made orders of the Labour Court) followed by writs of execution that could be implemented against the non-compliant firm by sheriffs of the court. Deetlefs did his job with an efficiency honed by his business school training, his understanding of clothing firms (he had previously been the founding chairperson of the Kei Clothing Employers Association) and background in labour law. He used the legislation and the NBC's resources to charge

Figure 6.4 Leon Deetlefs in a clothing workers' co-operative.*

* Copyright *Mail&Guardian* and Rogan Ward: https://mg.co.za/article/2013-02-01-textile-labour-leader-does-u-turn.

non-compliant firms not only for their failure to pay current minimum wages, but for amounts owing to workers in the past and for accumulated NBC levies.

Many writs were obtained, but not fully executed as NBC officials sought last minute agreements with firms over payments of dues and pension fund contributions owed to the NBC, as well as wages owed to workers. For firms that had been non-compliant for many years, the amounts owing in terms of back-pay and NBC contributions were substantial and self-evidently impossible to honour fully.[15] There was, therefore, some room for negotiation, although the high current cost of compliance remained the major sticking point. Some owners begged for time to implement the minimum wage whilst completing their existing orders and simultaneously making plans to shut down their companies. Some opened new businesses, sometimes in different locations, forcing the NBC to begin the process anew. They also leased machinery from other factories to avoid having these assets attached (confiscated). Others downsized to micro-enterprises (employing five or fewer workers) because such firms were automatically exempted from the NBC minimum wage. Some reorganized themselves as workers' co-operatives, because under the 2005 Co-operatives Act, members of workers' co-operatives did not qualify

[15] According to an audit done in September 2009, R40 million was owed in arrears payments to workers in non-compliant firms (Enslin-Payne, 2011).

as employees, meaning that the Labour Relations Act did not apply to them and hence that the NBC had no jurisdiction over workers' co-operatives.

Deetlefs told us in an interview (21 August 2014) that his legal strategy 'boxed in' non-compliant firms and that his strategy of enforcing compliance was responsible for 'taking out' about 45 per cent of the industry. His dogged pursuit of non-compliant firms was not without costs, however, as he was physically assaulted by employers and shot at by 'someone in a black Mercedes'. Deetlefs told us that when he left the NBC, there 'was not a single non-compliant firm that did not have a writ of execution' against them. He subsequently regretted his role in job destruction. He left the NBC to help labour-intensive producers in low-wage areas to restructure into workers' co-operatives in an effort to stay in business (Figure 6.4).

When the scale of job destruction became clear, the NBC, sometimes supported by SACTWU, began to hesitate before instructing sheriffs to implement the writs of execution. Deetlefs told us that the 'brakes came on' for the first time in 2004 after he had shut down forty firms. Representatives from the employer organizations that had voted for the higher minimum wages—and for the NBC to take action against non-compliant firms—started phoning him to ask if he could slow down the pace of obtaining writs of execution because they were worried about the very survival of the industry. Deetlefs said that employers and SACTWU would also sometimes intervene in an attempt to save particular firms. Employers and the union were, in Deetlefs' own words, trying to 'have their bread buttered on both sides', pushing up wages in general but begging for clemency for firms in which they had an interest. SACTWU, which he described as 'fanatical' in its bargaining position in the NBC and 'corrupt' in its attempts to save particular firms, would attempt to cut deals and influence compliance managers to prevent the writs from being executed in firms if many of its members stood to lose their jobs. Deetlefs heard reports of employers paying local union officials R1,000 a week to keep the NBC off their backs. In his opinion, the system had 'so many loopholes, so many double-standards'—but it also had the capacity to destroy large numbers of jobs, as the 2010 'compliance drive' illustrated publicly and dramatically.

When the NBC went on its 'compliance drive' in 2009/10, this simply meant that the NBC instructed sheriffs to execute existing writs obtained against non-compliant firms, to attach their assets and 'push them over the cliff', in Deetlefs' colourful language. The story of the compliance drive and its aftermath provides a concentrated lens on the role of bargaining councils in shaping employment. On one level, it demonstrated the power of bargaining councils to destroy jobs, especially at the low-wage, labour-intensive end of the industry, posing a direct threat to inclusive development. On another level, it showed that the politics of decent work fundamentalism is not straightforward, that the NBC, the government, and SACTWU were prepared to step back from the brink and negotiate various compromises. Even so, the enforcement of minimum wages sent a clear signal to the labour-intensive end of the industry that it was vulnerable and tolerated only in the short-term.

Most relatively low-wage, labour-intensive employers outside of Cape Town adopted a strategy of circumventing, as far as possible, the NBC. When discovered by NBC inspectors, many would shut down and some would open under new names elsewhere, essentially playing a cat and mouse game with the NBC. But the cat steadily prevailed, and many firms left the industry. In June 2011, five firms from Newcastle, together with the United Clothing and Textile Association, attempted a collective fightback by launching a judicial review application. They requested that the decision taken by the Minister of Labour at the end of 2010 to extend NBC-agreed minimum wages to them be set aside.[16] In the alternative, they sought to have declared unconstitutional the section of the Labour Relations Act that permitted the Minister to extend collective agreements without acting reasonably and having regard to the consequences for unemployment (Chen, 2011a). In 2013, the court ruled that the Minister of Labour had erred in accepting that the NBC was representative. The court found that the employers' associations that were party to the NBC did not employ a majority of even the registered employees in the industry. The court therefore set aside the Minister of Labour's extension of the collective agreement signed in the NBC.

As discussed in more detail below, the judgment bought the Newcastle clothing firms additional time, but unfortunately did nothing to resolve the underlying conflict. The Labour Relations Act gives the Minister of Labour the power, under a different section, to extend collective agreements, even if the parties to a bargaining council are not representative—which she did indeed do subsequent to the court judgment. The court did not rule on the question of the reasonableness of such action. The Cape Town-based union and employers continued to push for raised minimum wages in other parts of South Africa on the (correct) assumption that the Minister of Labour would continue to extend these wages across the country even though only a small minority of firms employing a minority of clothing workers were represented in the NBC.

National bargaining councils were established to bring employers and workers to a national negotiating table. In practice, the NBC in the clothing manufacturing industry provided an institutional mechanism through which some employers and the union could raise wages and impose them on other employers. Between 2003 and 2010, the NBC and Minister of Labour

[16] Case number 5642/2011 in the KwaZulu-Natal High Court.

repeatedly raised the minimum wages in the lower-wage areas like Newcastle. In 2000, minimum wages in clothing manufacturing in Newcastle were about half those in Cape Town (R192 and R390 per week respectively on average for the year). By 2011, after seven years of wage agreements in the NBC, they were at two-thirds the Cape Town level (R504 and R754 per week respectively).[17] This was achieved by the NBC pushing up non-metro wages at a much faster rate than wages in Cape Town. Indeed, up until 2010, real minimum wages in metro areas like Cape Town barely kept abreast of inflation (Figure 6.1). SACTWU wage negotiators were prepared to sacrifice real wage growth in an effort to save jobs in Cape Town—as they themselves recognized[18]—whilst destroying jobs in non-metro areas such as Newcastle. In dollar terms, however, wages rose from 2002/3 in all regions, with adverse consequences for competitiveness across the industry (Figure 6.6).

Metro-based employers were prepared to go along with the strategy as a means of constraining wage growth in their own factories. Even so, many jobs were also lost in the urban centres: the iconic former *Rex Trueform* factory that had provided jobs to the mothers of two of South Africa's future cabinet Ministers, was converted into a 'heritage' building repurposed for office space. The strengthening Rand between 2008 and 2010 put pressure on domestic clothing producers throughout the country. Employer organizations in the NBC supported the compliance drive not only to put pressure on any non-compliant competitors, but also to put pressure on SACTWU (by threatening imminent, multiple, job losses) to adopt a new wage model.

Some non-compliant firms applied to the NBC for exemptions from the minimum wage on grounds of financial hardship. The Labour Relations Act allows producers to apply for exemptions from sections of NBC agreements. The applications were turned down (Enslin-Payne, 2011). South Africa's bargaining councils rarely grant exemptions from the industry minimum wage, and the NBC seemed especially reluctant to do so. It even stopped hearing any exemption applications during part of 2010.

The NBC and the umbrella employers' association—the Apparel Manufacturers of South Africa (AMSA)—defended the compliance drive primarily as a struggle for survival by compliant firms, demonizing non-compliant firms in the process. The NBC compliance manager told reporters that non-compliant firms were 'taking business away from compliant firms whose existence is being threatened, so we cannot allow the situation to continue' (quoted in

[17] These figures are for the minimum wage for an experienced machinist. The minimum wages payable to trainee machinists were lower, but rose faster, as the NBC narrowed the gap between trainee and experienced machinists as well as the gap between lower-wage areas such as Newcastle and Cape Town.

[18] SACTWU Press Release, 'SACTWU and NCMA sew together wage agreement', 9 June 2005; http://sactwu.org.za/pr-and-news/archived-2005/71-sactwu-and-ncma-sew-together-wage-agreement.

Bisseker, 2010). Johann Baard, the head of AMSA, also attempted to frame the situation as a zero-sum game, claiming it was 'unconscionable' to 'sacrifice a complying industry employing tens of thousands of workers under conditions of "decent work" so that employees of non-compliant employers can remain employed in oppressive circumstances' (Bisseker, 2011). Baard here was echoing the views of some of AMSA's member firms.

We have argued that there is substantial dualism or differentiation in the South African clothing industry and that low-wage firms typically do not compete in the same product markets as the higher-wage firms (Chapter 2). Yet the industry is dynamic, and with the development of new competencies and flexible strategies by retailers and design houses, no product market niche is ever entirely safe. The question posed by the compliance drive was whether competition with non-compliant firms was indeed as threatening to the higher-wage producers as they maintained. We could find little evidence, however, to support the employers who dominated the NBC.[19] In one prominent case where a Cape Town-based firm lost a prospective contract to a Newcastle-based firm, the latter turned out to be compliant with the NBC's minima. In another case, a Cape Town employer complained about 'unfair' lower-wage competition from Newcastle firms, but then admitted that his main competitor was in fact in Lesotho. In this case, the Cape Town and Lesotho firms were both supplying a South African sporting apparel retailer. The Lesotho firm had a clear advantage in producing most of the cheaper, mass-produced lines, whilst the Cape Town firm retained the advantage in producing the more complex lines and short runs needed at short notice. The two firms competed fiercely, however, over contracts to produce lines in the middle of this spectrum. The case shows that higher-wage and lower-wage firms in different areas sometimes do compete directly, using different technologies to produce similar products. But even in these instances, Cape Town firms' higher productivity has allowed many of them to remain competitive. Using higher minimum wages to destroy lower-wage, labour-intensive clothing manufacturers in order to protect what appeared to us to be a small minority of higher-paying metro firms who may have, on occasion, found themselves in competition with lower-wage producers, was (and is) a very high price to pay in terms of net job destruction.

Labour-intensive producers are particularly sensitive to wage increases. According to the manufacturing census, wage costs in the clothing manufacturing industry constitute almost a fifth of total expenditure, almost double

[19] Neither producers nor buyers are willing to divulge publicly the details of producers' competitiveness. Our discussions with producers and buyers suggest that competition between compliant and non-compliant firms is limited. It is possible that talking to different producers or buyers would yield contrasting evidence. We are not aware, however, of any contrary evidence produced by any of our critics.

that for manufacturing as a whole (Table 4.3). The wage share is even higher in the lower-wage, labour-intensive firms in places like Newcastle. Four of the five Newcastle-based applicants in the High Court case had been in business since at least 2008 and for them, the proportion of total costs consumed by wages ranged between 35 per cent (a knitwear jersey producer) and 61 per cent (a cut-make-and-trim enterprise).[20] Raising minimum wages inevitably would have a substantial impact on such firms' profit margins, which were already tight in this highly competitive industry. We pick up their story in more detail below.

6.3.1 *Non-compliant Newcastle*

Non-compliant firms were concentrated overwhelmingly in KwaZulu-Natal and the Free State throughout the 2000s.[21] They were especially visible in Newcastle where they were located in two easily accessible industrial areas. The fact that many of the non-compliant firms in Newcastle were owned by people of 'Chinese' origin—that is, who had come from Taiwan, Hong Kong or China—may have made them more likely targets for both SACTWU's attention and the NBC's compliance drives as they were politically vulnerable and easily stereotyped. It is not an accident that the court case against the Minister of Labour and NBC was brought by five Chinese-owned firms as the first five applicants (the United Clothing and Textile Association being the sixth).

During the 1970s, Newcastle underwent a rapid process of industrialization. Manufacturing jobs expanded from 5,023 in 1970 to 19,514 in 1982, accounting for 49 per cent of the Gross Geographic Product (Robbins et al., 2004: 13). They were a crucial source of employment for people living in Madadeni and Osizweni, Newcastle's townships, many of whom were the victims of apartheid-era removals off white-owned commercial farms in the 1960s and 1970s.

The steel giant Iron and Steel Corporation provided over half of Newcastle's manufacturing employment. When the Corporation announced plans for further expansion of the steelworks, the Newcastle town council invested heavily in roads, housing, and related infrastructure, expecting a boom from the influx of skilled workers and manufacturers. But the Corporation cancelled these plans in 1979 and started downsizing its existing operations in the early 1980s. This left Newcastle with over 600 vacant houses, 2,000 serviced plots, and a shrinking industrial base (Hart, 2002: 146). The town

[20] Information obtained from firm-level annual financial reports.

[21] This section draws on secondary literature and on interviews with local government officials, factory owners and some of their workers.

council responded by developing a strategy to lure East Asian (initially Taiwanese) clothing firms to the area (Todes, 1998; Xu, 2017). By then, South Africa had established strong political and economic ties with Taiwan, a strategy born out of anti-communism in both countries and their status as pariahs in the international community (Pickles and Woods, 1989). Taiwanese investors were quick to respond to South African industrial decentralization incentives and were the mainstay of low-wage labour-intensive development in the bantustans.

Newcastle officials travelled to Taiwan, Hong Kong, and later also China. The key municipal official tasked with economic development learned basic Mandarin. His business card was printed in English on one side and in Chinese on the other. The strategy worked in part because of the generous subsidies on offer through the 1982 Regional Industrial Development Program, an apartheid-era industrial decentralization programme. Not all Chinese investors responded to these incentives, however, and many preferred to keep at arm's-length from the state. Other important economic inducements included cheap high-quality real estate, secure industrial areas and large supplies of lower-wage labour in the adjoining townships.

The first Chinese clothing firm established in Newcastle, *Amigo Clothing*, was a large export-oriented firm from Hong Kong, making jeans for the US market, which had been attracted by South Africa's decentralization incentives and by Newcastle's infrastructure (Xu, 2017). Machinery and equipment were imported from Hong Kong in May 1983, along with seventeen mechanics, and production kicked off in July that year (ibid.). Ten years later, Newcastle had the second largest Chinese population (mainly from Taiwan) in the country, with an estimated 1,000 Chinese residents and fifty-four large Chinese-owned factories (ibid.).

Chinese producers brought with them the skills and networks needed to operate at the very labour-intensive end of the clothing manufacturing industry (Todes, 1998). In this regard, Newcastle reflected the wider role played by Chinese business networks as industrial catalysts in sub-Saharan Africa (Bräutigam, 2003, 2009). Bräutigam et al. (2018) call this form of Chinese investment 'small geese travelling together in flocks'. By 1996, clothing and knitwear had become the mainstay of manufacturing in Newcastle, accounting for 11,295 jobs (Robbins et al., 2004: 15). The core of large Taiwanese firms soon attracted other, often smaller, family-linked firms to Newcastle, and a highly networked form of production soon developed. Knitting, assembly, and embroidery were often done in different firms, replicating the kinds of familial management systems and networks found in Taiwan (Hart, 2002: 183–4; Xu, 2017). Cut-make-and-trim operations also sprang up, producing basic items such as sleepwear, uniforms, jeans, skirts, and basic shirts, with factories often sharing orders, and outsourcing particular tasks. Xu identified three types of Chinese clothing firm in Newcastle: the large exporters (which by the mid-2000s were mostly out of business); the 'Chengyi' or cut-make-and-trim factories producing ready-to-wear garments; and the more capital-intensive 'Maoyi' factories producing jerseys and knitwear (Xu, 2017: 104–5).

Chinese immigration (initially from Taiwan and Hong Kong, but from 1998 also from Singapore and mainland China) continued long after the government's incentives were phased out in the early 1990s. A vibrant community developed, with many second-generation Chinese entrepreneurs taking over businesses or starting their own. Many were previously employed clothing workers. Notably *Luck Clothing*, set up in 1989 by Linda Shun (who had previously worked in a clothing firm in QwaQwa) was famous for recruiting supervisors and managers from China who subsequently set up their own clothing businesses in the area (Xu, 2017: 116–7). After diplomatic relations were established with mainland China in 1998, entrepreneurs from Shanghai and Jiangsu and Shandong Provinces came to Newcastle, often purchasing discounted machinery from the departing export firms (ibid.).

As of 2010, Newcastle had several Chinese restaurants, a Buddhist temple, a Chinese afternoon school, two Chinese chambers of business (one politically pro-Taiwan, the other with members from China, Taiwan, and Hong Kong), and a 'Welcome to Newcastle' obelisk at the city limits in Chinese and English (Figure 6.5). These East Asian immigrants retained strong links with their countries of origin, but many came to see Newcastle as their home in a very real sense. They owned houses and factories. They participated in local politics, with at least two having been elected as town councillors. Many became South African citizens and their children were born and schooled in South Africa.

But their journey had many twists and turns. The first economic shocks were felt in the early 1990s when government subsidies came to an end and WD 471, setting national minimum wages in clothing manufacturing (on a regionally differentiated basis) came into effect. Many clothing firms ignored the wage determination. By 1995, SACTWU had over thirty labour disputes with firms in Newcastle; it was in response to Newcastle firms in particular that its General Secretary, Ebrahim Patel, said he would 'eat these fly-by-nights for breakfast' (quoted in Hart, 2002: 165–6). Through the 1990s, Patel championed his decent work fundamentalism at national and international levels, a combination of industrial and labour market policy that sought to eliminate lower-wage producers such as the Newcastle employers (see Chapter 1 and further discussion in Chapter 7).

The second set of shocks to clothing manufacturing in Newcastle was trade liberalization (from 1995), the rise of Chinese imports, the appreciation of the Rand (from 2002) and the formation of the NBC (in 2003). The abrupt loss of competitiveness was disastrous for the large Taiwanese exporters. *Richfin*, a large Taiwanese-owned knitwear producer, applied to the Industrial Development Corporation (IDC) to reschedule a loan and, when refused, closed its doors, putting 1,660 people out of work. Already by this time the IDC had turned against relatively low-wage clothing firms, seeing them as part of an industrial segment not worth supporting. Despite representation from the Newcastle town council in an attempt to save the firm, the IDC called in the loan. Ironically, *Richfin*'s assets were sold at bargain basement prices (leaving the IDC out of pocket) to a Taiwanese producer who, with the support of a relocation grant from the Taiwan government, shipped the equipment to Taiwan where he set up a factory producing knitwear for the export market, including into South Africa.

Nova Clothing, one of the first firms to relocate to Newcastle from Hong Kong, was issued with a compliance order to pay legislated minimum wages and subsequently closed its doors, putting a further 1,600 people out of work. The owner had apparently instigated legal proceedings against the government over the creation of the NBC, but withdrew the action under pressure from SACTWU (including protest marches), and left South Africa.[22] He, like many other Chinese producers, was concerned about the power of the NBC to use the courts to confiscate property and assets of firms that were not paying the prescribed minimum wage (Robbins et al., 2004: 22–3). According to Chinese entrepreneurs in Newcastle, Wayne Chu, the owner of *Nova Clothing,* subsequently became one of the biggest importing agents in China for South African retailers *Mr Price* and *Edcon.*

Other large factories that closed during this period included *Welcome Textiles* and *Nantex,* which respectively put 450 and 2,000 people out of work. This signalled the effective death of Newcastle's clothing and textile export industry and the end of large-scale factory production. From 2003, almost all of the remaining producers were smaller family-owned clothing manufacturing operations, concentrated on the lower- and middle-income domestic market, competing directly with imports from countries like Lesotho and China. Many were knitwear firms in which men oversaw the first phase (the capital-intensive weaving of yarn into knitted fabric) and women operated the second phase (sewing knitted fabric into garments). John (Han-Wei) Chen, the first applicant in the Newcastle case against the NBC, operated precisely such a factory (Figure 6.5). His wife and his mother were involved in production, often working long hours on the factory floor. Although the knitting part of the factory is relatively capital-intensive, his operation was still very sensitive to wage increases, especially on the assembly side. Independent analysis of his financial records for the court case revealed that its net profit in 2010

[22] Information supplied by Ferdie Alberts, interviewed 14 June 2011 and 22 July 2018.

was R16,528 and that if he had paid the NBC minimum wage, he would instead have made a loss of R127,183 (Econex, 2011: 7).

Some Newcastle firms registered with the NBC, whilst others tried to avoid the NBC altogether. Most raised their basic wages somewhat over time, though the majority relied on piecework pay (outlawed in NBC agreements). Very few complied with all of the requirements of the NBC's collective agreements. Many failed to pay all of their dues (including the 'agency fee' to SACTWU, introduced in 2006, which raised labour costs by 10 per cent). Most failed to pay the steadily rising minimum wages.

As SACTWU has repeatedly emphasized, in some Newcastle firms working conditions were not compliant with the Basic Conditions of Employment Act (Gina, 2011; Kriel, 2012). In one particularly infamous case from 2001, a worker on a night shift gave birth prematurely to twins, both of whom died because no one could access the locked factory. This incident prompted the Department of Labour to inspect Newcastle clothing factories, finding other instances of abuse (Newman, 2005). SACTWU launched an 'Operation Clean-up' to end 'sweatshop conditions' in the area.

The Newcastle Chinese employers felt betrayed by the transformed policy environment and offended by what they perceived to be racist slurs (for example, being called 'fly-by-nights' when they regarded Newcastle as their home). They also felt that there was a failure to understand how difficult it

Figure 6.5 The Chinese in Newcastle. Left: John Chen and his wife inspecting production; middle: the Welcome to Newcastle obelisk; right: Alex Liu.*

* Permission granted by the Newcastillian, an online Magazine (Pixelfish Marketing).

was to compete at the labour-intensive end of the clothing manufacturing industry. In this highly competitive environment, missed deadlines could turn a small profit into a major loss as fines were imposed by large customers and orders cancelled. Some owners lived—and died—on their factory premises. Many new clothing firms began life as 'stable boyfriend/girlfriend' partnerships, typically a female line supervisor and a male sewing machine mechanic who split off from their previous employer to form their own business, often maintaining a close connection with the previous employer.[23] These entrepreneurs had a strong work ethic and were accustomed to working long hours, including through the night when deadlines loomed. They expected similar commitment from Newcastle workers and were highly resistant to raising wages unless this was demonstratively linked to higher productivity, resulting in tension and even abusive behaviour towards workers (Xu, 2017).

For SACTWU, wages much lower than NBC minima were 'simply irreconcilable with the work environment contemplated by our labour legislation and our Constitution' (Gina, 2011: paras 10–11). The union was also strongly opposed to the practice of many of Newcastle's Chinese employers of linking pay to productivity. One model entailed paying bonuses for production over and above a basic quota. Another was to offer low basic weekly wages but to supplement them with piecework payments. These practices could result in significant variation in earnings. According to wage records for 2011, take-home pay for workers employed by one of the applicants in the 2011 court case—a cut-make-and-trim firm—ranged from 15 per cent below the NBC minimum wage to almost double the minimum.[24] The union accepted that there would be job losses when non-compliant firms were closed but declared that this was justified in terms of ensuring that the industry only provided 'decent work' (Payne, 2011).

Some clothing firms in Newcastle responded by restructuring into workers' co-operatives. The typical approach was to separate the production and ordering sides of the firm and restructure the production arm into a workers' co-operative (controlled by a worker-mandated management committee) and maintain control of the ordering arm (restructured as a new company) which sourced orders for the workers' co-operative, paid for logistics and

[23] Xu reports that, as of early 2016, sixteen of the nineteen cut-make-and-trim firms in Madadeni's Ithala Industrial Estate were formed on the basis of such partnerships (2017).

[24] There was, therefore, no simple correlation between minimum weekly wages and total earnings, and not all workers would necessarily benefit if wages rose to the prescribed minimum if this meant the erosion of productivity-linked pay. Indeed, when John Chen attempted to increase his minimum wages to 70 per cent of the legal minimum, he could only do so by reducing his piecework bonuses. His most productive (and best-paid) workers resigned in protest at their reduced total earnings.

utilities, and leased machinery to the workers' co-operative where necessary (Xu, 2017: 162–3). Alex Liu, the chairman of the Newcastle Chinese Chamber of Commerce and Industry (henceforth 'the Chinese Chamber'), was one of the first movers (Figure 6.5). He shut down his clothing firm (*WinCool*) in 2008 but was prompted by his parents and ex-workers to start up again. He decided the only way this could be done was to help the workers set up a workers' co-operative (*Simunye*) which would fall under the 2005 Co-operatives Act rather than the NBC and to restructure *Win-Cool* as an order-sourcing mechanism (Payne, 2011). As of 2011, members of the workers' co-operative earned a basic income of R250 plus productivity-linked pay, which pushed earnings for some as high as R630 per week (well over the then NBC minimum wage of R489). The NBC, however, took a dim view of both the earnings and *WinCool/Simunye*'s structure, and took Liu to court several times (unsuccessfully).[25] The NBC was concerned that it was a disguised employment relationship or a sham co-operative, but was unable to convince the court.

The NBC compliance drive focused on clothing firms (including workers' co-operatives like *WinCool/Simunye*) in Newcastle and in the old bantustan areas. By the end of July 2010, the sheriffs had executed thirteen writs in metro areas and twelve in non-metro areas, nine of which were in Newcastle.[26] In August, the NBC ramped up the process, shutting down a further fourteen firms in Newcastle and QwaQwa (Khanyile, 2011). Employers and workers alike were alarmed by the precipitous job destruction. When the sheriffs shut down *Wintong Manufacturing* in Newcastle, factory workers protested vociferously and prevented sheriffs from confiscating the machinery and other assets (Dugger, 2010). The Chinese Chamber added its voice to the protest and eighty-five clothing firms closed in solidarity. SACTWU asked the courts to intervene, arguing that this amounted to an illegal lockout. Negotiations led to the reopening of the factories (including *Wintong*).

The crisis in Newcastle and elsewhere also prompted a series of national meetings between the Department of Labour, the NBC, AMSA, and various ad hoc representatives of firms that were not party to NBC agreements and were also not compliant with their terms (Chen, 2011a: para 54). Many of the non-party firms, mostly in KwaZulu-Natal, organized themselves into a new association, the United Clothing and Textile Association. (Deetlefs—once infamous for being the NBC's hatchet man—subsequently became the Chief Executive Officer of the new Association after he left the NBC in 2013

[25] In 2012–13, the trade unions pushed hard for abolishing the exemption of co-operatives from the Labour Relations Act. The 2013 Amendment clarified that members and non-members of co-operatives who fell under the Act's definition of employee would be covered by the Labour Relations Act, but this left open how 'employee' is to be defined.

[26] NBC, list of firms for priority writs of execution, undated, included as Annexure HC5 of Chen (2011a).

(Payne, 2013)). All parties to these meetings committed themselves to finding a solution that was acceptable to everyone. But they failed to find any such solution. The United Clothing and Textile Association proposed a new wage model for the entire industry to allow for lower minimum wages supplemented by piecework or productivity-linked pay. This, of course, was hardly 'new' as similar proposals had been made by the mostly KwaZulu-Natal-based employers during the negotiations in the run-up to the formation of the NBC. AMSA, which had been party to the compliance drive in the first place, concurred with the 'need for a new minimum wage dispensation in the industry because of the job losses and closures' and the imperative of reforming labour legislation.[27] This was rejected by SACTWU.

Later that month, SACTWU presented its 'Worst Employer Award' to the Chinese Chamber in the form of a broken brick, symbolizing employers who break, rather than build, 'decent work' in the clothing manufacturing industry.[28] SACTWU also, bizarrely, decided to celebrate a 'reduction in job losses' in October, on the grounds that the 30,000 jobs lost between 2007 and 2010 were 'fewer' than had been lost in the preceding three years.[29]

6.3.2 *Job Destruction Stalled*

By November 2010, 26 factories in Newcastle had been closed down (Chen, 2011a: para 52). The NBC proceeded to agree a new round of wage increases, submitting the collective agreement to the Minister of Labour so that she could extend the agreement to non-party employers countrywide. It is difficult to reconstruct precisely who knew what, and when, during the final weeks of 2010, but it seems that the combination of factory closures under the existing compliance drive and the prospective new round of wage increases focused attention again on the prospect of massive job destruction.

In December 2010, following substantial adverse publicity about job losses, Ebrahim Patel—by then the Minister of Economic Development—announced that the NBC and non-parties had accepted a proposal (the so-called '22 December resolution') for a phased period of compliance and a 'moratorium' on proceeding with writs of execution against non-compliant companies. Non-compliant firms would have to become 70 per cent compliant by 31 March 2011, 90 per cent compliant by 1 January 2012 and 100 per cent compliant by 30 April 2012 (Chen, 2011a: para 58). All arrears (in back-pay for workers, NBC levies, and so on) owed by non-compliant firms were suspended

[27] Minutes of the meeting chaired by Les Kettledas of the Department of Labour, 20 September 2010.

[28] http://sactwu.org.za/pr-and-news/archived-2010/161-worst-employeraward.

[29] SACTWU press release, 'Clothing and textile industry job losses slow down', 4 October 2010; http://www.cosatu.org.za/show.php?ID=4064.

and deemed payable only if the firm broke the phase-in agreement (or became non-compliant after 30 April 2012). Just two days later, however, the Minister of Labour gazetted the extension of the collective agreement, without any reference to phased transitions from non-compliance to compliance. Confusion reigned over the following months, as firms struggled to understand the minimum wage dispensation and whether the phasing-in agreement applied to the old or the new minimum wage levels. It nevertheless provided a breathing space for most firms, as enforcement activity declined.

The December 2010 'agreement' to phase in wage increases in non-compliant firms required that firms paid 70 per cent of the minimum wage by the end of March 2011. In mid-March, the *Financial Mail* reported that at least 250 clothing firms in Durban, Newcastle, QwaQwa, and Botshabelo would not be able to meet the 70 per cent target and 28,000 jobs were under threat (Bisseker, 2011). AMSA took the opportunity to push again for a new wage model for the clothing industry. Johann Baard told the reporter that 'the industry's cost structure does not match the prices the retailers want', adding that 'with almost half the industry non-compliant, it is clear that as an industry we have priced ourselves out of the market... Non-compliance reflects that the industry wage model has been overtaken by competitive global market realities' (quoted in Bisseker, 2011).

There is a certain irony here, given that AMSA and the NBC, which had managed to restrain real minimum wage growth in metro areas since 2000, had helped drive up labour costs in non-metro areas and for employers who were not represented at the NBC. In a later interview, Baard observed that AMSA's support for the compliance drive had been born out of frustration—and that this had been primarily with regard to the wage model in the industry rather than competition from low-wage firms. It appears that AMSA regarded the compliance drive primarily as a political weapon, to show the government and the wider trade union movement why their approach to minimum wage-setting needed to be more flexible. 'It is not that we are uncaring,' he said about the non-compliant firms, 'we are left with no alternative. It would be different if the unions, COSATU, the politicians and Luthuli House [ANC head office] had the will. We need to re-invent the wage dispensation in the country' (quoted in Planting, 2011).

Relations between the NBC and Newcastle firms worsened in March 2011 when, on the day that Alex Liu (who was also the deputy chair of the United Clothing and Textile Association) was attending a meeting with the NBC, sheriffs attached assets at his and eleven other Newcastle factories, for their failure to register with the NBC and pay over back-pay and outstanding NBC levies. Deetlefs, then still the NBC's compliance manager, denied that the timing had been deliberate, saying that 'Alex has been giving us the run-around' and that it had taken the NBC two weeks to find his new premises

(Enslin-Payne, 2011). Liu pointed out that the NBC had visited the premises in 2010 and knew exactly where it was.[30]

In July 2011, following the issue of further compliance orders, five Newcastle firms and the United Clothing and Textile Association launched their legal action against the Minister of Labour and the NBC. The firms were subject to ongoing harassment and intimidation, including threats from the sheriff to confiscate assets and close them down (Chen, 2011b). The Newcastle case became an important focus of attention because by mid-July, writs had been issued to 109 companies across South Africa, affecting 6,400 employees (Planting, 2011). A report for the KwaZulu-Natal Provincial Treasury found that full compliance with the NBC minimum wages would lead to the destruction of as many as 25,000 jobs (Coetzee, 2011), and the press reported the figure of 28,000 in early 2011 (Bisseker, 2011).

It is difficult to be precise about the total number of workers being paid less than the legal minima. The 2010 compliance drive entailed executing writs against firms employing more than 19,000 workers with respect to minimum wage violations, and firms employing another 2,000 workers with respect to non-compliance with benefits (especially pension fund contributions) or NBC levies. Almost 13,000 of these workers were in KwaZulu-Natal, and another 5,500 in the Free State (predominantly in former bantustan areas).[31] It is impossible to determine the precise number of jobs under threat as some workers may have been paid at or above the minimum wage and some producers might have been able to improve efficiency (for example, by shedding unskilled workers and becoming more capital-intensive) and stay in business (although with a smaller workforce, and probably producing different products). However, given existing low-profit margins, skills shortages and strong competition from countries like China, the situation was likely extremely threatening for most labour-intensive producers of basic clothing items in South Africa.[32]

The scale of potential job losses in 2010–11, if the new minimum wages were enforced, explains both the producers' responses—forming a new association and taking the Minister of Labour and NBC to court—as well as the subsequent hesitation on the part of the state and even the union with respect to enforcing compliance. As we have seen, Patel participated in the informal agreement at the end of 2010 to tolerate temporary non-compliance through

[30] Interview with Alex Liu, 24 July 2018.

[31] NBC, 'Prioritised compliance action list' (Excel spreadsheet, undated). These figures include only workers employed in firms known to the NBC. It is likely that most of the (predominantly informal) firms not known to the NBC were also paying below the official minimum wage—and jobs in these firms, too, would come under threat if or when they were identified by NBC officials or Department of Labour inspectors.

[32] Some firms switch from production to importing. In Newcastle, for example, several factory shops already stock more items imported from China than are produced on the premises.

a gradual phasing-in of the new minima (although this was not acknowledged in the Minister of Labour's extension of the NBC's 2010 collective agreement). In August 2011, the crisis in the clothing industry was the subject of a cabinet briefing, where the Minister of Finance (Pravin Gordhan) suggested that changes to labour policies might be necessary to prevent further job losses. His comments were subsequently endorsed by Trevor Manuel, a previous Minister of Finance and head of South Africa's National Planning Commission.[33] Their views, however, did not prevail. Rather, as discussed in Chapter 5, the ANC went on to set a national minimum wage in 2018 that was even higher than the NBC minimum wage for machinists in rural areas.

SACTWU, with support from COSATU, maintained that only high-wage, 'decent' work was acceptable but in practice became hesitant to insist on large-scale destruction of jobs in non-compliant firms. In late 2011 and into 2012, the union restrained the NBC from further action against non-compliant firms. When, in July 2012, AMSA sought a court order to compel the NBC to act on the 450 writs of execution that it had accumulated but not served on non-compliant firms, SACTWU initially opposed the application, explaining that it favoured 'living wages' but not factory closures. A few days later the union reversed its position, explaining that it did not want to give the impression that it condoned non-compliance (Planting, 2012). In subsequent wage agreements, SACTWU reverted once again to allowing phased-in wage increases for non-compliant firms. Non-compliant firms, providing they implemented other aspects of the collective agreement, were allowed to pay 80 per cent of the bargained wage. These were supposed to expire over an 18-month period but were continued in subsequent agreements and in practice firms that paid 80 per cent of the minimum wage were not pursued by the NBC.

The NBC's retreat in 2011/12 from its aggressive compliance drives of 2009–11 meant that job destruction stalled and then employment picked up. The state and union attributed this not so much to *de facto* tolerance of non-compliance as to the government's industrial policy. The DTI and union claimed that the DTI's industrial policies had 'effectively stabilized a deeply vulnerable sector' (DTI, 2012: 2) and achieved a 'significant slowdown in retrenchments in the industry'[34] (see also Vlok, 2011; Steyn, 2012). Whilst industrial policy incentives no doubt assisted the firms that benefitted from them, key to the turnaround was further depreciation in the exchange rate, which provided space for firms to absorb Rand denominated increased wages without loss of competitiveness. As can be seen in Figure 6.6, minimum wages

[33] http://mg.co.za/article/2011-08-25-cabinet-no-pravin-we-wont-relax-sas-labour-laws.

[34] SACTWU press release, 'Significant slowdown in clothing, textile and footwear job losses', 14 November 2011; http://sactwu.org.za/pr-and-news/archived-2011/210-significant-slowdown-in-clothing-textile-and-footwear-joblosses.

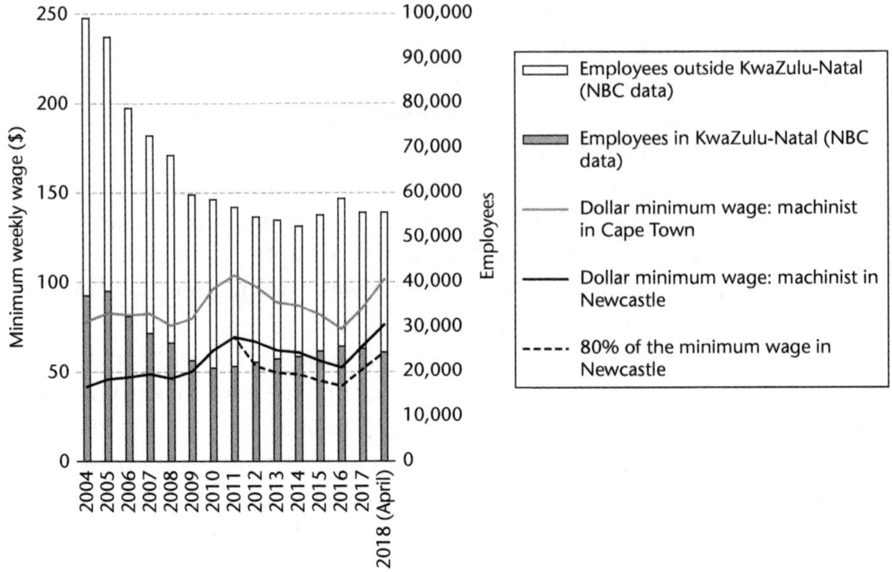

Figure 6.6 Minimum wages (dollar) and employment in the South African clothing manufacturing industry: 2004–2017.

Source: NBC data on employment, collective agreements, and South African Reserve Bank.

declined in dollar terms between 2011 and 2016. This facilitated an increase in employment and in real wages. Employment grew, but remained below pre-compliance-drive levels, and in 2017 declined again as the Rand appreciated, pushing up dollar wages.

Wages were clearly important in shaping employment in the South African clothing manufacturing industry. The 2009–11 compliance drive pitted mostly compliant Cape Town-based employers, the union, and the Minister of Labour against non-compliant employers in Newcastle, other parts of KwaZulu-Natal, and the Free State, with various government and ANC officials urging caution on the NBC and Minister of Labour. The episode exposed the logic inherent in South Africa's institutions for minimum wage-setting and the capacity of bargaining councils to enforce minimum wages. The parties to the NBC could use the mechanisms of collective agreements and (with the backing of the Minister of Labour) extensions to raise the minimum wages that non-party firms were obliged to pay and could then use the courts to enforce compliance. If non-compliant firms were unable to pay these raised wages, given strong international competition, the outcome was large-scale job destruction.

The NBC subsequently became more tolerant of firms paying at least 80 per cent of the minimum wage. But this did not mean the NBC stopped enforcing compliance. In January 2013, for example, it issued fifty writs of execution against non-compliant firms in KwaZulu-Natal, shutting fifteen factories (Payne, 2013). Entrepreneurs from Newcastle informed us that most compliance activity subsequently became targeted at individual firms, often on an informal basis allowing for the payment of bribes by 'rotten apples' (disreputable businesses) to make the problem disappear. They also complained that since 2017, the NBC had been putting pressure on the design houses not to provide orders to non-compliant firms. (Design houses now, apparently, ask to see certificates of compliance with NBC collective agreements or a certificate declaring that they are legitimate workers' co-operatives). High-profile compliance drives remained rare, although in May 2018, the provincial NBC, together with government officials from the provincial departments of economic development, labour, and home affairs conducted a series of 'raids' on Newcastle clothing factories to check to see if they were employing workers from Swaziland and Lesotho without the necessary documentation.

Chapter 2 argued that there was significant dualism in the sector given that high- and low-wage firms were able to co-exist because they targeted different product markets using different technologies. Such dualism was tolerated under apartheid but rejected by the post-apartheid democratic government as being emblematic of the low-wage, racially discriminatory apartheid regime. As noted in Chapter 1, post-apartheid industrial and labour policy has been shaped by decent work fundamentalism: the notion that relatively low-wage, labour-intensive development is an undesirable 'low-road' to growth, promising nothing but a race to the bottom. In this chapter we showed how the advent of industrial-level minimum wage-setting (through national collective bargaining) coincided with rising international competition to undermine employment. Industrial policy sought to stem the tide of job losses. In line with the prevailing decent work fundamentalism, incentives (to facilitate upgrading) were targeted at those firms that could afford the rising minimum wages, thereby contributing to an increasingly capital- and skill-intensive trajectory for an industry with a shrinking pool of workers.

Job losses in South African clothing manufacturing were, in short, the product of a home-grown institutionally driven process of structural adjustment away from labour-intensive development and inclusive growth. The South African case thus stands as an example of the potentially dystopic consequences of using the minimum wage as a lever to facilitate upgrading in high unemployment contexts.

In May 2018, the South African parliament passed a new national minimum wage law setting a wage floor of R20 per hour (R3,500 per month). As noted in Chapter 5, exceptions were made for low-wage work in agriculture, domestic service, and public works programs. No mention was made of labour-intensive manufacturing, especially clothing, where in Newcastle the minimum monthly wage was R3,158 for a qualified machinist (and R2,527 for those paying 80 per cent of the minimum). Strict application of the new minimum wage would thus likely have adverse implications for labour-intensive jobs in Newcastle—but only for the very few remaining conventional firms. The growth of workers' co-operatives has provided a loophole (perhaps temporary) that is protecting employment in Newcastle and could continue to protect it into the future.

6.3.3 *The Challenges Posed by the Growth of Workers' Co-operatives for the NBC*

Uncertainty over minimum wages and continued harassment by the NBC encouraged more and more Newcastle clothing firms to go the route Alex Liu went in 2009, namely to transform their businesses into new operations involving collaborations with workers' co-operatives. This meant closing the company, retrenching the workforce, assisting the retrenched workers to form a workers' co-operative and then forging new working relationships with that co-operative. The Chinese Chamber engaged the services of a labour consultant, to assist workers to set up workers' co-operatives correctly (with their own bank accounts, book-keeping, equipment or lease agreements, health and safety procedures, and a 'management committee' mandated by the members to accept work, allocate tasks and remuneration). As of July 2018, the Chinese Chamber was also planning a support/training facility for workers' co-operatives and hoped to engage collectively with retailers to facilitate better prices for the co-operatives. According to Chinese entrepreneurs in Newcastle, the typical pricing model on items that could be easily produced in workers' co-operatives entailed a 20 per cent cut for the design houses (acting as middle-men between the producers and the retailers). For an item of clothing retailing at, say, R100, the design house would be paid R50. Of that, the design house would make a profit of R10, spend R15 on material and pay R25 to the producers. The ordering arm of the partnership with the worker co-operative would take a cut (of between 30 and 50 per cent) to cover logistics, utilities and other costs, leaving the co-operative to decide how to organize production and allocate earnings to create the clothing item at a unit cost of between R12 and R15. As the workers' co-operative would have to produce, pack and place the retail price ticket on each item, there was transparency about the mark-ups and cost at each point. The Chinese Chamber hoped that by uniting the workers' co-operatives, they would be able to convince/pressurize the retailers and the design houses to improve producer prices. However, this strategy is always mediated by the presence of competition from imports and other domestic producers.

Of the 120 or so Chinese clothing factories in business in mid-2018, only nine were still conventional companies paying dues to the NBC. The rest had reconstituted themselves into new small sourcing operations (employing few, if any, wage workers) working in partnership with newly constituted workers' co-operatives. They thus stopped paying dues to the NBC, and workers (now members of workers' co-operatives) stopped paying dues to SACTWU. When in co-operative structures, the only deduction on remuneration is for the Unemployment Insurance Fund. Members of workers' co-operatives no longer have to contribute to the NBC pension and provident fund (though they can choose to stay in it) or to the trade union. This boosts their take-home pay, though for those who stop saving for retirement, this is a short-term benefit and implies a greater burden on the government's old age pension when they reach pensionable age.

Robert (Zhiliang) Han, the fourth applicant in the 2011 court case, had by 2018 transformed his business into a workers' co-operative. At the time of the court case, independent assessment of his financial position revealed that he had made a profit of R48,308 in 2010 and that if he had complied with the minimum wage, he would instead have made a loss of R1,677,870, a clearly unsustainable economic outcome (Econex, 2011: 4). His old business, 'Goldfinch, JCR Clothing' has been superceded by 'Goldfinch Workers Co-op'. The workers' co-operative has a certificate from the DTI (co-operatives fall under the jurisdiction of the DTI) because his main customer, *Mr Price*, wanted assurance that it was a correctly constituted workers' co-operative. Government officials have on several occasions questioned the workers to ensure that his operation is not a 'sham' co-operative, or a form of 'fronting'. As of July 2018, his workers' co-operative remained operational, with the management committee taking full responsibility for hiring and firing additional workers (it appears that the workers' co-operatives also sometimes hire workers, including from Lesotho). The workers' co-operative manages labour productivity (through piecework payment systems) and remuneration and he is satisfied with the quality produced by the co-operative of orders he sources for them. In 2011 he employed 203 workers. As of July 2018, the workers' co-operative had 290 members.

The growth of workers' co-operatives poses existential challenges for the NBC as workers are transformed from employees to members of co-operatives, thereby slipping through the regulatory net it weaves and controls. In October 2016, the NBC went to the Labour Court asking for a declaratory order regarding the 2005 Co-operatives Act—specifically that members of workers' co-operatives were subject to the Labour Relations Act and hence under the control of the NBC. The judgment handed down in February 2017 found against the NBC, arguing that the Labour Relations Act only applied to 'employees' as defined in the Act (such as workers hired by workers' co-operatives) and thus a blanket declaratory order could not be issued. The judge found that:

> One of the main objects of labour law is to ensure equity in the relationship between individual employees and their employers, with it being accepted that the latter possess considerable social and economic power over the former. However, if the relationship between the parties to production have transcended the traditional employment hierarchies, where those providing their labour also jointly own the enterprise, share in any surplus and have a democratic say in the running of the operation, then, in my view, labour law should not and does not apply.
>
> (Judgment by Judge Whitcher, on case no D20/16 in the Durban Labour Court, 15 February 2017, paragraph 22)

The judge also commented that nothing in the judgment 'should be taken to condone sham co-operatives who adopt the form of a workers' co-operative to circumvent labour law' (paragraph 36) and that such misuses require inspection on a case-by-case basis. The NBC took the matter on appeal. The appeal court upheld the judgment, emphasizing that the Labour Relations Act would apply to workers hired by workers' co-operatives, but not to members of workers' co-operatives (Case DA04/2017 in the Durban Labour Appeal Court, judgment by Judges Hlophe and Savage, paragraph 15).

Undeterred, the NBC took the case to the Constitutional Court (which it also lost), complaining inter alia that the growth of workers' co-operatives has 'far reaching implications for the continued existence of the applicant' (paragraph 15 of the NBC's appeal). The NBC argued that there were 199 workers' co-operatives in the clothing industry in KwaZulu-Natal as of January 2016 and that this number increased sharply to 259 by April 2016 and had risen to 'approximately 400' by June 2018, the date of the application (paragraphs 16 to 18). The NBC complained that about half of the employers previously registered with the NBC in the Free State province had converted to workers' co-operatives and if the precedents set by the Labour Court and the Appeal Court remained unaltered, there would be no reason why this would not 'spread to other industries' (paragraph 18).

The growth of workers' co-operatives in the South African clothing manufacturing industry is both a response to aggressive enforcement of overly high minimum wages and an opportunity for workers to have a greater say (if not complete control over) production and distribution. As discussed further in Chapter 7, it also opens the door for more progressive and participatory practices.

7

The Political Economy of Upgrading

Trade Union Strategy and Industrial Policy in South Africa

Chapter 6 explained how industrial policy, wage-setting institutions and trade union strategy combined to undermine labour-intensive growth in South Africa's clothing manufacturing sector. We highlighted the role of the NBC and SACTWU's strategy of narrowing regional wage differentials by driving up minimum wages fastest in lower-wage areas. This chapter explores SACTWU's strategy in more detail, suggesting that its attitude towards lower-wage firms was shaped not only by ideology but also by a set of political–economic interests. South Africa's policy of 'black economic empowerment' (BEE) enabled SACTWU to morph into an organization that was part trade union, part financial investment vehicle and finally part capitalist, providing additional incentives to support an industrial strategy oriented towards higher wages for fewer workers rather than a labour-intensive trajectory for the clothing industry.

7.1 Trade Unions and the State

In the 1980s and early 1990s, South Africa's trade unions mobilized for political change, challenged managerial despotism on the shop floor and secured improved working conditions and higher wages (Baskin, 1991; von Holdt, 2003; Philip, 2018). After the transition to democracy, the political influence of unions expanded, both through the participation of COSATU in the Tripartite Alliance with the governing ANC and the South African Communist Party, and through the participation of union members, shop stewards and officials in ANC and South African Communist Party structures. The National Economic, Development and Labour Council, provided organized labour with another platform for influencing policy, but this ultimately proved less important than direct connections between trade unionists, the governing party and the government (Nattrass, 2014a).

Trade unions expanded their institutional power through corporatist institutions, especially the bargaining councils. The trade unions' organizational capacity also expanded. By the early 2000s, COSATU and its affiliates had more than 1,800 full-time officials, a dedicated parliamentary office and a research wing (Webster and Buhlungu, 2004). At the same time, critics charged, workplace organization weakened, and unions' officials with their many perks became more-and-more distanced from the unions' members, resulting in wildcat strikes and exacerbating challenges of 'ungovernability' in the workplace (Bramble and Barchiesi, 2003; Buhlungu, 2010; Buhlungu and Tshoaedi, 2012). COSATU disputed such analyses (COSATU, 2010), but events in the mining sector in 2012–14 gave these criticisms credence. Disaffected platinum mineworkers defected from the National Union of Mineworkers, hitherto the largest union in COSATU, and joined the rival Association of Mineworkers and Construction Union. This shaped the context leading up to the Marikana Massacre in August 2012 (Alexander, 2013), and a long and bitter strike in the first half of 2014. Strategic and ideological disputes within COSATU eventually led to the formation of a breakaway rival trade union federation, the South African Federation of Trade Unions, in 2017. The new Federation was more vocal in its criticisms of government economic policy than COSATU, and more socialist in its rhetoric. SACTWU remained in COSATU.

SACTWU had particularly strong connections into the state and had significant influence on labour and industrial policies. As discussed in Chapter 6, employers in the clothing industry argued in various 'tri-partite' policy forums (that is, including representation from business, labour and the government) that labour productivity needed to be raised and they pushed for a new wage model that would allow individual workers' earnings to be linked to their individual productivity through 'scoring' and piecework systems. SACTWU favoured an alternative strategy, notably to use labour market and industrial policies to raise productivity through skills development and the upgrading of industrial processes (which in practice mostly meant mechanization) to accommodate higher wages (Chapter 6).

As early as 2000, at a Clothing and Textiles Sector Jobs Summit convened to address the challenge of job losses, SACTWU demanded supportive industrial policies, 'decent work for all', action against illegal imports, and support for a 'buy local' campaign (Bennett, 2003: 31–3). What SACTWU did not anticipate was the rise of Chinese production. As discussed in Chapters 4 and 6, Chinese clothing exports transformed clothing manufacturing worldwide, capturing not only South Africa's export markets but also much of South Africa's domestic market. We have argued that this benefitted South African consumers but at the cost of sharply reduced employment in the clothing manufacturing industry. When SACTWU was formed in 1989 it had 198,000 members, mostly in the major metropolitan areas. By the early 2000s this had dropped to little more than 100,000, of which about 72,600 were in clothing manufacturing (Bennett, 2002: 6; Bennett, 2003: 14). NBC data suggest that SACTWU's membership in clothing firms registered with the NBC fell from 64,885 in 2003 to 57,231 in 2012 to a mere 51,865 by 2018.

As discussed in Chapter 6, the crisis in clothing manufacturing led to protracted discussions in the early 2000s between government, producers, and retailers but SACTWU remained aloof from this process. As Maree et al. observed, SACTWU specifically, and COSATU more broadly, adopted a strategy of 'strategic ambivalence' which allowed them to avoid interest mediation or compromises with business whilst retaining a 'private voice in the corridors of power and decision-making' (2000: 84). Rather than engaging in the Customized Sector Plan process, SACTWU relied on its direct links to Alec Erwin, a former union organizer in the clothing and textile sector, who served as minister of the DTI from 1996 to 2004. For example, it was under direct pressure from SACTWU that the government concluded a two-year agreement with China (the 'China Restraint Agreement' of 2007–8) restricting the importation of certain garments even though this angered retailers, thereby undermining attempts to 'co-ordinate' domestic supply chains (Morris and Levy, 2016).

SACTWU's general secretary, Ebrahim Patel, exerted considerable influence more broadly through COSATU and the various corporatist forums in which the unions participated. Patel had been the chief labour negotiator during the democratic transition, was a key architect of the Labour Relations Act and was influential also in the ILO, co-authoring key documents on decent work (discussed in Chapters 1 and 3). His strategy for the clothing sector became the model for labour market and industrial policy generally, and he helped to bring the ILO's ideology of 'decent work', with modifications, to South Africa.

In 2009, Patel was appointed Minister of Economic Development in Jacob Zuma's first government (or 'comrade minister' as SACTWU called him[1]). Within two weeks, he and Rob Davies (a member of the central committee and politburo of the South African Communist Party and Zuma's new Minister of Trade and Industry) were faced with the threatened closure of *Frame Textiles* in KwaZulu-Natal. Patel and Davies began talks with the state-owned IDC (that was initially housed in Davies' department and subsequently moved under the control of Patel's Department of Economic Development) to rescue the company (Donnelly, 2009). The IDC had initially declined requests to assist *Frame Textiles*, but under political pressure reconsidered the issue, including working with a prospective (but unnamed) 'Asian investor' to buy

[1] See http://hci.co.za/clothing-textile/frame-unravels-while-it-awaits-government-rescue/.

into the company. Davies explained that government was 'trying to defend strategic industrial capacity' and 'create the conditions to build on this and progressively shift the growth path to one which yields decent work and sustainable livelihoods' (quoted in Ensor, 2009). *Frame Textiles* was nonetheless closed when the 'Asian investor' walked away (Le Roux, 2009). It was rumoured that the attempted bailout had been strongly criticized by other South African firms who claimed that the entire industry needed assistance and preference should not be given to a single firm.

The episode thus speaks to the tension between efforts to protect and build a domestic supply chain (running from textiles to clothing manufacturing, to retail), and efforts to support clothing manufacturers by inter alia enabling producers to import textiles as cheaply as possible. South Africa's industrial policy allows duty-free imports of textiles for clothing manufactures producing for export, but those producing for the domestic market are still required to show that South African textile producers cannot meet their requirements before they can use imported material in production for the domestic market. Despite such tariff protection (and efforts such as those discussed above) to save *Frame*, the South African textile industry has proved disappointing to policymakers and clothing manufacturers alike.

SACTWU was influential not just through its contacts with government ministers. In the 1990s and 2000s, SACTWU accumulated massive financial assets, assisted fundamentally by the government's BEE policies. SACTWU became the major shareholder of Hosken Consolidated Investments (HCI), the most successful of South Africa's trade union investment funds. As of March 2014, SACTWU owned shares worth R5.8 billion and was receiving over R50 million a year in dividends. As discussed in more detail below, SACTWU ceased to play a straightforward role as a trade union organizing in the working class and its relationship with the state was complicated by its dual role as union and investor. Its financial income affected the incentives facing the union, dovetailing with its preference for a more capital- and skill-intensive industry. SACTWU's economic incentives were complicated further by its part ownership of *Seardel*, which, aside from owning a low-wage factory in Lesotho, also owned *Frame Textiles*, the firm that Patel tried to bail out weeks after he stepped down as general secretary of SACTWU. Thus, at the time, Patel was widely regarded in the clothing industry as attempting to intervene on the part of SACTWU in both its role as a union *and* an investor (Bisseker, 2009).

7.2 Union Investment Funds: Workers as Capitalists?

SACTWU used state power not only to try to transform the clothing and textiles industries to raise productivity and permit much higher wages, but also to acquire financial assets.[2] In this regard, it benefitted substantially from BEE policies, which expanded opportunities for an emerging black elite, but also for largely 'black-owned' organizations, including trade unions.

BEE is a key feature of post-apartheid South Africa (Tangri and Southall, 2008; Cargill, 2010). As Southall (2007) has argued, it was a logical development of the history of the ANC and the nature of South Africa's democratic transition. Yet it was not without its tensions and contradictions, especially regarding the involvement of unions. BEE deals typically took the form of debt-financed transfers of share ownership, which were advantageous for beneficiaries when stock markets were rising because the debt could easily be repaid out of dividends and capital gains. It thus worked very successfully during the booming 2000s.

Supporters argued that BEE deals offered trade unions the chance to accumulate substantial strike funds, give workers a greater say over investment decisions and potentially transform the economy in progressive directions (Southall and Tangri, 2006: 132; see also Golding, 1997; Vlok, 1999; and Dexter, 1999). Others, however, worried that this was regressive in that the strategic focus of South African unionism supposedly came 'to resemble a combination of narrow workerism and "social capitalism"' (McKinley, 1999: 85). As discussed below, the focus of union investment on high-end property, media, hotels, and especially casinos indicates that there was often not much 'social' about the form of capitalism in which it typically engaged.

In 1997, a COSATU-appointed inquiry voiced its concern that the line between unions and investment companies was becoming blurred and that officials were gaining financially from fees and cheap shares (September Commission, 1997: chapter 4). It recommended that the goals of union investment vehicles be 'radically broadened' beyond considerations of profitability and more closely aligned with the strategic perspective of the union movement (ibid.). But in practice, most union investment vehicles prioritized profitability and by the early 2000s had accumulated financial assets, mostly in financial services, information technology, and especially in media and casinos (Southall and Tangri, 2006: 133–4).

Union investment in the gambling/gaming industry is in direct opposition to COSATU's policy on gambling. In its 2007 submission to the National Gambling Amendment Bill, COSATU stated:

> We are opposed to any form of legalisation of gambling. We view gambling as a self-destructive vice that does a lot of harm to society. It gives false hope and promises to people that they can escape the misery of poverty, instead often plunging them into debt and deeper poverty. Instead of directing resources to

[2] This section draws on Nattrass and Seekings (2015).

> productive investment, gambling takes away from the poor to the rich. It promotes greed. John Maynard Keynes once said that the only people who win from gambling in the long run are those who operate the gambling. (2007: 2)

Not all union investment managers agreed. As discussed in more detail below, SACTWU obtained a significant stake in the gambling industry through its relationship with HCI.

The National Union of Mineworkers' Mineworkers Investment Corporation, and the SACTWU's SACTWU Investment Group (housed in HCI) were the most successful union investment vehicles, contributing significantly to trusts aimed at benefitting union members and their families through educational bursaries and social programmes (Southall and Tangri, 2006: 133; Cargill, 2010). Of the two, SACTWU Investment Group was by far the most successful in financial terms: whereas the Mineworkers Investment Corporation leveraged an initial loan of R3 million in 1995 to achieve financial assets worth R1.4 billion by 2010, SACTWU Investment Group leveraged a loan of R2 million to achieve financial assets of R4 billion over the same period (Cargill, 2010: 138). Other union investment companies, notably companies set up by the National Union of Metalworkers of South Africa and the South African Railway and Harbour Workers Union were less successful (Vlok, 1999; Southall and Tangri, 2006: 133). In Cargill's assessment, most union investment vehicles 'muddled along, maintaining small portfolios with little apparent market interest in them as BEE partners' with some acquiring 'dubious reputations' in the process (2010: 141).[3] By the mid-2000s, SACTWU and the National Union of Mineworkers accounted for more than 90 per cent of union company investment interests, an outcome COSATU attributed to a rising stock market, BEE deals and being able to 'take advantage of opportunities in regulated telecommunications and casino industries on extremely favourable terms' (COSATU, 2006).

SACTWU also managed six pension funds (for members in different subsectors), but with less success. In 2011 it transpired that much of the money had been channelled to a failed luxury property development via an unsecured loan to a business co-owned by an ex trade-unionist turned politician that subsequently went bankrupt. SACTWU suspended its deputy general secretary (who was the trustee of three of the five funds) and took legal action against various people involved, including the former national benefits co-ordinator for SACTWU (Underhill, 2012). SACTWU later reported that it had used

[3] Some disreputable practices backfired on the union movement. For example, COSATU's investment arm, *Kopano Ke Matla* suppressed criticism from within COSATU of a fishing company it owned (Cargill, 2010: 147–8) and in 2014 it was revealed that *Kopano Ke Matla* had defrauded COSATU in a property sale and had conducted an unapproved pension fund administration business resulting in the disappearance of millions of Rands (Welz, 2015: 6–7).

R200 million of its own financial assets to replenish half of the retirement funds that had been lost (Paton, 2013). The episode illustrates that financial management is fraught with danger as well as opportunities. It was fortuitous that SACTWU's independent wealth could be mobilized to compensate, at least in part, the workers' pension funds that had been mismanaged under its watch.

From 2007 (excepting 2009, following the financial crash), the market value of SACTWU's shares in HCI and *Seardel* per member exceeded the annual earnings of an experienced machinist in Cape Town, that is, for a worker earning the highest NBC minimum wage (see Figure 7.1). Between 1999 and 2005, about R120 million in financial dividends from these shares were channelled by SACTWU to fund its social programmes including support for schools and shelters for victims of domestic violence (HCI, 2005: 14–15). SACTWU also funded sport and recreational activities for its members, provided bursaries for tertiary education for their children, a housing loan scheme at rates below those of commercial banks, and guarantees for members to access loans through the National Housing Trust. As of 2005, SACTWU members had obtained over R100 million in housing loans through this scheme (ibid.: 15).[4]

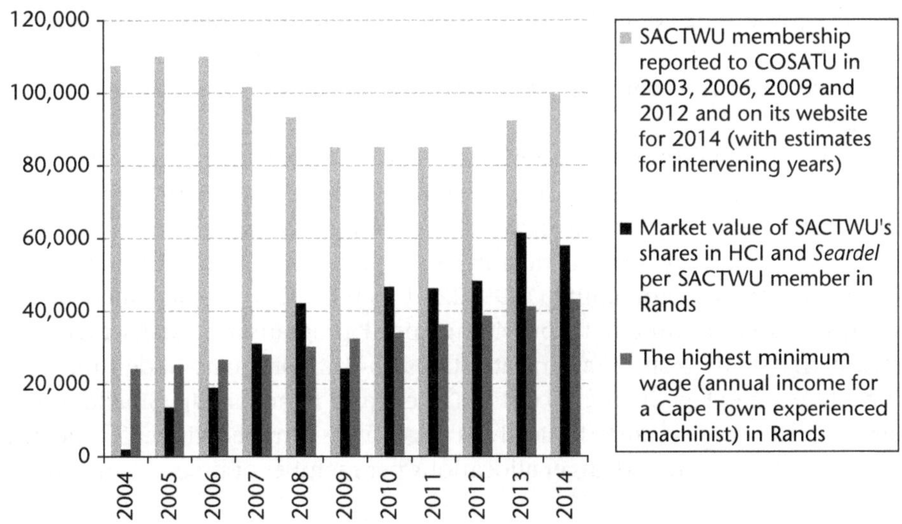

Figure 7.1 SACTWU's HCI and *Seardel* share value per member, and total membership.
Source: Data on membership available at: http://cosatu.org.za/docs/reports/2012/report.pdf; Data on *Seardel* was obtained from: http://*Seardel*.co.za/investor-relations (as of July 2015) but this website no longer exists. Data on HCI available at: http://hci.co.za/financials/.

[4] For SACTWU membership and social programmes see: www.sactwu.org.za/union

Figure 7.2 SACTWU's Black Rock Casino, Hotel, and Entertainment Complex, Newcastle.

In 2013, SACTWU's dividend payment from HCI alone was R54 million, rivalling its income from membership fees. Assuming it had 92,361 members at the time[5] and that the members paid on average R12 per week in fees (i.e. mid-way between the maximum fee of R15.20 and the minimum of R9.10) this implied an income stream from membership fees of about R53 million.[6] This suggests that by the time the Chinese entrepreneurs challenged SACTWU and the bargaining council in court over the extension of minimum wages to them, SACTWU probably had more of an (economic) interest in the Newcastle casino that it owned through Tsongo (Figure 7.2), than in Newcastle clothing workers.

Significant investment income in relation to membership fees affects the incentive structure facing unions. As Faulkner pointed out in 1999 in relation to 'business unionism' in the other countries, it 'decreases the need for organising campaigns to extend membership' potentially also harming union democracy and accountability (1999: 22). In SACTWU's case, its independent wealth and commitment to providing social programmes for its members meant that aside from retaining its status as the dominant trade union on the NBC, it had few, if any, incentives to expand membership. Smaller numbers of better-paid workers (typically in larger firms) implied higher fee income per organizing effort and larger allocations per member of investment-funded

[5] According to http://www.sactwu.org.za, SACTWU claimed a membership of 99,697 in 2014 (checked 25 November 2014) and it reported a figure of 85,025 for 2012 to the COSATU conference. Assuming membership grew steadily in the intervening years, this implies a membership of 92,361 in 2013. SACTWU does not put its accounts in the public domain, hence the estimate for fee income.

[6] This does not include the 'agency fees' that, since 2006, have been deducted off the wages of *all* workers registered with the NBC and sent to SACTWU as a result of the NBC agency shop agreement with SACTWU.

social programmes. SACTWU historically had higher rates of organization in larger firms, with limited membership in the smaller cut-make-and-trim operations (Webster et al., 2008: 86) and this trend is likely to continue, especially in the face of widespread transformation of smaller firms into workers' co-operatives (discussed later).

HCI provides a lens for exploring the tensions and choices facing union investment vehicles over whether, and when, to prioritize profits and when to act strategically to save jobs of union members. As discussed below, HCI, under pressure from SACTWU, made a substantial investment in the clothing and textile industry through its involvement with *Seardel*, then South Africa's largest employer in the clothing industry. In this regard, HCI differed from the Mineworkers Investment Corporation, which has a shareholder's compact preventing it from taking a direct stake in any company in the mining, energy, and construction sectors where the National Union of Mineworkers organizes workers.[7] SACTWU, like the chemical workers' union, has been happy to invest in its own backyard (Cargill, 2010: 145). The advantage is that SACTWU can—and has—acted to save jobs for its members that might otherwise be lost. The potential disadvantage is that it results in the kind of conflict of interest the Mineworkers Investment Corporation sought to avoid. As we show below, SACTWU's strategy to save jobs in the clothing firms it owned was assisted by government subsidies and related support. But even so, HCI struggled to save *Seardel*, eventually selling the remaining apparel units directly to SACTWU. It was only because of its significant investment through HCI that SACTWU had the resources to buy the factories outright and to sink an additional R25 million into a 'design centre' to boost innovation and fashion.[8] This wealth was a consequence of its participation in casino capitalism in both a figurative and literal sense through its stock market earnings and investment in casinos.

7.3 The Rise of HCI: Trade Unions Take Advantage of Casino Capitalism

In 1997, SACTWU and the National Union of Mineworkers acquired control of HCI, thereby creating the biggest union-controlled investment company on the Johannesburg Stock Exchange (Golding and Copelyn, 2007: 6). According to Marcel Golding, former deputy general secretary of National Union of Mineworkers and then chairman of HCI, the objective was to improve the wealth and savings of workers, to provide employment opportunities and to contribute

[7] http://mic.co.za/investment-sectors.
[8] http://iol.co.za/capetimes/sactwu-invests-r25m-to-grow-jobs-1.1676743#.VHHkkcnp-Zd.

to the transformation of the economy (Golding, 1997). He and John (Jonny) Copelyn, the former general secretary of SACTWU and chief executive officer of HCI, launched an investment strategy that made them both Rand billionaires and which would transform SACTWU from a working-class union into an independently wealthy entity (Nattrass and Seekings, 2015). They used HCI's BEE status (largely courtesy of the National Union of Mineworkers and SACTWU having predominantly black members) to obtain loans and shares. They also acted as opportunistic equity investors, picking stocks that benefitted from the dotcom and technology stock bubble of the late 1990s. Then, having what they describe as the 'good sense and luck' to take their profits months before the market crash of 2000 (ibid.), Golding and Copelyn were able to repay HCI's debt and provide shareholders with a substantial dividend.

Golding and Copelyn also bought a 25 per cent stake in e-TV (South Africa's only private TV station), invested additional resources and eventually gained full control of it. Most shareholders, however, were unhappy with this move. In 2002, Copelyn and Golding sold HCI's shares in telecommunications and offered disgruntled shareholders a cash exit. Approximately 73 per cent of the total share capital of HCI was returned—including from the National Union of Mineworkers' Mineworkers Investment Corporation—leaving SACTWU and HCI management as the major shareholders. The following year, e-TV revenues increased by 43 per cent (thanks to the football World Cup) and HCI started expanding and consolidating its holdings in casinos and hotels through its subsidiary, *Tsogo Investment Holdings*, a BEE holding company. It was later alleged in court documents that SACTWU used these financial assets for political and economic advantage, notably putting pressure on e.TV to provide publicity for Ebrahim Patel and to prevent any mention of *Tsogo* in a programme featuring gambling addiction (Golding, 2014: paras 63 and 67).[9]

From 2003 to 2007, HCI grew on the back of the global economic boom and rapidly rising stock markets in South Africa and abroad. It obtained economic interests in a range of sectors including mining, gas (in the US), agriculture, traffic monitoring equipment etc. In 2004 HCI bought Cape Town's *Golden Arrow* Bus Service for R250 million, angering COSATU because a rival bid by a

[9] This allegation was made in 2014 court documents (pertaining to a dispute between Golding and the HCI board which ended in Golding's resignation). Golding stated that his relationship with Copelyn had deteriorated because of 'concerted pressure' from SACTWU and its persistent attempts 'to influence the editorial direction of e.TV news in order to further its agenda' (Golding, 2014: para 43). Golding argued that pressure had worsened in 2013/14 in the run-up to the elections and especially after a politically connected SACTWU representative joined the board of HCI (ibid.: para 44). Former ANC government minister Barbara Hogan resigned from the board of HCI along with Golding, also citing dissatisfaction with SACTWU's behaviour (Hogan, 2014). The intricacies of the corporate power struggle aside, the documents provide a window into the way that power can, and has, been wielded through union investment vehicles in support of economic interests and political allies.

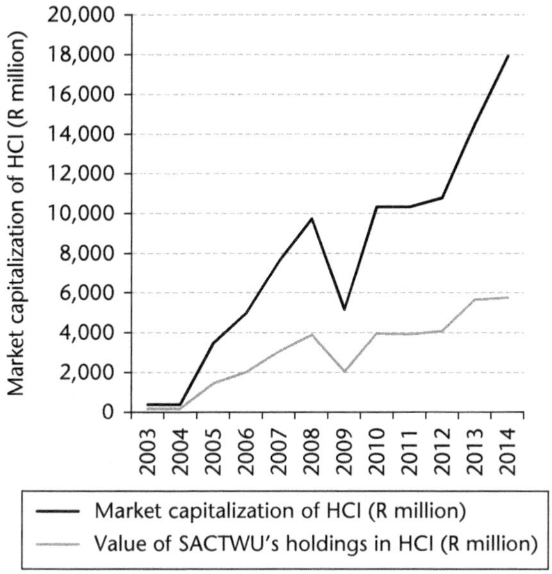

Figure 7.3 Market Capitalization of HCI from 2003 to 2014.
Source: Data from financial reports available at: http://hci.co.za/financials/.

workers' co-operative which had already invested R100 million with the company had been overlooked (Southall and Tangri, 2006: 127–8). By 2007, HCI was 'rated the number one financial services company in terms of broad based black economic empowerment ownership and the fifth overall empowerment company on the JSE [Johannesburg Stock Exchange]' (Golding and Copelyn, 2007: 6). HCI's market capitalization had increased twenty-fold, and SACTWU's share had increased seventeen-fold (Figure 7.3). By this time, HCI's earnings were fuelled primarily by gambling, high-end property and e-TV.

The 2008 global financial crash made a dent on market capitalization and no dividends were paid that year. Instead, HCI used the downturn in stock prices to gain a 75 per cent stake in *Tsogo*, thereby orienting the company even further towards gaming. Also that year, HCI took control of *Seardel*, South Africa's premier employer in the clothing and textile industry.

7.3.1 *HCI and* Seardel

Seardel Investment Corporation originated in 1957 when Aaron Searll bought a small company employing fifteen people to make nurses' caps and bras. Eleven years later, he incorporated the business into an investment holding company, branching into lingerie. The company expanded into clothing production (purchasing *Bonwit* clothing from *Woolworths* in 1989 and gaining full control of *Bibette* clothing in 1996), toys, travel and property (gaining full control of *Prima Toy and Leisure Group* in 2001) and electronics (obtaining a controlling stake in *Sharp Electronics* in 1981). *Seardel* also moved upstream in the clothing value chain into textiles, eventually obtaining full control of the textile company *Frame Group Holdings* in 2001 (*Seardel*, 2004: 9).

By 2008, when Searll relinquished ownership of *Seardel* and Copelyn became chairman, it had grown to employ 15,000 people with a turnover of R3.9 billion and was the largest clothing and textile group in Southern Africa (Searll, 2008: 4). In 2009, *Seardel* opened a new subsidiary in Lesotho, *NyeNye Clothing*. At almost exactly the same moment, *Seardel* announced that it intended to close one of its subsidiaries in Cape Town, *Intimate Apparel*, with the loss of 800 jobs. Because HCI owned 71 per cent of *Seardel*, and SACTWU owned a 40 per cent share in HCI, the union was compromised by this indirect shift in operations from higher-wage Cape Town to lower-wage Lesotho. SACTWU's Andre Kriel was forced to argue that *Seardel* was motivated by a concern to save jobs in the wider region, not simply to make a profit. *NyeNye Clothing*, he said, paid 'above the legal minimum wage' in Lesotho, 'and complies with all other Lesotho labour laws. Our role, together with our Lesotho counterparts, is to advance our agenda for decent work in southern Africa, including in Lesotho'. As other observers noted, however, compliance with the minimum wage in Lesotho meant paying wages a lot lower than in the non-compliant firms in South Africa, which the union was determined to close down (Lombard, 2009).

But by this stage the company's South African textile and clothing production units were making such a loss that the company was threatened with bankruptcy. As can be seen in Figure 7.4, *Seardel*'s apparel and household textiles division made losses of R162 million in 2008, significantly overwhelming the small contribution to profitability from other arms of the business.

The decline of *Seardel*'s clothing operations started in 2003/4 when an appreciating Rand sharply increased clothing imports (Chapter 6). This, coupled with wage pressure, forced *Seardel* to retrench 10 per cent of its clothing and textile workforce. In its annual report for 2004, *Seardel* recorded its hope that the new NBC in the clothing sector would come up with a 'sensible agreement on a flexible wage model as both compliance and regulated flexibility should feature in our labour market policies' (Lazarus and Searll, 2004: 6). Despite being cautiously optimistic about industrial relations, and noting that 'agreement exists in principle at the NBC with the representative trade union, SACTWU, on the need to be globally competitive and to develop "new generation" wage agreements focusing on labour productivity', *Seardel*'s management complained that 'insufficient progress has actually been made' (*Seardel*, 2004: 19–20). In an attempt to gain some respite, the company

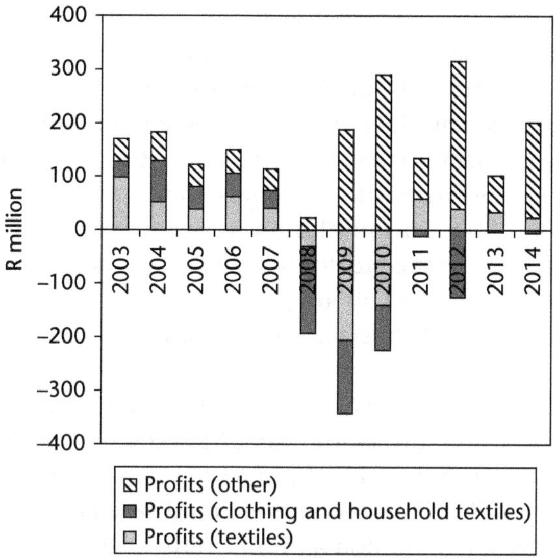

Figure 7.4 Profits generated by the different business segments of *Seardel*.

Source: Annual reports were available at: http://*Seardel*.co.za/investor-relations (as of July 2015). This website no longer exists. *Seardel* does not report profits by business segment. Profits were estimated by multiplying return on tangible assets by tangible assets for each business segment).

moved its Durban garment producing facilities to Ladysmith to benefit from the lower minimum wages allowed in such non-metro areas.

SACTWU responded by purchasing shares in *Seardel* (attaining 19.3 per cent of N-ordinary shares in 2005) and Copelyn was installed on the board. Copelyn had some experience running clothing firms, through *Zenzeleni Clothing*. *Zenzeleni* had been established by SACTWU as a workers' co-operative in the late 1980s with finance provided as part of a retrenchment package to employ 300 retrenched textile workers (Southall and Tangri, 2006: 133; Cargill, 2010: 137). When it ran into trouble, in 1992, Copelyn was brought in to help recapitalize and restructure the business along more commercial lines, and in the process had to lay-off 150 workers (Cargill, 2010: 137). The fate of presiding over retrenchments was to befall him again in *Seardel*.

In 2005, *Seardel*'s management complained about a COSATU nation-wide strike in support of its campaign to encourage retailers to buy local, noting that it 'is difficult to understand how strikes can assist in saving jobs when the industry is under such intense competition from Rand strength in the export market and from imports domestically' (*Seardel*, 2005: 20). The following year it complained about the inability of the NBC to facilitate 'the adoption of a coherent labour cost structure which reflects the highly competitive nature of clothing manufacturing' (*Seardel*, 2006: 20), as well as the slow progress that was being made in the consultative process towards a Customized Sector Plan.

In 2007, the company noted that the Plan had been 'finally ratified' after encountering 'many delays and setbacks' but complained bitterly that wage pressure was becoming unbearable; wage increases were 'difficult to justify unless linked to clear productivity improvement initiatives' (*Seardel*, 2007: 20). In 2008, as *Seardel*'s apparel business crashed into the red, dragging the entire corporation down with it, management stated that it would only implement the 12.5 per cent minimum wage increase set for the non-metro areas by the NBC when forced to do so by the legal extension of the agreement to them by the Minister of Labour (*Seardel*, 2008: 11). As further job losses were announced, SACTWU mobilized its position in HCI to effect a bail out of *Seardel*.

In 2008/9 a massive rights issue, pitched at 50c a share and underwritten by HCI, saved *Seardel* from liquidation. About R200 million of the R300 million used to acquire the 70 per cent stake in *Seardel* came from SACTWU (Crotty, 2012). Not even SACTWU's intervention could save *Frame Textiles*, which by that stage was losing R30 million a month (Ensor, 2009). According to Golding and Copelyn, the decision to close *Frame* after the failed bailout effort 'rocked relations with our major shareholder, SACTWU, but still seemed unavoidable to us' (Golding and Copelyn, 2009: 6–7). Instead, they put their efforts into improving productivity and performance in the remaining clothing and textile production units.

HCI's investment strategy had been focused, up until this point, on taking advantage of BEE deals and maximizing shareholder value. Its move to rescue *Seardel* marked something of a break in strategy and was almost certainly the result of pressure from SACTWU. Not all financial commentators thought that this was a good idea. Golding and Copelyn were particularly incensed by one analyst's assessment that HCI shares should be discounted because management was displaying a 'lack of focus' by purchasing an asset in the troubled clothing industry (cited in ibid.: 6). They retorted by stating that they 'were confident that the assets we have amassed in HCI are top-class assets that anyone should be proud to own' (ibid.: 6).

An appreciating Rand between 2008 and 2011 made the planned turnaround very difficult as import competition intensified. In 2010, Golding and Copelyn warned that despite the management team in *Seardel* having 'worked like a Trojan to turn that business around' it would be 'silly to underestimate the difficulties of returning all the businesses in the group to sustainability' (2010: 7). It was only the injection of significant government funding in the form of R78 million of production incentives that saved *Seardel* from running at a loss that year (Hassenfuss, 2011). HCI blamed 'persistent customs fraud, inequitable wage structures across the region, the strong Rand and some internal operating shortcomings' for continuing losses in the apparel division but expressed hope that new branding initiatives such as 'obtaining the local and international rights to procure, manufacture, distribute and sell apparel and accessories under the 46664 [Nelson Mandela's prison number] brand name' would help the firm enter higher value-added markets (HCI, 2011: 20).

Despite the depreciation of the Rand from 2012, *Seardel*'s apparel production unit continued to drain *Seardel*'s coffers (as the financial analyst, mentioned earlier and to which Golding and Copelyn had taken great exception, suspected would be the case back in 2008). Indeed, *Seardel* would have made a loss in 2012 if it had not been for the injection of R192 million into *Seardel* as the result of a settlement of a long-running legal dispute with previous shareholders (HCI, 2012: 23). According to HCI, the competition faced by *Seardel*'s apparel division from 'imports out of lower wage paying countries and manufacturers from within South African borders that do not pay the prescribed minimum wages meant that rising input costs could not be recovered in higher prices for products supplied' and that 'the resultant losses were of such a magnitude that it left no alternative but to rationalise the business unit' (HCI, 2012: 21). It announced that it would be closing *Intimate Apparel* (retrenching 800 workers) in Cape Town, a decision SACTWU described as a 'bolt out of the blue' (Hartley, 2012).

As employment and output contracted in the clothing and textile units (see Figure 7.5), *Seardel* relied increasingly on the distribution of branded products, property, and leisure activities. As shown in Figure 7.6, this coincided with rising average wages for the remaining workers in the company, higher asset-to-employee ratios (as the business became more capital-intensive as a whole) and rising profitability. In this regard, *Seardel* was a microcosm of the restructuring taking place in the clothing industry (and wider economy) involving the shedding of relatively unskilled jobs and shifting towards more capital-intensive employment.

It was also a microcosm of how the benefits of South Africa's pro-capital upgrading trajectory and related industrial policies benefitted primarily an elite. As COSATU complained when it became clear that *Seardel* was going to close *Intimate Apparel*:

> *Seardel* as a group has taken millions of Rand from government programmes to shore up their company and they were meant to restructure the operations and make it more effective. The money seems to have been pocketed as the cars and bonuses of directors are as extravagant as always and the companies are still struggling. (COSATU, 2012)

Indeed, according to *Seardel*'s accounts, the company received about R643 million in production subsidies between 2001 and 2014 in what ultimately turned out to be a largely futile attempt by the state to save clothing and textile production in *Seardel* and other firms.

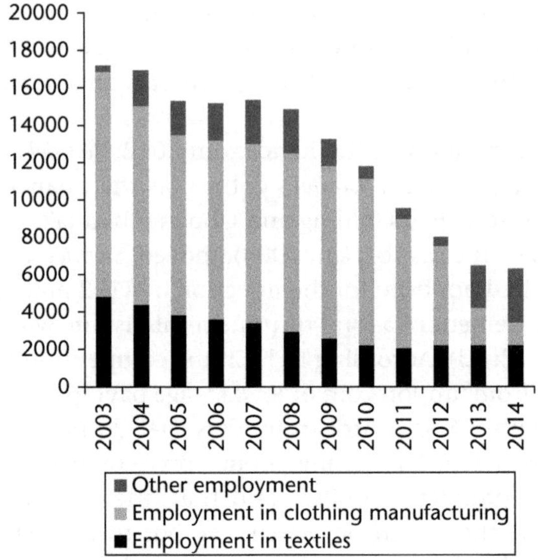

Figure 7.5 Employment in *Seardel.*

Source: Annual reports were available at: http://*Seardel*.co.za/investor-relations (as of July 2015). This website no longer exists. *Seardel* reported aggregate data only. A breakdown of employment by sectors was available for the years 2010, 2011, and 2012 (*Seardel,* 2012: 15) and annual reports mentioned staff numbers by sector occasionally, but not systematically. Some of the data was thus imputed using available information and trends.

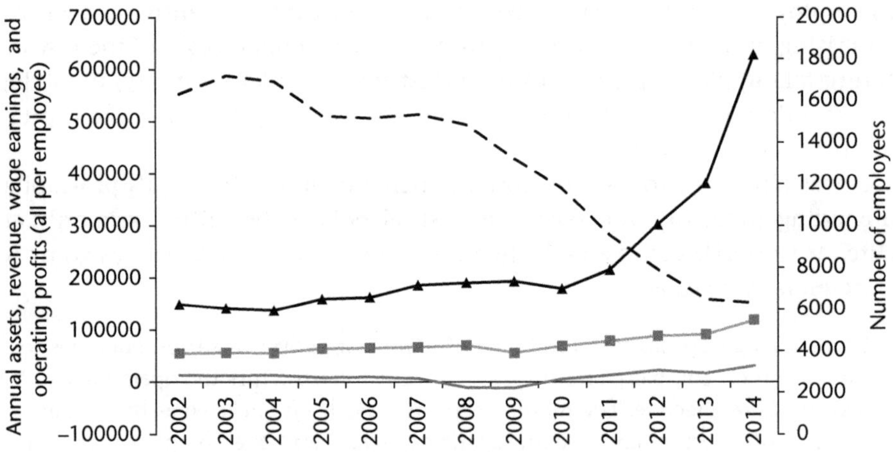

Figure 7.6 *Seardel*: Key Economic Indicators from 2003 to 2014.

Source: Data were obtained from financial reports available at: http://www.*Seardel*.co.za/investor-relations (as of July 2015). This website no longer exists.

In 2014, HCI threw in the towel with regard to the clothing business, no longer prepared to test its shareholders' patience with the ongoing losses. It sold its remaining clothing manufacturing units (accounting for 2,000 jobs) directly to *Trade Call Investments*, an investment company co-owned by SACTWU and the Managing Director, Herman Pillay (Matsilele, 2014). It also sold the Lesotho operation (*NyeNye Clothing*) to a firm leaving South Africa, finally ridding SACTWU of the embarrassment of owning a low-wage producer in Lesotho that had benefitted directly from the destruction by NBC inspectors of low-wage competition in South Africa. HCI bailed out the remainder of *Seardel* with a R5 billion rights issue and consolidated its media operations into *Seardel* (HCI, 2014). This left HCI with a 78 per cent stake in what was left of *Seardel*, that is, largely a media and property investment platform, entirely devoid of the economic base in clothing production upon which Aaron Searll originally built the company. SACTWU retained a 3 per cent holding of N-ordinary shares in *Seardel*.

This episode illustrates how difficult it has proven to be for South African clothing manufacturing companies, even those like *Seardel* with committed management and massive government support, to survive in the face of the squeeze between strong international competition and wage pressure. Despite substantial government assistance in the form of incentives and grants, SACTWU's strategy as both union and owner ultimately resulted in decent work for the few (at least in its South African-owned enterprises) at the cost of job destruction in *Seardel* and across the South African clothing industry.

7.4 Workers as Capitalists or Co-owners?

The history of the post-apartheid clothing manufacturing industry is emblematic of the consequences of an upgrading trajectory which, with the help of industrial policy incentives and the enforcement of rapidly rising minimum wages, results in a pro-capital outcome (Chapter 3) in which average wages rise for a shrinking pool of employed workers in an increasingly skill- and capital-intensive sector. The development trajectory for clothing manufacturing was reflected across the post-apartheid economy as real wages and the profit share rose at the cost of stagnant and even falling employment (Nattrass, 2014a). Factors unique to particular sectors (such as drought in agriculture and the depletion of mineral resources in mining) contributed to this outcome as did increased international competition across the economy. Yet, trade union strategy and industrial policy were decisive in precluding a dualist outcome for South Africa that could have facilitated some 'downgrading' and the expansion or even just the preservation of labour-intensive production. The winners of the South African growth path were those (typically more skilled) workers who kept their jobs, and firms that were either in, or could move into, more capital- and skill-intensive activities, assisted by industrial policies.

One of the consequences of this growth path is that the South African trade union movement has come to represent predominantly skilled workers in relatively protected sectors, notably government. COSATU's own surveys show that unskilled and semi-skilled workers comprised 60 per cent of COSATU unions' membership in 1994, but only 22 per cent in 2009 (Bischoff and Tshoaedi 2012: 52). Relatively skilled workers have a clear interest in high-wage, high-productivity (upgrading) trajectories; labour-intensive development is not their concern. Their approach is justified by a discourse of decent work fundamentalism and economic upgrading as the *only* acceptable growth strategy.

'High road' growth policies are not simple technical choices. Ideas and interests affect how they resonate within society and whether they are adopted by the state (Schmidt, 2008). The ideological power of decent work fundamentalism, and the political appeal of growth through industrial 'upgrading' rather than via 'sweated labour', cannot be overemphasized. Yet the blurring of the boundaries between trade union and business strategy in the clothing and textile industries raises further questions about the role of industrial policy and its intended beneficiaries. As shown above, SACTWU was successful at mobilizing government industrial policy assistance, but this did not prevent substantial job losses or the payment of executive bonuses, or its expansion of SACTWU's manufacturing capacity into lower-wage regions outside of South Africa, thereby posing a threat to the South African firms on whom it had contributed to forcing high and rising minimum wages.

In 2015, SACTWU further undermined efforts to develop a domestic value chain (linking textile producers, clothing manufacturers, and retailers) by purchasing a textile factory outside the country. SACTWU, through *Trade Call Investments*, purchased *Star Knitwear* in Mauritius supposedly to 'spearhead our plans to promote our speed to market strategy as we plan to revive the South African clothing and Textile Industry'.[10] Yet in practice, owning *Star Knitwear* enabled SACTWU to act like a typical clothing manufacturer: to source textile inputs as cheaply as possible on a regional basis and at the cost of local textile firms. In 2018, the *Business Day* reported that the Nelson Mandela centenary 'Madiba' T-shirt was produced by *Star Knitwear* using cotton grown in Madagascar and spun, knitted, and dyed in Mauritius (Ardé, 2018). South African textile producers cried foul, pointing out that the fabric could have been made in South Africa. The managing director of *Trade Call Investments* (and co-owner with SACTWU) responded by saying that the

[10] http://www.tciapparel.co.za/our-history/.

company had invested in Mauritius because South African knitters 'lacked capacity and weren't cheap' whereas the factory in Mauritius allowed them to 'invest in integrated supply chains' with 'quick turnaround time' to reduce 'dependency on China' (quoted in ibid.). A Durban-based knitter and garment manufacturer, however, responded that there was spare capacity in the South African textile sector, that staff were being put on short-time and even retrenched and hence that South African manufacturers should:

> abide by agreements to support the local industry, pay fair wages and source materials ethically. You can't boast about Madiba T-shirts being made locally when it damages the local industry. Madiba's image on that T-shirt is made of words like 'integrity' and 'accountability'. (Quoted in Ardé, 2018)

SACTWU's General Secretary denied that their knitting operation in Mauritius posed any competitive threat to South African knitters, but his protestations rang hollow in the face of outrage from South African textile producers who pointed out that minimum wages were lower in Mauritius and that Mauritian businesses could pay on a piecework basis, whereas they were hamstrung by collective agreements with SACTWU preventing this (ibid.). The strong whiff of hypocrisy around SACTWU stems from its attempt to play both sides of the capital/labour divide and its apparent preference for making profits for its members over creating jobs in South Africa.

7.4.1 *SACTWU and the Challenge of Co-operatives*

SACTWU's direct engagement as an investor and manufacturer is one model—business unionism—for how workers can engage more directly in production through the ownership of factories. Worker-owned firms, or co-operatives, is another model. SACTWU has experimented with workers' co-operatives (such as *Zenzeleni Clothing*) but over time has become increasingly suspicious of them, initially through its own negative experiences running them, and later because of the shift to workers' co-operatives in places like Newcastle.

In the mid-1980s, the National Union of Mineworkers, the National Union of Metalworkers of South Africa, SACTWU and other unions set up workers' co-operatives to provide jobs for retrenched members and as an alternative to the more hierarchical capitalist firm (Philip, 2018). SACTWU's *Zenzeleni* workers' co-operative initially produced t-shirts and then expanded into t-shirt printing, and the mining and metalworkers unions set up t-shirt printing co-operatives. They all targeted the 'solidarity market' (notably, hoping to get orders from COSATU), but found that this market was not big enough for all of them and that, besides, buyers demanded that they be competitive in terms of both price and quality (Philip, 2018: 59). As Philip comments: 'Even within the solidarity market of the trade union movement, the co-ops could not escape the price-setting mechanisms of the wider market' (2018: 60). There were some notable successes amongst the ex-mineworkers' co-operatives (such as consumer co-operatives to buy and sell chickens, and agricultural co-operatives growing and selling produce to local shops), yet the overall experience was one of failure, prompting the National Union of Mineworkers to move into more conventional forms of small business development. Many co-operatives struggled with cashflow and other managerial functions, a problem exacerbated by suspicion towards management, seeing it as emblematic of the very authoritarianism of the capitalist firms they were trying to avoid (Philip, 2018: 57–66).

Having initially regarded the co-operative movement as a potentially progressive development, SACTWU hardened its stance towards workers' co-operatives when they emerged in clothing manufacturing as a last-ditch effort to avoid being driven entirely out of business by the NBC. Precisely because they originated as defensive efforts to avoid harassment from the NBC, SACTWU regards them as 'sham co-operatives'—and, as discussed in Chapter 6, SACTWU and the NBC made a concerted, but failed, attempt to ensure that labour law applied to members of workers' co-operatives. The NBC argued that the labour law should apply to both members of, and workers hired by, workers' co-operatives on the grounds that 'individual employees/ members are no more insulated from exploitation by the co-operatives than were the co-operatives another form of juristic entity, such as in most instances, the Close Corporation or Company under whose auspices the worker co-operative business was previously conducted' (NBC Constitutional Court appeal, para 52). The courts disagreed.

Many of the new co-operatives may well be 'sham', yet as judges from the Labour Court through to the Appeal Court and then the Constitutional Court argued, the legal framework for workers' co-operatives provides the institutional architecture for genuine worker control. Hence, when properly set up, even those co-operatives that were initiated by employers seeking to circumvent the NBC, transferred real decision-making power to workers and changed the relationship between them and their previous employer in a fundamental way. As the judge in the NBC's failed legal case noted, the Labour Relations Act affords protection for those working 'for' rather than 'with' others:

> A legitimate and properly constituted co-operative is characterised by the values of collective self-help, self-reliance, self-responsibility, democracy, equality and social responsibility. At its heart is the impulse of members to voluntarily associate with each other and to apply democracy as the basis of organisational decision-making. This is reflected in the provision of the COA [2005 Co-operatives Act] dealing with shareholding and the allocation of surpluses, requiring regular meetings, and instituting the general membership of the co-operative as the highest decision-making body of the organisation. Members of a workers' co-operative may

> be employed in a very wide sense but, in legitimate co-operatives, these members are not working *for* another person in the same way a wage-earner is. They do not place their capacity to work at the disposal of others. They are working *with* others for themselves in an enterprise they jointly own and collectively control.
>
> (Judgment by Judge Whitcher, on case no D20/16 in the Durban Labour Court, 15 February 2017, paragraph 23)

The growth of workers' co-operatives in the clothing manufacturing industry suggest that there is a remaining route to labour-intensive development, and one which potentially also provides a more dignified and empowering source of employment than low-wage employment, even if earnings in workers' co-operatives are also low. In a capitalist firm, the employer owns the machinery and leases or owns the factory, and it is the employer who decides whether to take on a cut-make-and-trim contract given existing wages and productivity in the firm. When workers are formed into co-operatives, they decide collectively whether to take on a contract, how to divide up the work and the income they receive from it. The old employer-turned-contracting-agent remains relatively powerful to the extent that s/he is better placed than the workers' co-operative to obtain orders and leverage existing relationships with design houses, international textile suppliers and the like. Some old employers lease machinery to the workers' co-operatives, others simply build this into the costs when negotiating their fee for sourcing orders. Yet, as the workers' co-operative gains experience, there is no reason why members could not displace their old employer, purchase their own machinery, lease their own factories. This, in turn, provides incentives to the employer to forge long-term, collaborative relationships with the workers' co-operatives, including providing training and assisting the co-operatives plan (and even execute) the production of orders. Workers and their old employers understand that the management/sourcing fee is something that can be bargained over. Allowing a relatively large cut to cover utilities, logistics (notably transporting the finished products to retailers), sourcing orders, and the like, can be advantageous for the workers' co-operative as it removes some of the managerial functions that the old mineworkers' co-operatives struggled with, allowing the workers' co-operatives to concentrate solely on organizing work effort and allocating pay. Even so, the possibility that the workers' co-operative might walk away from the deal, or work directly with design houses, serves to restrain management fees, making egregious exploitation less likely.

According to one of the Newcastle Chinese employers who opted to assist his workers restructure as a workers' co-operative, his earnings are now lower, but his life much improved by the change:

> I now earn slightly less than before. Not too bad. But it feels so good because I am hassle free from the unions and NBC. To deal with these guys [unions and NBCs], it

> just takes so much time and energy that I could in no way focus on my business... Well, if you talk to the co-op members, they will tell you that they don't necessarily get more than workers in other regular factories. Because with piecework pay, those 'quick hands' can earn a considerable wage. Here, we are not doing piece rate, they themselves [the managing team] decide on the allocation of the actual wages. But they are smart. They know who should be rewarded, and who should not. I am glad that I did this. This probably the way of doing factories in the future.
>
> (Quoted in Xu, 2017: 47)

The idea that workers are better able to monitor themselves, especially when obtaining a share of profits and once they have a fuller understanding of the economics of their business, has a long pedigree in economics, beginning with John Stuart Mill. He, like the Newcastle entrepreneur quoted above, thought that profit-sharing arrangements were the way of the future and that they would encourage greater labour productivity, eventually outcompeting conventional capitalist factories (Mill, 1848, book 4, chapter 7). He was overly optimistic about the power of co-operative forms to transform the entire capitalist order. As the Fabian socialists Beatrice and Sidney Webb pointed out a century ago, co-operatives tend to fail because of inadequate work discipline (and/or inability to manage the labour process), insufficient knowledge of the market, and a reluctance/inability to adapt (discussed in Philip, 2018: 47–8). Yet when marketing and the sourcing of orders can, in effect, be outsourced to the old employer, and when production systems are clear and understood (and can be adapted, perhaps, with the support of technical assistance provided by the old employer), then some of these incentive problems fall away. Worker-owned firms can be competitive where workers engage in mutual monitoring, have 'residual claimancy' (that is, a share of the profits) and have developed strong norms of reciprocity (including the preparedness to punish shirkers) (Carpenter et al., 2009). Workers' co-operatives in the clothing manufacturing industry can have these features: cut-make-and-grim contracts have clear deadlines and, in setting up the work process, members of the workers' co-operatives understand what rates of output are required, and line-based production allows for both monitoring by team leaders and mutual monitoring within the line itself.

We have spoken to members of workers' co-operatives in Newcastle, and they were, for the most part, cautiously optimistic about the model. They are typically small operations, mostly working with their old employers to source work. Their production systems are very basic and labour-intensive. For example, Figure 7.7 shows members of a workers' co-operative where production targets and tallies are noted on chalkboards, and machinists manually push bundles of partly completed garments down the line. Mutual monitoring is evident, but some team leaders worried that their workers' co-operative still lacked key skills, notably how best to lay out production lines for each job,

Figure 7.7 Members of a labour-intensive clothing workers' co-operative in Newcastle (bottom picture is of the management committee).

and how to price their work to win the contract and make a profit. Some workers' co-operatives hire Chinese line supervisors to assist them with both tasks (or have this managerial function provided for them by their old employers). These line supervisors are still known to 'shout', but members of workers' co-operatives experience this as helpful, rather than abusive.

Members of low-earning labour-intensive workers' co-operatives are, some would charge, simply exploiting themselves. This is a key ideological reason behind SACTWU's general distrust of workers' co-operatives, yet the challenge workers' co-operatives pose for the NBC (and thus also to SACTWU's power to set minimum wages with dominant employer organizations) provides a probably far greater incentive for union bosses to oppose workers' co-operatives.

Workers' co-operatives should not be dismissed simply as disguised forms of exploitation or as necessarily unprogressive and inimical to decent work. Members of workers' co-operatives are positioned to make informed choices about participating in low-earnings activities—knowing the economics of the situation and determining whether particular jobs are worth bidding for. They are buffeted by the same forces of market competition as workers in capitalist firms, but stand in a different relationship to the profit-making process. Even though their options are limited, they are empowered in the sense of understanding the business better and by being able to make real choices about production and distribution. It is 'decent work' in this sense, even if also low-earning. A strategy of inclusive dualism would direct industrial policy assistance to such firms as well as to the more skill- and capital-intensive operations where this assists competitiveness.

8

Conclusion

Dualism, Unemployment, and the Perils of Decent Work Fundamentalism

Decent work fundamentalism—that is, the use of rising minimum wages to boost labour productivity by destroying labour-intensive jobs—undermines inclusive development in surplus labour countries. In the first half of the book, we showed that the growth of large-scale, chronic and open unemployment in a set of developing countries points to the ongoing relevance of Lewis's 'dualist' model of economic development. In the presence of surplus labour, inclusive development requires job creation. Labour-intensive sectors such as clothing manufacturing can provide much-needed jobs and have been of crucial importance in the growth paths of many successful developing economies. In the second half of the book we examined the case of the clothing manufacturing industry in South Africa, where decent work fundamentalism not only impeded job creation but resulted in job destruction in places where they were desperately needed.

Decent work fundamentalism is underpinned by three propositions: (1) raising productivity is essential for economic growth and development; (2) labour-intensive growth necessarily leads to a 'race to the bottom' with falling real wages; and (3) promoting decent work through enforcing large increases in minimum wages alleviates poverty and inequality. We have argued that these propositions require more nuance and pay insufficient attention to the need for job creation in surplus labour countries. Following Lewis, we argued instead for a more diversified (or 'dualist') development strategy accommodating a range of wages and production technologies.

The first proposition—on the relationship between productivity growth and development—is correct but frequently misapplied. Productivity growth is essential for sustainable development, but the definition and measure of productivity are crucial. In surplus labour countries, the appropriate measure of productivity is not output per employed worker (labour productivity) but rather output per available worker (that is, output per person in the labour force, including the unemployed as well as the employed). When new labour-intensive manufacturing jobs are created, the employment elasticity of growth increases as the manufacturing sector becomes more labour-intensive and average labour productivity falls. This is desirable in a surplus labour country because more people are productively employed and per capita income rises.

The second proposition—on the purported 'race to the bottom'—is widely and greatly exaggerated. It is of course true that many jobs in tradable sectors have moved from high-wage countries (especially in Europe and North America) to lower-wage countries (including China). As wages in China grew, so production has relocated to Bangladesh, Cambodia, Vietnam, and elsewhere. However, there is no reason to believe that the growth of labour-intensive sectors such as clothing manufacturing harms other, more capital- and skill-intensive sectors, or even higher-wage firms in the same sector. Using the clothing manufacturing industry as a lens, we challenged the notion that low-wage producers necessarily pose a competitive threat to higher-wage producers in the same country and in the same sector. Clothing manufacturing is typically differentiated (or dualistic), with a range of production technologies and product markets. This means that it has been, and remains, feasible for relatively low-wage clothing producers (typically targeting the lower-income mass market of basic clothing products) to coexist, in the same country, alongside higher-wage producers (typically targeting the higher and more fashionable end of the consumer market). The Southern African case confirms that profitable opportunities for participating in global and regional value chains are structured by rules governing international trade, proximity to end markets and other factors. It also shows, however, that labour costs matter for competitiveness and continue to underpin the potential for generating jobs through labour-intensive growth.

The third proposition—on promoting decent work through minimum wage increases—holds in full-employment economies. Increasing wages faster at the bottom end of wage distribution worked well in post-war social democracies and in the co-ordinated market economies of Europe to narrow wage inequality and boost labour productivity. Active labour and industrial policies ensured that those who lost their jobs could rely on state-sponsored retraining programmes and on social security (Nattrass, 1999; Hall and Soskice, 2001). But the strategy has proven disastrous in South Africa, a surplus labour economy. Raising minimum wages incentivizes employers to raise labour productivity through implementing more skill- and capital-intensive technologies. In a context where unemployment is relatively low and the workforce is generally skilled, this reinforces a relatively high-wage, high-skilled growth path. But in the context of high unemployment, a skills shortage and labour- and industrial policies biased against labour-intensive firms, the result—as demonstrated by the case of the South African clothing manufacturing industry—can be significant net job destruction and rising unemployment.

The history of the global clothing industry demonstrates the power of Lewis-like growth to promote development and reduce poverty. The Lewis growth model remains relevant because of the persistence of surplus labour—and the rise of large-scale, open unemployment in countries in Southern Africa and elsewhere. This does not mean that Lewis-like growth is, on its own, a panacea for the growing reality of unemployment. Fostering labour-intensive firms and sectors can only be part of a strategy for confronting the scourge of unemployment and is consistent with development policies to raise labour productivity elsewhere to ensure a suitably diversified economy. Nor does the Lewis growth model require disregard for job quality and working conditions—indeed, it is consistent with the 'better work' initiatives in Bangladesh following the Rana Plaza disaster. The Lewis model is not, however, consistent with decent work fundamentalism, that is, driving up minimum wages irrespective of labour market conditions.

The South African clothing manufacturing industry provides a salutary lesson of what can happen when decent work fundamentalism prevails. Not only were minimum wages in the non-metropolitan areas increased massively and rapidly, especially after the formation of the NBC in 2003, but enforcement was stepped up (notably during the 'compliance drive' of 2009–2011). The systematic enforcement of increased minimum wages, set by a minority of employers together with a trade union that protected the interests of its core membership, destroyed jobs in the labour-intensive end of clothing manufacturing. It revealed starkly how the level of the minimum wage and its enforcement can matter profoundly for employment. Belated efforts to provide lower-wage producers with some relief slowed down the destruction of jobs, in an implicit recognition that decent work fundamentalism was bad for employment. Yet higher minimum wages continued to be extended across the industry. The prospects for labour-intensive production came to depend on the survival of newly formed workers' co-operatives whose members were exempt from the minimum wage legislation.

Policies biased against labour-intensive development in the Southern African surplus labour countries, where both unemployment and inequality are high, pose serious problems for distribution. Simulations suggest that a 10 percentage point reduction in unemployment would reduce South Africa's Gini coefficient by 2 percentage points (Anand et al., 2016). To put this in perspective, a similar reduction in inequality by increased welfare spending (rather than job creation) would require a 40 per cent increase in government transfers, amounting to 11 per cent of government expenditure or about 3 per cent of GDP (ibid.: 20).

The South African case study drew attention to the institutional mechanisms that facilitated decent work fundamentalism and impeded Lewis-like growth. In South Africa, the 'extension' of collective agreements on minimum wages by the Minister of Labour to all firms in the industry was crucial to job destruction in the clothing manufacturing industry. This issue of extensions has long been controversial in South Africa, as we noted in Chapter 1). When the Labour Market Commission in the mid-1990s recommended that the Minister of Labour be required to consider potential employment losses before extending bargaining council agreements to non-parties, opposition from organized labour resulted in the government rejecting the proposal. Instead, the bargained minimum wage became a lever at industrial level to raise average labour productivity, including through the destruction of lower-productivity, lower-wage jobs in sectors such as the clothing manufacturing industry.

In the South African context, a strategy of inclusive dualism would retain minimum wages, but remove the automatic extension of industry-level minimum wages to non-parties in dualistic industries where this would destroy jobs or impede job creation. Collective bargaining is good for industrial peace, for providing collective resources (such as industry-specific pension schemes and training programmes) and for strengthening the bargaining power of labour. Workers need a voice and trade unions can provide a forum for workers to negotiate any potential trade-off between wages and employment. Extending collective agreements to non-party firms, however, is neither a necessary condition for collective bargaining nor a desirable one in a surplus labour country given the social and economic costs of job destruction. When workers in non-compliant firms in Newcastle sought to prevent sheriffs of the court from entering their workplaces to shut them down, they were also revealing how the national union, SACTWU, was failing to represent their interests. Extending and enforcing collective agreements on non-parties undermined both industrial democracy and inclusive development.

The South African government's decision, in May 2018, to set a national minimum wage (for implementation in 2019) at a level higher than the minimum wage for machinists in the clothing manufacturing industry was testimony to the power of decent work fundamentalism in shaping the national agenda. As noted in Chapter 5, the government's national minimum wage proposals exempted the government's own public works programmes (the wage for public works programmes was set at just over half the national minimum) to maximize job creation within a budgetary envelope, but similar exemptions were not provided for labour-intensive firms in the private sector. The extent to which the national minimum wage constrains potential labour-intensive growth in the future depends on the rate at which it is increased and on whether workers in non-compliant firms complain about underpayment—and on how these complaints are acted upon.

How surplus labour countries can best resolve their unemployment crisis is a fundamentally contextual issue. For surplus labour countries long embroiled in civil strife or wars with neighbours (Libya, the West Bank and Gaza), political solutions to the conflict are likely to be paramount. For oil-rich, politically oppressive Gabon, the challenges include overvalued exchange rates (the persistent problem of commodity exporters) as well as democratization. For the post-communist countries (Armenia, Bosnia and Herzegovina, Macedonia, and Montenegro) ongoing challenges of economic restructuring towards more efficient forms of production are also obviously important. For all these countries, tolerance of lower-wage, lower-productivity work (that is, tolerance of dualism) as a means of job creation could help address the unemployment problem and assist in the development of small businesses but is unlikely to resolve it in the foreseeable future.

In discussing the surplus labour countries, we highlighted the Southern African cluster of high-unemployment countries (Botswana, Lesotho, Namibia, South Africa, Swaziland, and Mozambique). All, with the exception of Swaziland, which is a traditional monarchy, are democratic countries where development strategy was a matter of choice, although obviously moulded by political and economic interests and shaped/constrained by history. Climate also matters in that the possibility for the kind of intensive, smallholder agriculture evident in settings like Vietnam and Cambodia are not possible across the vast arid or semi-arid spaces of Southern Africa. Open unemployment in Southern Africa is thus also the result of the inability of the subsistence peasant sector to provide the kind of social safety net—or dual economy—as assumed in the Lewis model. Mozambique (the only low-income country in the cluster of Southern African surplus labour countries) is better suited climatically to growing a peasant sector. Lesotho, which recently became classified as a middle-income country, lost its fertile agricultural territories ('the conquered territories') to South Africa in the nineteenth century, leaving it with mostly steep mountainous regions suitable for little other than livestock husbandry. Continuing its (Lewis-like) strategy of promoting clothing production and other light manufacturing is thus essential for addressing unemployment. Its preferential access to advanced capitalist country markets (AGOA) and its role within regional value chains supplying low-cost clothing items into the South African market, is advantageous in this respect.

8.1 The Challenge of Rising Unemployment Across Africa

The challenges of surplus labour are especially severe in Southern Africa, but open unemployment is no longer confined to this part of Africa. Unemployment is increasing across Africa, the result of the coincidence of both rising numbers of young entrants to the labour market and a generally low employment-intensity of economic growth (Page, 2013; Filmer and Fox, 2014). The combination of population growth, landlessness and stagnant demand for labour has generated growing anxiety across the continent over open unemployment, especially amongst young men and women. Surplus to their families' agricultural needs and without access to land themselves, young people migrate to towns and cities, where they are seen to pose political and social threats. The need for Lewis-like growth and the perils of decent work fundamentalism now extend across much of Africa.

Concern over unemployment amongst young people has a long history in Africa. In the twentieth century colonial, and then post-colonial, states worried intermittently about unemployment amongst 'youth' in the growing but still small urban areas. In growing towns such as Dar es Salaam, the late colonial state repatriated unemployed 'undesirables' to rural areas—just as, more notoriously, the apartheid state did in South Africa. After independence, amidst continued rapid urbanization, the post-colonial state in Tanzania similarly denounced 'unproductive' and idle youth and sought to repatriate them to rural areas (Burton, 2006, 2007). In reality, however, the perceived threat posed by unemployed young people in towns was small. Across most of Africa, most young people lived in the countryside, where they followed their parents into peasant agriculture and livestock husbandry, sometimes interspersed with episodes of employment as migrant workers.

The real challenge of youth unemployment emerged across most of Africa only in the 2000s. Urbanization rates had slowed markedly in the 1980s and 1990s, as structural adjustment policies constricted urban economies. In the 2000s, fuelled by renewed economic growth, rapid population growth, and deepening landlessness in rural areas, urbanization accelerated once again, with the result that unemployment amongst urban youth apparently rose despite economic growth. Anxiety was reflected in publications such as the World Bank's 2007 *World Development Report*, which focused on the 'next generation' (World Bank, 2006), and its 2008 study of *Youth in Africa's Labor Market* (Garcia and Fares, 2008). The United Nations Economic Commission on Africa (UNECA) published its first *Africa Youth Report* in 2009 (UNECA, 2009). As the World Bank emphasized, Africa had the youngest population of all the world's regions, with 200 million people aged between 12 and 24. Moreover, it reported, 18 million young people were unemployed in Sub-Saharan Africa (as of 2003) (Garcia and Fares, 2008).

The decision of the UN General Assembly in 2009 that 2010–11 would be the International Year of the Youth focused further organizational attention on the issue of youth (un)employment. The African Union (AU) adopted a Youth Decade Plan of Action for 2009–18. In 2011, the AU devoted a summit (in Malabo, in Equatorial Guinea) to the theme of 'Accelerating Youth Empowerment for Sustainable Development'. The UNECA published a second *Africa Youth Report* (UNECA, 2011). In the first half of 2012, the ILO launched a programme of national meetings on youth employment.

The actual statistics on youth employment and unemployment are, at best, uneven. The ILO reports that the youth unemployment rate in Sub-Saharan Africa is about 11 per cent whilst in North Africa it is close to 30 per cent.[1] Whatever the data on current unemployment rates, the perception was widespread by the mid-2000s that the future entry into the labour market of young African men and women would result in a deepening unemployment crisis. This could be viewed as either a challenge (how to realize the 'demographic dividend'?) or a threat (to social and political stability). The prominence of young people in political turmoil (including in Tunisia and Côte d'Ivoire) was widely noted, amidst references made to a 'ticking time-bomb' (ADB, 2016: 125; see also Filmer and Fox, 2014: 1–2).

According to estimates by the ILO, between 2015 and 2050, the labour force will grow by 789 million individuals in Sub-Saharan Africa and another 86 million in North Africa. In the rest of the world, overall, the labour force would hardly grow at all (with growth in South and South-east Asia offset by contraction in China and Europe) (Losch, 2016). Population growth slows with economic development, but policies matter too. There is a strong association globally between the establishment and intensity of family planning programmes and the decline in fertility rates after adjusting for changes in per capita income, urbanization, infant mortality, female labour force participation and educational attainment (de Silva and Tenreyo, 2017: 220). Africa's rapidly rising labour force is partly a consequence of the failure of African governments to ramp up their family planning policies prior to the late 1990s (ibid.: 218).

Unsurprisingly, youth employment has continued to be prominent on the AU's agenda. In 2014–15 the AU developed strategies around the theme of 'Employment, Poverty Eradication and Inclusive Development'. The AU adopted a Declaration and Plan of Action in Addis Ababa in January 2015 (at the same time as the AU adopted its *Agenda 2063* vision statement).[2] The AU recognized that Africa has the youngest population in the world, with millions of young people entering the labour market every year. Job creation and the reduction of unemployment (including especially youth unemployment) were integral to the AU's vision. The AU lacked, however, any clear vision of

[1] https://www.ilo.org/global/about-the-ilo/multimedia/maps-and-charts/enhanced/WCMS_600072/lang–en/index.htm.

[2] The Declaration was supposed to have been adopted at a summit in Ouagadougou in 2014, and was dubbed the Ouagadougou +10 declaration, referring to an earlier, 2004 declaration. But the Ebola outbreak prevented this, and the declaration was adopted in 2015 in Addis Ababa instead.

how to achieve these goals. Flagship projects included transport, internet and related e-commerce and e-learning, and even an outer space strategy.

The AU's failure to formulate a clear strategy whilst punting ultra-modernist, Wakanda-like[3] fantasies reflects a broader lack of consensus as to what needs to be done to avert further rises in (youth) unemployment in Africa. The basic challenge is how to raise productivity—especially in the low-productivity, labour-intensive agricultural and informal sectors—at the same time as expanding employment rapidly in the more modern labour-intensive sectors.

There is widespread agreement that labour has either been 'stuck in agriculture... despite the sector's decline as a share of GDP' or has been shifting from low-productivity agriculture to low-productivity 'household enterprises', that is, self-employment in the informal economy (Fox and Thomas, 2016: i22; see also Rodrik, 2016). McMillan and Headey (2014) estimate that the average output per worker in agriculture across Sub-Saharan Africa was, in 2005, barely above the US$1/day (extreme) poverty line that was in wide usage at that time. Labour productivity outside agriculture was perhaps eight times higher. This was, as McMillan and Headey emphasized, a classically Lewisian case of surplus labour and economic dualism—except that dualist development remained stunted because there had been too little structural change and the subsistence agricultural sector continued to account for most employment. In most countries, twice as many people remained in agricultural employment as were in all non-agricultural sectors combined.

Faced with the structural problem of exclusive dualism, that is, a dualist economy that continued to deny most people, including especially young people, the benefits of economic growth, some organizations and researchers emphasized primarily labour supply-side measures as a way of effecting structural change. UNECA (2011) argued that the problem was the shortage of good jobs and of youth with appropriate skills, not an absence of jobs per se. UNECA held up the utopian vision of an apparently uniformly high-skill, highly formal employment, contrasted with the supposed dystopia of labour-intensive production. The ILO similarly emphasized education and skills development and a strategy of 'formalizing' employment. It is clear that its priority in Africa remains 'building and strengthening labour market institutions that enable the realization of the goal of decent work for all' (ILO, 2015b: 2). As pointed out in Chapter 3, the goal of work for all has been, for the ILO, secondary to the goal of decent work (for whoever is actually working).

The Food and Agriculture Organization of the United Nations (FAO) emphasized that 'sustainable agriculture and rural development' were

[3] In the film 'Black Panther', Wakanda was an African country with the most sophisticated technological capacity on the planet.

essential to absorb the many young people—11 million in 2014 alone, across Africa—who were entering the labour market.[4] Given the importance of agriculture and currently low levels of productivity, raising the productivity of agriculture must be integral to economic growth if poverty is to be reduced, as the FAO argues strongly. But, as Collier and Dercon (2014) note, increased agricultural output through increased labour productivity will surely result in a declining proportion of the growing labour force being engaged in agriculture, making the need for employment growth in other sectors even more urgent (Fox and Thomas, 2016: i17).

Other organizations and researchers have advocated a more Lewis-like growth path. The World Bank emphasizes the importance of both raising productivity in the informal economy (including peasant agriculture) and job creation in labour-intensive, export-oriented manufacturing. In a study of the potential for light manufacturing to generate labour-intensive growth in Africa, World Bank researchers argued that rising real wages in China were opening up opportunities for African countries (Dinh et al., 2012). The Chronic Poverty Action Network similarly emphasized the importance of economic diversification into labour-intensive sectors—such as clothing manufacturing—at the same time as investing in education and health (Mariotti and Shepherd, 2016). Page (2013) emphasized that young men and women need more skills, even if they are to enter labour-intensive sectors. Others have pointed to the potential for labour-intensive digital services (including business process outsourcing), tourism and other 'industries without smokestacks' such as horticultural exports to provide a potential engine for growth in Africa (Newfarmer et al., 2018).

The AU itself acknowledged the importance of labour-intensive manufacturing and services in the reduction of unemployment, but its vision of the future remained the ILO's modernist world of skilled labour. Probably influenced by the ILO, it reiterated the goal of *decent* work more than the goal of *more* work. The result of such an approach can only be further reduction in the employment-intensity of economic growth. The pace of economic growth will need to be extraordinarily rapid if Africa's surplus labour is to be absorbed into high-skill and high-productivity work. This is an impossible fantasy. The inevitable result of relying exclusively on such an approach is that labour will continue to leave the agricultural sector, especially if productivity in agriculture rises; urbanization will continue, perhaps accelerating; and more and more people, especially young people, will remain excluded from the economy.

The alternative, across Africa, is inclusive dualism through a Lewis-like development strategy. Surplus labour—including both low-productivity labour in

[4] José Graziano da Silva: https://agriorbit.com/african-rural-youth-unemployment-needs-attention/.

smallholder agriculture and the rising numbers of openly unemployed urban youth—would be absorbed into labour-intensive sectors where productivity is higher than in smallholder agriculture. The high-skill, high-productivity sectors imagined by the AU might also be encouraged (where this makes sense in terms of competitiveness), but it would be foolish to rely on them alone. Promoting skills development and encouraging job creation across a wider range of sectors, including labour-intensive sectors such as clothing manufacturing, offers the only feasible route to a more inclusive development or growth path.

8.2 The Potential for Labour-intensive Development in Africa

Labour-intensive industrialization might be desirable in Africa and there have been successes—notably Ethiopia which has cheap hydro-energy, high-quality cotton, and a growing clothing industry—but there are many obstacles relating to the relatively high cost of doing business in Africa, notably logistical and infrastructural challenges, problems of governance and access to finance, skills shortages etc. (Dinh et al., 2012; Harrison et al., 2014; Rodrik, 2016; World Bank, 2017a).

Some of these constraints may be overcome in Special Economic Zones (see Bräutigam and Tang, 2014) offering some hope for the development of export-led employment growth, including in clothing manufacturing. Producing for export remains crucial for large-scale sustained employment growth given the economies of scale involved. Rodrik (2015) has shown that only those low-wage Asian developing countries that were able to grow their exports managed to buck the pattern of 'premature deindustrialisation' evident elsewhere.

Our discussion of the global clothing industry highlighted how countries like China and subsequently other low-income Asian countries (notably Bangladesh) were able to benefit from Lewis-like growth and have been able to improve job quality and diversify into more sophisticated product lines primarily for export. Long-standing connections with retailers in the advanced capitalist countries (such as *Walmart*'s relationship with clothing producers in Bangladesh), and the role of supply chain co-ordinators like *Li & Fung* in managing the flow of clothing output internationally, seems to favour existing players to the exclusion of new entrants.

Yet the global clothing manufacturing industry has been very dynamic. The major existing players were all new entrants, some in the very recent past. Moreover, it has not proved impossible for African countries to break into this highly competitive global market. Most African countries (but not South Africa) qualify for the third country fabric provision under AGOA, allowing them to import yarns and fabrics and still gain duty-free access to the US market. This gives them a competitive advantage over Asian exporters (which as of 2015 faced an average tariff into the US market of 11.4 per cent) making them an attractive destination for clothing manufacturers also wishing to import fabric and yarns (Williams, 2015). The rise in Chinese wages since the mid-2000s as the country reached the Lewis tipping point (when surplus labour is absorbed) provides further incentives for Chinese investors and clothing manufacturing companies to move production to lower-wage countries, including in Africa. The growth of regional markets in East and Southern Africa opens further opportunities for labour-intensive growth spearheaded by the clothing manufacturing sector. African countries might collectively press for even more preferential access to European and North American markets, arguing explicitly that facilitating Lewis-like growth in Africa is better than large aid programmes. For example, preferential access under AGOA might be extended to middle-income African countries with surplus labour such as South Africa.

Clothing employment in Africa has been facilitated by foreign direct investment from Taiwan, China, Korea, and elsewhere in the global South. Investment from Taiwan enabled Lesotho to participate in international value chains, and investment from Mauritius and South Africa tied Lesotho into regional value chains, targeting especially the growing South African market. The Ethiopian clothing industry grew initially on investment from Turkey, followed by a much larger second wave of investment in the mid-2010s, driven by apparel companies from India, Korea, Taiwan, and Sri Lanka.

Kenya provides another illustration of how a domestic clothing industry can leverage foreign capital to participate in both international and regional value chains. Between 2000 and 2003, employment in clothing manufacturing rose from 5,565 to 36,348, then declined following the end of the MFA and the 2008 financial crisis to stabilize at around 24,000 by 2010 (Kamau et al., 2013). Kenya has a rapidly growing clothing manufacturing industry, with 70 per cent of clothing firms targeting the US market, enabling Kenya to account for just over a third of total African clothing exports to the US under AGOA (Wang et al., 2018). Chinese investment in Kenya has also been encouraged by excess capacity in China, resulting in the transport of both second hand machinery and experienced workers to East Africa (ibid.). Firms targeting the export market tend to install advanced machinery to meet the production quality standards required by US and EU buyers, whereas those producing for the growing regional market use the older, less expensive equipment and more labour-intensive technologies (ibid.).

Similar differentiation is evident in Ethiopia, where foreign direct investment in the clothing and textile sectors targets both the export and regional market (Bräutigam et al., 2018: 15). Such differentiation was encouraged also by government policy to support both import substitution and export production which has helped the development of locally owned clothing firms by subsidizing the cost of learning to export as well as building a national supply chain from cotton to textile to clothing manufacturing (Staritz and Whitfield, 2017; Whitfield and Staritz, 2017).

Export-oriented industrialization (facilitated by supportive industrial policy including the creation of export processing zones) enables production at scale and hence offers an important route for labour-intensive job creation. Yet import-substituting firms can also provide employment, as well as help develop the local manufacturing sector (the so-called 'missing middle' of small- and medium-sized firms), and generate backward and forward linkages using relatively simple machinery (Bräutigam et al., 2018: 20–4). The growth in regional markets in the global South has created opportunities beyond the established advanced capitalist countries for participating in new (regional) value chains and exploiting growing domestic markets.

However, even the most optimistic projections indicate how difficult it will be to generate the growth in industrial employment required to deal with rising unemployment. Fox et al. (2013) modelled an optimistic scenario in which African countries were gifted the same employment elasticity of growth as the early Asian industrializers, as well as accelerated industrial growth rates. The model predicted that this would generate an additional 7 million industrial jobs over five years. This pace of job creation could make a big difference to some parts of Africa but overall would be insufficient to absorb all of the new entrants into African labour markets.

Opportunities for labour-intensive growth lie not only with light manufacturing, but also in services. As Newfarmer et al. point out, a great deal of 'back-office' operations and accounting in manufacturing have been 'spun off and subcontracted', and this redrawing of the boundary between manufacturing and services is in part responsible for observed 'premature de-industrialisation' (2018: 7). Kenya, for example, was an early entrant into the business process outsourcing market and there are now over fifty firms providing services such as data processing, digitization, transcription and call centres (Ngui and Kimuyu, 2018). However, another early entrant, Senegal, failed to turn this into a sustainable growth engine. Having been able to attract better-qualified employees than in France at one-tenth the price, the number of call centres fell from thirty-five in 2000 to just nine by 2016 because of slow internet speed and high infrastructural costs (English, 2018). The extent to which these sorts of 'fourth industrial revolution' type services can generate significant jobs, on a sustained base, remains to be seen.

For the high-unemployment countries of Southern Africa, tourism is another potential source of employment creation. After Morocco, South Africa, Botswana, Kenya, Mozambique, and Namibia account for the most tourists in Africa (UNWTO, 2015) – a testimony to their scenery, wildlife, and climate. Tourism is the most labour-intensive of South Africa's services (Bhorat et al., 2018) and has strong linkages into accommodation, restaurants, crafts, guiding etc. Wilderness is diminishing around the world, but in Africa, there remains space and opportunities to protect it. Developing eco-tourism and providing people with incentives to keep these spaces wild through providing them with access to employment opportunities associated with tourism could contribute both to job creation and green growth.

Most of Africa will struggle over the next twenty or more years with the combination of a rapidly growing labour force and a predominant sector—agriculture—which will be pushed to become more productive and thus able to absorb relatively few new working men and women. The scale of the challenge will far exceed the maximum possible job creation through labour-intensive industrialization, in clothing manufacturing and similar sectors. Combined with growth in labour-intensive non-industrial sectors—including business services and tourism—labour-intensive industrialization could, however, make a substantial difference. The alternative, if the employment elasticity of growth remains low or even falls further with intensified emphasis on promoting decent work at all costs, is deepening inequality.

The South African case reveals some of the political challenges to expanding labour-intensive sectors. South Africa's state institutions were designed primarily to raise labour productivity and wages amongst white insiders under apartheid. These same institutions have now been appropriated by trade unions representing the interests of their mostly black African members. Moreover, the history of apartheid tainted labour-intensive employment with the stigma of exploitation and discrimination. The post-apartheid political imperative of racial redress also opened up opportunities for trade unions to become major investors, shifting their interests even further away from job creation (as discussed in Chapter 7 with regard to SACTWU). Decent work fundamentalism has extended its reach deep into South African politics. Furthermore, South Africa's electoral and party system effectively disempowers unemployed voters whilst civil society organizations mobilize primarily around municipal services not job creation. The result is a political environment distinctly unfavourable to job creation in labour-intensive sectors (Seekings and Nattrass, 2016).

The political landscape is less unfavourable elsewhere in Africa where decent work fundamentalism has less political muscle. Elites are more anxious about the instability that results from rising 'youth unemployment'. Expanding low-productivity, low-wage employment is probably good politics. Yet, as is clear in documents produced by the AU, modernist fantasies have considerable appeal to elites. Presidents, ministers, and technocrats appear to imagine that they will lead their countries immediately into a high-tech, high-skill, and high-wage future.

8.3 Social Protection and Surplus Labour in Southern Africa

The cases of Botswana, Namibia, and South Africa—the three upper-middle-income surplus labour countries in Southern Africa—point to social protection (or welfare) programmes as an alternative basis for inclusion in a differentiated economy (that is, for inclusive dualism). All three countries have extensive social protection systems, including social assistance programmes reaching large numbers of poor people as well as contributory programmes for the semi-privileged minority of the population enjoying mostly skilled or white-collar formal employment. These social assistance programmes (including old-age pensions, disability and child grants, and workfare programmes) provide a partial safety net for the poor. The three countries' systems differ in terms of generosity, with South Africa being the most generous and Botswana the most parsimonious. Even in Botswana, however, the result is a weak form of inclusive dualism, comprising higher-wage, higher-productivity employment (and related benefits) for one part of the population and modest social assistance to another.

The safety net is incomplete, even in these countries. There are large holes through which many poor people fall. Whilst these states support various categories of people who are unable to support themselves (especially the elderly, the disabled and children), they provide only limited coverage to able-bodied, working-age adults who cannot support themselves because they are unemployed. In South Africa, many unemployed women receive child support grants on behalf of their children, and unemployed people try to persuade doctors that they are disabled and deserve a disability grant. The only cash transfers to young men, however, are through workfare programmes, which reach only a minority of the unemployed. Proposals to extend the social safety net through, for example, the introduction of a Basic Income Grant (BIG), have been rejected by governments in both South Africa and Namibia (Matisonn and Seekings, 2003; Haarmann et al., 2012; Seekings and Matisonn, 2012).

It is unclear, however, whether there is much fiscal space for increasing welfare through a tax-financed BIG in South Africa, let alone elsewhere. Social assistance already reaches more than half of all households in South Africa and the South African welfare state is already generous by Southern standards, doing a great deal to reduce poverty (Seekings and Nattrass, 2016). In any event, the ruling ANC consistently resisted proposals for a BIG, preferring to channel assistance to the 'deserving poor' (Seekings, 2008). In Namibia, there was significant social mobilization in favour of a BIG in the early 2000s (as well as support for it from the Namibian Tax Commission) and donor money was raised for a pilot project. The project showed significant gains in reducing child malnutrition, encouraging savings and payments of clinic and school fees (Haarmann et al., 2009). However, the government opted to target the destitute directly through in-kind benefits such as a food bank—a strategy that proved both inefficient and poorly targeted (Katjangua, 2018).

The politics of why a BIG has not been introduced in South Africa or Namibia is instructive about the political–economic factors underpinning non-inclusive development in both countries. Starting in the early 2000s the idea of unconditional cash transfers—of just 'giving money to the poor'—gained traction within the international development community and in Sub-Saharan Africa (Garcia et al., 2012; Ferguson, 2015). In Namibia and South Africa broad civil society coalitions supported the idea of a tax-funded BIG to alleviate poverty, but in both cases the coalitions were fragile over the issue of who would pay for it. In South Africa, Le Roux (2002) argued that a BIG should be financed through an increase in value-added tax (VAT) to ensure that the overall tax and spending was progressive (high spenders would pay more in VAT than they received from the grant). This proposal, however, was resisted by organized labour. COSATU argued that a BIG should be financed by higher income and wealth taxes on the very rich so that its members (the employed) would be net beneficiaries rather than net contributors under the VAT-financed model (Seekings and Matisonn, 2012). In Namibia, the national Tax Commission estimated that a modest VAT-financed BIG would cost between 2 and 3 per cent of GDP, that there was fiscal space for this and that 85 per cent of Namibians would be net beneficiaries (NAMTAX, 2002, reprinted in 2005). Like its counterpart in South Africa, the Namibian trade union movement was concerned about potential increased taxes for its members and in 2010 announced that it was pulling out of the Namibian BIG coalition. The trade union leadership was forced to rescind this decision when faced by a revolt amongst the delegates at the next congress—but its support for the BIG remained tepid and eventually withered to nothing in the face of continued resistance to the grant by the Namibian government.

Resistance by organized labour—that is, mostly higher-waged skilled and white-collar workers—to proposals that a BIG might be financed in ways that posed any additional tax burden on them is an understandable response to what is a kind of 'catch-22' for employed workers in developing countries with high unemployment and limited if any public support for the unemployed. There is a universal old-age pension in South Africa and Namibia and many unemployed people get by through living with old-age pensioners. Wage earners find themselves in a similar position to pensioners in being expected to support unemployed kin and their families. This so-called 'black tax' is often used as an argument for tax relief for the (black) middle class (essentially the formally employed, in skilled or white-collar occupations), for higher minimum wages and against low-wage work. Similarly, employed workers are understandably resistant to labour market reforms that might make it easier for firms to fire workers or allow for downward wage flexibility. In principle, workers would be better off if labour-intensive growth facilitated job creation, thereby reducing social claims on their income. In practice, workers are incentivized to prioritize the gains they have made over the hypothetical benefits of labour market reforms (faster employment growth) which even if realized might not accrue to their own households.

Precisely because unemployment is high in South Africa and wage earners find themselves at the centre of a de facto kin-based social safety net, the case has been made for keeping average wages high and subsidizing the wage costs of employers (Levinsohn, 2008). The South African government initiated an employment tax incentive for young workers in 2014. Prior to its initiation, it was generally acknowledged that its redistributive impact would vary depending on sector and the wage elasticity of the demand for labour (Burns et al., 2013). Subsequent evaluations have not revealed any clear effects on employment (Ebrahim et al., 2017).

The alternative to providing grants (whether a BIG or income support for the unemployed) is to provide income-earning opportunities through a public works programme. Botswana, South Africa, and Namibia provide workfare through such programmes, typically involving the construction and maintenance of gravel roads and rural infrastructure, providing lower-wage short-term job opportunities as a form of relief for the unemployed (Odhiambo et al., 2015). The South African government's Expanded Public Works Programme (EPWP) provides lower-wage, short-term job opportunities for poor people and there have been calls to expand it into a larger programme akin to the Indian Employment Guarantee Scheme (e.g. Philip, 2012). The reach of South Africa's EPWP is limited, in part, by high administrative costs of as much as 50 per cent of total expenditure[5]—without taking into account the human resources required on the part of government departments to apply to the department of public works for access to EPWP funding for proposed projects, or for monitoring and accounting for that spending. It is, in other words, a very resource-intensive process, rendering it a poorly targeted effort (Odhiambo et al., 2015).

In Botswana, workfare programmes have long been central to the country's welfare state. Workfare was introduced first as an emergency drought relief measure, in the 1960s, providing very modest support to men or women (and their dependents). Workfare was later institutionalized and expanded, and provides an indispensable if very thin social safety net. Whilst the elite and middle classes denounce workfare for fostering 'dependency' (i.e. on government 'handouts'), their importance to poor voters protects the programme from cutbacks (Hamer, 2016; Seekings, 2016b).

[5] Expanded Public Works Programme, Third Quarter Report 2017, available at: http://epwp.gov.za/documents/Reports/Year14-17-18/Q3-2017-18/Q3_2017_18%20Annexure_A-E.pdf.

Across most of Southern Africa, in both countries with extensive social assistance programmes (such as South Africa and Botswana) and those without (such as Zambia or Malawi), elites tend to view programmes through conservative lenses. (Male) elites are generally anxious about dependency, consequent 'laziness' and possible undermining of (patriarchal) family relations. Elites may accept that people who cannot support themselves—most clearly, the elderly—should be supported by the state, but insist that able-bodied, working-age adults should only be supported through workfare programmes, and even these have their critics. The basic mantra is that people should 'not get something for nothing'. There is evidence that many ordinary citizens also hold such views (Kalebe-Nyamongo and Marquette, 2014; Seekings, 2017, 2018). Electoral competition rarely provides an incentive to political parties or candidates to promise major reforms. In societies that still have a large peasant-farming sector (such as Zambia or Malawi), elites and voters alike tend to prefer subsidies to farmers over social assistance programmes (Dawson and Fouksman, 2017; Seekings, 2018).

Whilst social protection *can* provide an alternative basis for inclusive dualism, expanding the social safety net through cash transfers and workfare is likely to be constrained by both political and economic imperatives. It is imaginable that provision for the elderly, disabled, and children will expand. It is also possible that expanded workfare programmes will provide a slightly fuller safety net for the unemployed, but the challenge of rising unemployment will far exceed the feasible scope of even workfare. Employment guarantees (such as in rural India) are not even on the policy agenda in Africa. 'Inclusion' through welfare or workfare is important, but is no substitute for inclusion through job creation, even in lower-productivity, lower-wage, labour-intensive firms and sectors.

8.4 Conclusion

The scale of the challenges facing surplus labour economies in Southern Africa and elsewhere—including, increasingly, across much of Africa—induces pessimism. The number of unemployed men and women in Southern Africa is already daunting: Successive cohorts of men and women have already experienced chronic unemployment, sometimes punctuated with short episodes of work. Across Africa, more than ten million young people enter the labour market every year, with ever diminishing prospects of employment in agriculture and poor prospects in informal employment. At the same time that peasant farming and informal employment provide a shrinking safety net, political and fiscal constraints limit the expansion of a social safety net based on welfare or workfare. The future promises dualistic economies characterized by large islands of privilege amidst a sea of poverty. Rising unemployment renders this an exclusive form of dualism. Africa seems likely to retain the distinction of being the part of the world where poverty and extreme poverty persist and inequalities grow.

The expansion of labour-intensive, non-agricultural sectors is a necessary element in the package of changes that will mitigate, although probably not prevent entirely, this gloomy future. The clothing manufacturing industry is the premier example of such a sector. Lower-wage employment in clothing manufacturing has been a key component of economic growth and development across much of the global South. It is perhaps the only manufacturing sector to have been barely affected by widespread technological change. Until it is possible to automate the sewing machine, that is, replace machinists, clothing manufacturing will continue to offer an opportunity to surplus labour economies to raise productivity and reduce poverty by transforming people languishing in unemployment or low-productivity smallholder agriculture into semi-skilled workers.

For Africa to follow the lead of many other economies in realizing the opportunity of labour-intensive industrialization through clothing manufacturing requires improved infrastructure and a favourable and stable business environment. The South African experience shows that it requires also the avoidance of decent work fundamentalism. Whilst health and safety should be prioritized, wages regulated (even through a national minimum wage), and fairer supply chains and 'better' work promoted, minimum wages should not be raised to levels that preclude labour-intensive industrialization and development. In economies such as South Africa's, workers' co-operatives provide an opportunity for working women and men to choose for themselves how to manage the trade-off between earnings and employment. But these should not be the only source of labour-intensive employment. Lewis's insight that development can be dualist (differentiated) and inclusive, improving the lives of the poor, remains relevant across much of Africa, and hence to the challenge of poverty-reduction on a global scale.

References

Aaronson, D., French, E., Sorkin, I., and To, T. 2018. 'Industry Dynamics and the Minimum Wage: A Putty-Clay Approach', *International Economic Review*, 59 (1), 51–84.

Abras, A. L. G. 2012. 'Success and Upgrading after the End of the MFA', in G. Lopez-Acevedo and R. Robertson (eds), *Sewing Success? Employment, Wages and Poverty Following the End of the Multi-fibre Arrangement* (Washington, DC: World Bank), 87–135.

ADB, 2016. *Africa's Youth in the Labour Market*, African Development Report 2015, Chapter 2 (Abidjan: African Development Bank).

Adelzedeh, A. 2016. *A National Minimum Wage: Quantification of Impact*. Presentation to the School of Economics at University of Cape Town, July.

Alam, M. S., Selvanathan, E. A., and Selvanathan, S., 2017. 'Determinants of the Bangladesh Garment Exports in the Post-MFA Environment', *Journal of the Asia Pacific Economy*, 22 (2), 330–52.

Alam, S. and Natsuda, K. 2016. 'The Competitive Factors of the Bangladeshi Garment Industry in the Post-MFA Era', *Canadian Journal of Development Studies*, 37 (3), 316–36, DOI: 10.1080/02255189.2016.1157457.

Alexander, P. 2013. 'Marikana, Turning Point in South African History', *Review of African Political Economy*, 40 (138), 605–19.

Allen, R. 2009. 'The Industrial Revolution in Miniature: The Spinning Jenny in Britain, France and India', *Journal of Economic History*, 69 (4), 901–27.

Altenburg, T. and Assmann, C. (eds). 2017. *Green Industrial Policy. Concept, Policies, Country Experiences* (Geneva, Bonn: UN Environment; German Development Institute/Deutsches Institut für Entwicklungspolitik).

Altman, M. 1994. *An Industrial Strategy for the Clothing Sector, Industrial Strategy Project* (Cape Town: Development Policy Research Unit, University of Cape Town, UCT Press).

Altman, M. 1996. 'Labour Regulation and Enterprise Strategies in the South African Clothing Industry', *Regional Studies*, 30 (4), 387–99.

Altman, M. and Valodia, I. 2006. 'Introduction: Where to for the South African Labour Market? Some Big Issues', *Transformation*, 60, 1–5.

Amin, S. 1977. *Imperialism and Unequal Development* (Brighton: The Harvester Press).

Anand, R., Kothari, S., and Kumar, N. 2016. 'South Africa: Labour Market Dynamics and Inequality', IMF Working Paper, No. 16/137. Available at: https://www.imf.org/external/pubs/cat/longres.aspx?sk=44078.0.

ANC, 1990. *Discussion Document on Economic Policy*, September (ANC Department of Economic Planning).

Anstey, M., 2004. 'National Bargaining in South Africa's Clothing Manufacturing Industry: Problems and Prospects of Multi-Employer Bargaining in an Industry under Siege', *Industrial Law Journal*, 25 (October), 1829–64.

Ardé, G. 2018. 'Mandela centenary T-shirt should surely be 100% South African', *Business Day*, 21 June. Available at: https://www.businesslive.co.za/bd/opinion/2018-06-21-mandela-centenary-t-shirt-should-surely-be-100-south-african/.

Arnold, D. and Hartman, L. 2005. 'Beyond Sweatshops: Positive Deviancy and Global Labour Practices', *Business Ethics: A European Review*, 14 (3), 206–22.

Arnold, D. and Hartman, L. 2006. 'Worker Rights and Low Wage Industrialization: How to Avoid Sweatshops', *Human Rights Quarterly*, 283, 676–700.

Atkinson, A. B., Piketty, T., and Saez, E. 2011. 'Top Incomes in the Long Run of History', *Journal of Economic Literature*, 49, 3–71.

Avdagic, S. and Salardi, P. 2013. 'Tenuous Link: Labour Market Institutions and Unemployment in Advanced and New Market Economies', *Socio-Economic Review*, 11 (4), 739–69.

Baah-Boateng, W. 2015. 'Unemployment in Africa: How Appropriate is the Global Definition and Measurement for Policy Purpose', *International Journal of Manpower*, 36 (5), 650–67.

Backer, K. and Miroudot, S. 2013. 'Mapping Global Value Chains', OECD Trade Policy Papers No. 159. Available at: http://dx.doi.org/10.1787/5k3v1trgnbr4-en.

Baldwin, R. 2014. 'Multilateralising 21st Century Regionalism', OECD Global Forum on Trade, 11 February. Available at: http://www.oecd.org/tad/events/OECD-gft-2014-multilateralising-21st-century-regionalism-baldwin-paper.pdf.

Barker, H. A. F. 1962. *The Economics of the Wholesale Clothing Industry of South Africa, 1907–1957* (Johannesburg: Pallas Publications).

Barnes, J. 2005. *A Strategic Assessment of the South African Clothing Sector*, Report for NEDLAC, 29 July. (Hillcrest: Benchmarking and Manufacturing Analysts).

Barnes, J. 2018. 'Status Quo Analysis of the South African R-CTFL Value Chain', (Hillcrest: Benchmarking and Manufacturing Analysts).

Barrientos, S., Gereffi, G., and Pickles, J. 2016. 'New Dynamics of Upgrading in Global Value Chains: Shifting Terrain for Suppliers and Workers in the Global South', *Environment and Planning*, 48 (7), 1214–19.

Barrientos, S., Gereffi, G., and Rossi, A. 2011a. 'Economic and Social Upgrading in Global Production Networks: A New Paradigm for a Changing World', *International Labour Review*, 150 (3–4), 319–40.

Barrientos, S., Mathur, K., and Sood, A. 2010. 'Decent Work in Global Production Networks: Challenges for Vulnerable Workers in the Indian Garments Sector', in A. Posthuma and D. Nathan (eds), *Labour in Global Production Networks in India* (Oxford: Oxford University Press), 127–45.

Barrientos, S., Mayer, F., Pickles, J., and Posthuma, A. 2011b. 'Decent Work in Global Production Networks: Framing the Policy Debate', *International Labour Review*, 150 (3–4), 297–317.

Baskin, J. 1991. *Striking Back: A History of COSATU* (Johannesburg: Ravan Press).

Bean, J. S. and Boyer, G. R. 2009. 'The Trade Boards Act of 1909 and the Alleviation of Household Poverty', *British Journal of Industrial Relations*, 47 (2), 240–64.

Bell, T. 1983. 'The Growth and Structure of Manufacturing Employment in Natal', Institute for Social and Economic Research *Occasional Paper* 7 (Westville: University of Durban).

Bell, T. 1986. 'The Role of Regional Policy in South Africa', *Journal of Southern African Studies*, 12 (2), 276–92.

Bennett, M. 2002. *Organising Workers in Small Enterprises: The Experience of the Southern African Clothing and Textile Workers' Union*. Geneva: International Labour Office. Available at: http://www.ilo.org/public/libdoc/ilo/2002/102B09_301_engl.pdf.

Bennett, M. 2003. *Organising in the Informal Economy: A Case Study of the Clothing Industry in South Africa*. Geneva: International Labour Office. Available at: http://www.ilo.org/public/libdoc/ilo/2003/103B09_4_engl.pdf.

Bentolila, S. and Saint-Paul, G. 2003. 'Explaining Movements in the Labor Share', *Contributions to Macroeconomics*, 3 (1), 1–31.

Bernal, S. 2009. 'The Informal Labor Market in Colombia: Identification and Characterization', *Desarrollo y Sociedad* (63), 145–208.

Bernal-Verdugo, L. E., Furceri, D., and Guillaume, D. 2012. 'Labor Market Flexibility and Unemployment: New Empirical Evidence of Static and Dynamic Effects', *Comparative Economic Studies*, 54 (2), 251–73.

Betcherman, G. 2015. 'Labor Market Regulations: What Do We Know about Their Impacts in Developing Countries?', *The World Bank Research Observer*, 30 (1), 124–53.

Bhorat, H., Goga, S., and Van Der Westhuizen, C. 2012. 'Institutional Wage Effects: Revisiting Union and Bargaining Council Wage Premia in South Africa', *South African Journal of Economics*, 80 (3), 400–14.

Bhorat, H., Kanbur, R., and Mayet, N. 2012. *The Impact of Sectoral Minimum Wage Laws on Employment, Wages and Hours of Work in South Africa* (Cape Town: Development Policy Research Unit).

Bhorat, H., Kanbur, R., and Stanwix, B. 2017. 'Minimum Wages in Sub-Saharan Africa: A Primer', *The World Bank Research Observer*, 32 (1), 21–74.

Bhorat, H., Rooney, C., and F. Steenkamp. 2018. 'Understanding and Characterizing the Services Sector in South Africa: An Overview', in Newfarmer, R., Page, J., and Tarp, F. (eds). 2018. *Industries Without Smoke-Stacks: Industrialization in Africa Reconsidered* (Oxford: Oxford University Press), 275–295.

Bhorat, H. and Van der Westhuizen, C. 2009. 'A Synthesis of Current Issues in the Labour Regulatory Environment', *Working Paper* No. 09/135, Development Policy Research Unit, University of Cape Town (February).

Bischoff, C. and Tshoaedi, M. 2012. 'The Experience of Conducting a Longitudinal Study: the COSATU Workers' Survey, 2008', in S. Buhlungu and M. Tshoaedi (eds), *COSATU'S Contested Legacy: South African Trade Unions in the Second Decade of Democracy* (Cape Town: HSRC Press).

Bisseker, C. 2009. 'Friends in high places', *Financial Mail*, 28 May. Available at: http://www.hci.co.za/clothing-textile/friends-in-high-places/.

Bisseker, C. 2010. 'Workers not going down without a fight', *Financial Mail*. Available at: http://www.bizcommunity.com/Article/196/462/51033.html.

Bisseker, C. 2011. 'Slow strip or redress?', *Financial Mail* (17 March).

Black, A. and Hasson, H. 2016. 'Capital Intensive Industrialisation and Comparative Advantage: Can South Africa Do Better in Labour Demanding Manufacturing?', in A. Black (ed.), *Towards Employment Intensive Growth in South Africa* (Cape Town: Juta).

Black, A. and Roberts, S. 2009. 'The Evolution and Impact of Industrial and Competition Policies', in J. Aron, B. Kahn, and G. Kingdon (eds), *South African Economic Policy Under Democracy* (Oxford: Oxford University Press), 211–43.

Blackburn, S. 1991. 'Ideology and Social Policy: The Origins of the Trade Boards Act', *The Historical Journal*, 34 (01), 43–64.

Boccara, B. and Moll, P. 1997. 'Labor Market Flexibility and Industrial Councils in South Africa', Unpublished paper, World Bank, (May).

Bond, P. 1991. *From Commanding Heights to Community Control* (Johannesburg: Ravan Press).

Bourguignon, F. 2015. *The Globalization of Inequality* (Princeton, NJ: Princeton University Press).

Bowles, S. and Boyer, R. 1995. 'Wages, Aggregate Demand, and Employment in an Open Economy: An Empirical Investigation', in G. Epstein and H. Gintis (eds), *Macroeconomic Policy after the Conservative Era: Studies in Investment, Saving and Finance* (Cambridge: Cambridge University Press), 143–71.

Bramble, T. and Barchiesi, F. (eds). 2003. *Rethinking the Labour Movement in the 'New South Africa'* (Aldershot: Ashgate).

Braude, J. and Menashe, Y. 2011. 'The Asian Miracle: Was it a Capital-intensive Structural Change?', *The Journal of International Trade & Economic Development*, 20 (1), 31–51, DOI: 10.1080/09638199.2011.538183

Bräutigam, D. 2003. 'Close Encounters: Chinese Business Networks as Industrial Catalysts in Sub-Saharan Africa', *African Affairs*, 102 (408), 1063–467.

Bräutigam, D. 2009. *The Dragon's Gift: The Real Story of China in Africa* (Oxford: Oxford University Press).

Bräutigam, D. and Tang, X. (2014), '"Going Global in Groups": Structural Transformation and China's Special Economic Zones Overseas', *World Development*, 63: 78–91.

Bräutigam, D., Xiaoyang, T., and Xia, Y. 2018. 'What Kinds of Chinese "Geese" are Flying to Africa? Evidence from Chinese Manufacturing Firms', China–Africa Research Initiative, *Working Paper* No. 17, August.

Brenton, P. and Hoppe, M. 2007. 'Clothing and Export Diversification: Still a Route to Growth for Low-Income Countries?', World Bank, Policy Research *Working Paper* No. 4343 (Washington, DC: World Bank).

Broecke, S., Forti, A., and Vandeweyer, M. 2017. 'The Effect of Minimum Wages on Employment in Emerging Economies: A Survey and Meta-Analysis', *Oxford Development Studies*, 45 (3), 366–91.

Brown, R. 2006. 'On Labour Market Dualism in the Lewis Model: A Comment', *The Manchester School*, 74 (3), 350–4.

Buhlungu, S. 2010. *A Paradox of Victory: COSATU and the Democratic Transformation in South Africa* (Pietermaritzburg: UKZN Press).

Buhlungu, S. and Tshoaedi, M. 2012. 'A Contested Legacy: Organisational and Political Challenges Facing COSATU', in S. Buhlungu and M. Tshoaedi (eds), *COSATU's*

Contested Legacy: South African Trade Unions in the Second Decade of Democracy (Cape Town: Human Sciences Research Council Press), 1–31.

Burchell, B., Sehnbruch, K., Piasna, A., and Agloni, N. 2014. 'The Quality of Employment and Decent Work: Definitions, Methodologies, and Ongoing Debates', *Cambridge Journal of Economics*, 38 (2), 459–77.

Burns, J. 1998. *Wage Disparities in the South African Clothing Industry*. Unpublished report, University of Cape Town.

Burns, J., Edwards, L., and Pauw, K. 2013. 'Revisiting Wage Subsidies: How Pro-Poor is a South African Wage Subsidy Likely to Be?', *Development Southern Africa*, 30 (2), 186–210.

Burton, A. 2006. 'Raw Youth, School-Leavers and the Emergence of Structural Unemployment in Late-Colonial Urban Tanganyika', *Journal of African History*, 47 (3), 363–87.

Burton, A. 2007. 'The Haven of Peace Purged: Tackling the Undesirable and Unproductive Poor in Dar es Salaam, ca. 1950s–1980s', *International Journal of African Historical Studies*, 40 (1), 119–51.

Butcher, K. and Rouse, C. 2001. 'Wage Effects of Unions and Industrial Councils in South Africa', *Industrial and Labour Relations Review*, 54 (2), 349–74.

Cargill, J. 2010. *Trick or Treat: Rethinking Black Economic Empowerment* (Johannesburg: Jacana).

Caro, F. and Martinez-de-Albéniz, V. 2015. 'Fast Fashion: Business Model Overview and Research Opportunities', in N. Agrawal and S. Smith (eds), *Retail Supply Chain Management: Quantitative Models and Empirical Studies*, 2nd edn (New York: Springer), 237–64.

Carpenter, J., Bowles, S., Gintis, H., and Hwang, S. H. 2009. 'Strong Reciprocity and Team Production: Theory and Evidence', *Journal of Economic Behavior & Organization*, 71 (2), 221–32.

Cattaneo, O., Gereffi, G., Miroudot, S., and Taglioni, D. 2013. 'Joining, Upgrading and Being Competitive in Global Value Chains', World Bank Policy Research *Working Paper* No. 6406. Available at: http://econ.worldbank.org/external/default/main?pagePK=64165259&piPK=64165421&theSitePK=469382&menuPK=64166093&entityID=000158349_20130409182129.

CCTC. 2012. *Annual Yearbook. Cape Clothing and Textile Cluster*, Cape Town.

Chamon, M. and Kremer, M. 2009. 'Economic Transformation, Population Growth and the Long-Run World Income Distribution', *Journal of International Economics*, 79 (1), 20–30.

Chan, C. K. C. and Hui, E. S. I. 2014. 'The Development of Collective Bargaining in China: From "Collective Bargaining By Riot" to "Party State-Led Wage Bargaining"', *The China Quarterly*, 217, 221–42.

Charmes, J. 2012. 'The Informal Economy Worldwide: Trends and Characteristics', *Margin: The Journal of Applied Economic Research*, 6 (2), 103–32.

Checchi, D. and Garcia-Peñalosa, C. 2010. 'Labor Market Institutions and the Personal Distribution of Income in the OECD', *Economica* 77 (307), 413–50.

Chen, H. 2011a. 'Founding Affidavit, 6 June 2011', Case number 5642/2011, High Court of South Africa, Pietermaritzburg.

Chen, H. 2011b. 'Founding Affidavit, 25 November 2011', Case number 11023, High Court of South Africa, Pietermaritzburg.

Child, K. 2018. 'Crashing Edcon Seeks Relief From Mall Rents', *Sunday Times*, 16 December.

Chiu S. W. K., Ho K., and Lui T. 1997. *City-States in the Global Economy: Industrial Restructuring in Hong Kong and Singapore* (Boulder, CO: Westview).

Cling, J., M. Razafindrakoto and Roubaud, F. 2009. 'Export Processing Zones in Madagascar: The Impact of the Dismantling of Clothing Quotas on Employment and Labor Standards', in R. Robertson, D. Brown, G. Pierre, and L. Sanchez-Puerta (eds), *Globalization, Wages, and the Quality of Jobs: Five Country Studies* (Washington, DC: World Bank), 237–64.

Coakley, M. and Kates, M. 2013. 'The Ethical and Economic Case for Sweatshop Regulation', *Journal of Business Ethics*, 117 (3), 553–8.

Coe, N. M., Dicken, P., and Hess, M. 2008. 'Global Production Networks: Realizing the Potential', *Journal of Economic Geography*, 8 (3), 271–95.

Coe, N. M. and Henry Wai-Chung Yeung, H. 2015. *Global Production Networks: Theorizing Economic Development in an Interconnected World* (Oxford: Oxford University Press).

Coetzee, C. 2011. Newcastle Labour Relations Dispute, Report for KwaZulu-Natal Provincial Treasury (9 February).

Colclough, C. and McCarthy, S. 1980. *The Political Economy of Botswana: A Study of Growth and Distribution* (Oxford: Oxford University Press).

Coleman, N. 2012. 'Towards New Collective Bargaining, Wage and Social Protection Strategies: Learning from the Brazilian Experience', Concept paper presented at the University of Cape Town Conference on Strategies to Overcome Poverty and Inequality, 4 September, Cape Town, South Africa. Available at: http://www.ilo.org/actrav/WCMS_234488/lang–en/index.htm.

Collier, P. and Dercon, S. 2014. 'African Agriculture in 50 Years: Smallholders in a Rapidly Changing World?', *World Development*, 63, 92–101.

Collier, P. and Venables, A. J. 2007. 'Rethinking Trade Preferences: How Africa Can Diversify its Exports', *World Economy*, 30 (8), 1326–45.

Conway, P. and Shah, M. 2011. *Incentives, Exports and International Competitiveness in Sub-Saharan Africa: Lessons from the Apparel Industry* (Washington, DC: World Bank). Available at: https://openknowledge.worldbank.org/handle/10986/12779. License: CC BY 3.0 IGO.

COSATU. 2006. *Secretariat Report to the Ninth Congress*, 21 September. Available at: http://www.cosatu.org.za/show.php?ID=2150.

COSATU. 2007. *COSATU Submission on the National Gambling Amendment Bill*. Submitted to the Portfolio Committee on Trade and Industry. Available at: http://www.cosatu.org.za/docs/subs/2007/gambl.pdf.

COSATU. 2010. 'COSATU's response to Prof Buhlungu', Press release, 10 February.

COSATU. 2012. 'COSATU condemns Seardel Group closures', 9 February. Available at: http://www.cosatu.org.za/show.php?ID=5835.

Coughlin, P., Rubin, M., and Darga, L. 2004. 'The SADC Textile and Garment Industries: Towards a Global Vision', in D. McCormick and C. Rogerson (eds), *Clothing and Footwear in African Industrialisation* (Pretoria: Africa Institute of South Africa), 18–77.

Crivelli, E., Furceri, D., and Toujas-Bernate, J. 2012. 'Can Policies Affect Employment Intensity of Growth? A Cross-Country Analysis', IMF *Working Paper*, August 2012.

Crotty, A. 2012. 'SACTWU fights Seardel job losses that lift value', in *Business Report* (22 February). Available at: http://www.iol.co.za/business/news/sactwu-fights-seardel-job-losses-that-lift-value-1.1239623#.VHR83cnp-Zc.

Dawson, H. and Fouksman, E. 2017. '"Don't Give Money to the Lazy": The Moral Functions of Wage Labour and the Rejection of Cash Transfers by the Poor in South Africa', unpublished paper.

De la Hey, M. and Beinart, W. 2017. 'Why Have South African Smallholders Largely Abandoned Arable Production in Fields? A Case Study', *Journal of Southern African Studies*, 43 (4), 753–70.

De la Torre, J. 1984. *Clothing-Industry Adjustment in Developed Countries* (London: Macmillan).

De Silva, T. and Tenreyro, S. 2017. 'Population Control Policies and Fertility Convergence', *Journal of Economic Perspectives*, 31 (4), 205–28.

Deaton, A. 2013. *The Great Escape: Health, Wealth and the Origins of Inequality* (Princeton, NJ: Princeton University Press).

Department of Finance (DOF). 1996. *Growth, Employment and Redistribution: A Macroeconomic Strategy*. Available at: http://www.treasury.gov.za/publications/other/gear/chapters.pdf.

Dexter, P. 1999. 'Union Investment Companies: Business Unionism or Union Business?', *South African Labour Bulletin*, 23 (6), 82–4.

Di Filippo, A. 2009. 'Latin American Structuralism and Economic Theory', *Cepal Review*, 98, 175–196.

Dinh, H., Palmade, V., Chandra, V., and Cossar, F. 2012. *Light Manufacturing in Africa: Targetted Policies to Enhance Private Investment and Create Jobs* (Washington, DC: World Bank).

Donnelly, L. 2009. 'Patel lends a hand to former employer', *Mail&Guardian*, 26 May. Available at: http://mg.co.za/article/2009-05-26-patel-lends-a-hand-to-former-employer.

DTI (Department of Trade and Industry). 2009. 'Rescue Package: Clothing and Textiles', Media release, 28 April. Available at: http://www.ifashion.co.za/index.php?option=com_content&task=view&id=1742&Itemid=237.

DTI. 2010. 'Production Incentives Guidelines for 2010/11', Media release, 17 May. Available at: http://www.ifashion.co.za/index.php?option=com_content&view=article&id=2761&catid=139.

DTI. 2011. *Industrial Policy Action Plan 2011/12–2013/14*, February. South African Department of Trade and Industry. Available at: http://www.dti.gov.za/DownloadFileAction?id=561.

DTI. 2012. *Progress Report on Implementation of the Industrial Policy Action Plan (IPAP) for the Financial Year April 2011 to March 2012*. Available at: http://www.thedti.gov.za/news2013/ipap_2013-2016.pdf.

Dugger, C. 2010. 'Wage laws squeeze South Africa's poor', *New York Times* (26 September).

Ebrahim, A., Leibbrandt, M. and Ranchhod, V. 2017. 'The Effects of the Employment Tax Incentive on South African Employment', UNU-WIDER *Working Paper* No. 2017-5 (Helsinki: UNU-WIDER).

Econex. 2011. *Economic Report on the Impact of the Extension of the Collective Agreement to Non-Parties*, revised version August. Unpublished report.

Edwards, L. 2005. 'Has South Africa Liberalised its Trade?', *South African Journal of Economics*, 73 (4), 754–75.

Elkan, W. 1973. *An Introduction to Development Economics* (Harmondsworth: Penguin Books).

English, E. P. 2018. 'Senegal: A Service Economy in need of an Export Boost', in Newfarmer, R., Page, J., and Tarp, F. (eds). 2018. Industries Without Smoke-Stacks: Industrialization in Africa Reconsidered (Oxford: Oxford University Press), 254–274

Enslin-Payne, S. 2011. Bargaining Council Cracks Down on Clothing Industry, *Business Report* (24 March).

Ensor, L. 2009. 'Frame Rescue "about Safeguarding Industry"', *Business Day*, 5 June. Available at: http://www.hci.co.za/clothing-textile/frame-rescue-about-safeguarding-industry/.

Euromonitor International. 2013. *Apparel in South Africa*. Cape Town: Euromonitor.

Fang, T. and Lin, C. 2015. 'Minimum Wages and Employment in China', *IZA Journal of Labor Policy*, 4 (1), 1–30.

Faulkner, S. 1999. 'Investing in Ourselves: A Cautionary Tale', *South African Labour Bulletin*, 23 (4), 18–22.

Fei, J. C. H. and Ranis, G. 1961. 'A Theory of Economic Development', *American Economic Review*, 51 (4), 533–65.

Feinstein, C. 2005. *An Economic History of South Africa: Conquest, Discrimination, Development* (Cambridge: Cambridge University Press).

Feldmann, H. 2009. 'The Unemployment Effects of Labor Regulation around the World', *Journal of Comparative Economics*, 37 (1), 76–90.

Ferdows, K., Lewis, M. A., Machuca, J. A. D. 2004. 'Rapid-Fire Fulfillment', *Harvard Business Review*, 82 (11), 104–10.

Ferguson, J. 2015. *Give a Man a Fish: Reflections on the New Politics of Distribution*. Durham, NC: Duke University Press.

Fernandez-Stark, K., Federick, S., and Gereffi, G. 2011. *The Apparel Global Value Chain: Economic Upgrading and Workforce Development*, (Durham, NC: Duke University Press).

Fields, G. S. 1975. 'Rural–Urban Migration, Urban Unemployment and Underemployment and Job Search Activity in LDCs', *Journal of Development Economics*, 2 (2), 65–188.

Fields, G. S. 2003. 'Decent Work and Development Policies', *International Labour Review*, 142 (2), 239–62.

Fields, G. S., 2004. 'Dualism in the Labor Market: A Perspective on the Lewis Model After Half a Century', *The Manchester School*, 72 (6), 724–35.

Fields, G. S. 2006. 'Labour Market Dualism in the Lewis Model: Reply', *The Manchester School*, 74 (3), 355–9.

Filmer, D. and Fox, L. 2014. *Youth Employment in Sub-Saharan Africa* (Washington, DC: World Bank).

Fisher, A. 2010. 'The Great China Currency Debate: For Workers or Speculators', G-24 *Policy Brief* No. 56, 26/05/2010. Available at: https://www.g24.org/wp-content/uploads/2016/01/G24-Policy-Brief-56-26-5-2010.pdf.

Fox, L. and Thomas, A. 2016. 'Africa's Got Work to Do: A Diagnostic of Youth Employment Challenges in Sub-Saharan Africa', *Journal of African Economies*, 25 (s1), i16–36.

Fox, L., Thomas, A., Haines, C., and Munoz, J. 2013. 'Africa's Got Work to Do: Employment Prospects in the New Century', IMF *Working Paper* (Washington, DC: International Monetary Fund).

Frank, A. 1978. *Dependent Accumulation and Under-development* (London: Macmillan).

Frederick, S. and Staritz, C. 2012. 'Developments in the Global Apparel Industry after the MFA Phaseout', in G. Lopez-Acevedo and R. Robertson (eds), *Sewing Success? Employment, Wages and Poverty Following the End of the Multi-fibre Arrangement* (Washington, DC: World Bank), 41–86.

Freeman, R. B. 2009. Labor Regulations, Unions, and Social Protection in Developing Countries: Market Distortions or Efficient Institutions? (NBER *Working Paper* No. w14789) (Cambridge, MA: National Bureau of Economic Research).

Friedman, S. 1987. *Building Tomorrow Today: African Workers in Trade Unions, 1970–1984* (Johannesburg: Ravan Press).

Galenson, W. and Leibenstein, H. 1955. 'Investment Criteria, Productivity, and Economic Development', *The Quarterly Journal of Economics*, 69 (3), 343–70.

Garcia, M. and Fares, J. (eds). 2008. *Youth in Africa's Labor Market* (Washington, DC: World Bank).

Garcia, M. and Moore, C. M. 2012. *The Cash Dividend: The Rise of Cash Transfer Programs in Sub-Saharan Africa* (Washington, DC: World Bank).

Gawande, K., Hoekman, B., and Cui, Y. 2014. 'Global Supply Chains and Trade Policy Responses to the 2008 Crisis', *World Bank Economic Review*, 29 (1), 102–28.

Gelb, S. 2010. 'Macroeconomic Policy and Development: From Crisis to Crisis', in B. Freund and H. Witt (eds), *Development Dilemmas in Post-Apartheid South Africa* (Pietermaritzburg: University of KwaZulu-Natal Press), 32–62.

Gereffi, G. 1994. 'The Organization of Buyer-Driven Global Commodity Chains: How US Retailers Shape Overseas Production Networks', in G. Gereffi and M. Korzeniewicz (eds), *Commodity Chains and Global Capitalism* (Westport, CT: Praeger), 95–122.

Gereffi, G. 2014. 'Global Value Chains in a Post-Washington Consensus World', *Review of International Political Economy*, 21 (1), 9–37.

Gereffi, G. and Fernandez-Stark, K. 2011. *Global Value-Chain Analysis: A Primer.* (Durham, NC: Duke University Press).

Gereffi, G. and Güler, E. 2010. 'Global Production Networks and Decent Work in India and China: Evidence from Apparel, Automotive and Information Technology Industries', in A. Posthuma and D. Nathan (eds), *Labour in Global Production Networks in India* (Oxford: Oxford University Press), 103–26.

Gereffi, G., Humphrey, J., and Sturgeon, T. 2005. 'The Governance of Global Value Chains', *Review of International Political Economy*, 12 (1), 8–104.

Gerschenkron, A. 1962. *Economic Backwardness in Historical Perspective: A Book of Essays* (Cambridge, MA: Belknap Press of Harvard University Press).

Gibbon, P. 2004. 'South Africa and the Global Commodity Chain for Clothing: Export Performance and Constraints', in D. McCormick and C. Rogerson (eds), *Clothing and Footwear in African Industrialisation* (Pretoria: Africa Institute of South Africa), 148–92.

Gibbon, P. 2008. 'Governance, Entry Barriers, Upgrading: A Re-Interpretation of Some GVC Concepts from the Experience of African Clothing Exports', *Competition & Change*, 12 (1), 29–48.

Gibson, B. and Van Seventer, D. 2000. 'Real Wages, Employment and Macroeconomic Policy in a Structuralist Model for South Africa', *Journal of African Economies*, 9 (4), 512–46.

Gina, S. C. 2011. 'Affidavit, 8 December', Case number 11023, High Court of South Africa, Pietermaritzburg.

Godfrey, S. 1997. 'Why do Employers Bargain at Particular Levels? A Longitudinal Study of Western Cape Clothing Employers' Perceptions and Behaviour with Regard to Levels of Collective Bargaining, 1991–1995', Unpublished M.A. thesis, University of Cape Town.

Godfrey, S. 2015. 'Global, Regional and Domestic Apparel Value Chains in Southern Africa: Social Upgrading for Some and Downgrading for Others', *Cambridge Journal of Regions, Economy and Society*, 8 (3), 491–504.

Godfrey, S. and Macun, I. 1992. 'The Politics of Centralised Bargaining', *South African Review* 6, 388–402.

Godfrey, S., Maree, J., Du Toit, D., and Theron, J. 2010. *Collective Bargaining in South Africa: Past, Present and Future?* (Cape Town: Juta).

Godfrey, S., Maree, J., and Theron, J. 2006a. 'Regulating the Labour Market: The Role of Bargaining Councils', *Industrial Law Journal*, 27, 731–52.

Godfrey, S., Maree, J., and Theron, J., 2006b. 'Flexibility in Bargaining Councils: The Role of Exemptions', *Industrial Law Journal*, 27, 1368–86.

Godfrey, S., Maree, J., and Theron, J., 2006c. 'Conditions of Employment and Small Business: Coverage, Compliance and Exemptions', *Working Paper* No. 06/106, Development Policy Research Unit, University of Cape Town.

Golding, M. 1997. 'Pioneers or Sellouts? Exploring New Lands', *South African Labour Bulletin*, 21 (3), 85–90.

Golding, M. 2014. 'Affidavit', Case number 933/2014 (Cape Town: Labour Court). Available at: http://www.enca.com/south-africa/golding-challenges-hci-suspension-cites-ulterior-motive.

Golding, M. and Copelyn, J. 2007. *HCI Annual Report 2007* (Report of Chairman and Chief Executive Officer), 6. Available at: http://www.hci.co.za/Pages/annualreport2007.pdf.

Golding, M. and Copelyn, J. 2009. *HCI Annual Report 2009* (Report of Chairman and Chief Executive Officer), 6–7. Available at: http://www.hci.co.za/reports/2009HCI_Annual_Report.pdf.

Golding, M., and Copelyn, J. 2010. *HCI Annual Report 2010.* (Report of Chairman and Chief Executive Officer), 6–7. Accessed December 24, 2014. http://www.hci.co.za/reports/2010_HCI_Annual_Report.pdf

Gollin, D. 2014. 'The Lewis Model: A 60-Year Retrospective', *Journal of Economic Perspectives*, 28 (3), 71–88.

Golub, S. and Hayat, F. 2014. 'Employment, Unemployment and Underemployment in Africa', WIDER *Working Paper* No. 2014/014, World Institute for Development Economics Research.

Gustafsson, B. and Makonnen, N. 1993. 'Poverty Remittances in Lesotho', *Journal of African Economies, 2* (1), 49–73.

Haarmann, C., and Haarmann, D. 2012. 'Namibia: Seeing the sun rise – the realities and hopes of the basic income grant pilot project'. In C. Pateman and M. Murray (eds), *Horizons of Reform: Basic Income Solutions around the World* (London: Palgrave Macmillan), 33–57.

Haarmann, C., Haarmann D., Jauch, H., Shindondola-Mote, H., Nattrass, N., van Niekerk, I., and Samson, M. 2009. *Making the Difference! The BIG in Namibia*, (Windhoek: DfSD, ELCRN).

Hall, P. and Soskice, D. 2001. 'An Introduction to Varieties of Capitalism', in P. Hall and D. Soskice (eds), *Varieties of Capitalism: The Institutional Foundations of Comparative Advantage* (Oxford: Oxford University Press), 1–67.

Hamer, S. 2016. '"Our Father's Programmes": Political Branding Around Social Protection in Botswana, 2008–2014', CSSR *Working Paper* no. 370 (Cape Town: Centre for Social Science Research, University of Cape Town).

Hansard, 1909. 'Trade Boards Bill', *House of Commons, Debate: 28 April 1909*, 4, cc342–411. Available at: http://hansard.millbanksystems.com/commons/1909/apr/28/trade-boards-bill.

Harris, J. and Todaro, M. 1970. 'Migration, Unemployment and Development: A Two-sector Analysis', *American Economic Review*, 40, 126–42.

Harrison, A., Lin, J., and Xu, L. 2014. 'Explaining Africa's (Dis)advantage', *World Development*, 63: 59–77.

Harrison, A. E. and Scorse, J. 2003. 'Globalization's Impact on Compliance with Labor Standards', in S. M. Collins and D. Rodrik (eds), *Brookings Trade Forum 2003* (Washington, DC: Brookings Institution Press), 45–82.

Harrison, K. 1997. 'Industrial Response to Globalisation within a Medium-sized Town: A Focus on the Clothing Manufacturing Sector in Port Shepstone', *Transformation* 32, 79–101.

Harriss-White, B., with Rohra, S., and Singh, N. 2011. 'Revisiting Technology and Underdevelopment: Climate Change, Politics and the "D" of Solar Energy Technology in Contemporary India', in V. Fitzgerald, J. Heyer, and R. Thorpe (eds), *Overcoming the Persistence of Inequality and Poverty* (London: Palgrave Macmillan), 92–126.

Hart, G. 2002. *Disabling Globalization: Places of Power in Post-Apartheid South Africa* (Berkeley, CA: University of California Press).

Hart, G. and Todes, A. 1997. 'Industrial Decentralisation Revisited', *Transformation*, 32, 31–53.

Hart, V. 1994. *Bound by our Constitution: Women, Workers and the Minimum Wage* (Princeton, NJ: Princeton University Press).

Hartley, A. 2012. 'SACTWU appalled by *Seardel* decision', *Cape Times*, 7 February. Available at: http://www.iol.co.za/capetimes/sactwu-appalled-by-seardel-decision-1.1228821#.VHSS18np-Zd.

Hassenfuss, M. 2011. '*Seardel* on a steep access: Relief granted', *Financial Mail*, 20 October. Available at: http://www.hci.co.za/clothing-textile/seardel-on-a-steep-access-relief-granted/.

Hausmann, R., Rodrik, D., and Velasco, A. 2008. 'Growth Diagnostics', in N. Serra and J. Stiglitz (eds), *The Washington Consensus Reconsidered: Towards a New Global Governance*, 324–55 (Oxford: Oxford University Press).

Hayter, S., Fashoyin, T., and Kochan, T. 2011. 'Review Essay: Collective Bargaining for the 21st Century', *Journal of Industrial Relations*, 53 (2), 225–47.

HCI (Hosken Consolidated Investments). 2005. *HCI Annual Report 2005*. Cape Town: Hosken Consolidated Investments. Available at: http://www.hci.co.za/Pages/HCI_2005_Annual_Report.pdf.

HCI. 2011. *Annual Report for 2011*. Available at: http://www.hci.co.za/reports/2011_HCI_Annual_Report.pdf.

HCI. 2012. *Annual Report for 2012*. Available at: http://www.hci.co.za/reports/HCI_2012_INTEGRATED_REPORT.pdf.

HCI. 2014. *Annual Report for 2014*. Available at: http://www.hci.co.za/reports/hci_integrated_report_2014.pdf.

Henderson, J., Dicken, P., Hess, M., Coe, N., and Yeung, H. W. C. 2002. 'Global Production Networks and the Analysis of Economic Development', *Review of International Political Economy*, 9 (3), 436–4.

Hirsch, A. 2005. *Season of Hope: Economic Reform under Mandela and Mbeki* (Pietermaritzburg: University of KwaZulu-Natal Press).

Hirschsohn, P., Godfrey, S., and Maree, J. 2000. 'Industrial Policy-Making in the Auto, Textile and Clothing Sectors: Labour's Strategic Ambivalence', *Transformation*, 41, 55–88.

Hirway, I. 2010. 'Labour Market Adjustment and Female Workers: Global Production and Expiry of Quotes in India's Textile and Garment Industry Sector', in A. Posthuma and D. Nathan (eds), *Labour in Global Production Networks in India* (Oxford: Oxford University Press), 166–89.

Hobson, J. A. and Durbin, E. F. M. 1933. 'Underconsumption. An Exposition and a Reply', *Economica*, 42, 402–27.

Hofmeyr, J. 1994. 'Reform of the Labor Market in South Africa', *South African Journal of Economic History*, 9 (1), 13–30.

Hogan, B. 2014. 'Why I have resigned from the Board of HCI', *GroundUp*, 28 October. Available at: https://www.groundup.org.za/article/why-i-am-resigning-board-hci_2391/.

Hood, T., 1843. *Song of the Shirt*. Available at: http://www.victorianweb.org/authors/hood/shirt.html.

Humphrey, J. and Schmitz, H. 2002. 'How does Insertion in Global Value Chains Affect Upgrading in Industrial Clusters?', *Regional Studies*, 36 (9), 1017–27.

ILO (International Labour Organization), 1972. *Employment, Incomes and Equality: A Strategy for Increasing Productive Employment in Kenya* (Geneva: International Labour Organization).

ILO, 1976. *World Employment Programme: Research in Retrospect and Prospect* (Geneva: International Labour Organization).

ILO, 2005. 'The ILO and the Follow-up of the World Summit on Social Protection', Background paper for the United Nations Commission on Social Development, February 2005 session. Available at: http://www.ilo.org/wcmsp5/groups/public/—dgreports/—wcsdg/documents/genericdocument/wcms_079464.pdf.

ILO. 2009. 'Report of the Director-General: Decent Work' (Geneva: International Labour Organisation).

ILO. 2011. Brazil: *An Innovative Income-Led Strategy* (Geneva: International Labour Organization). Available at: http://ilo.org/global/publications/books/WCMS_153768/lang–en/index.htm.

ILO. 2014. *World of Work Report 2014: Development with Jobs* (Geneva: International Labour Organization).

ILO. 2015a. *Global Wage Report, 2014/5: Wages and Income Inequality* (Geneva: International Labour Organization). Available at: http://www.ilo.org/global/research/global-reports/global-wage-report/lang–en/index.htm.

ILO. 2015b. *Transforming Africa through Decent Work for Sustainable Development* (Addis Ababa: International Labour Organization).

ILO. 2017. *Towards Safer Working Conditions in the Bangladesh Ready-Made Garment Sector* (Bangladesh: International Labour Organization). Available at: http://www.ilo.org/dhaka/Whatwedo/Publications/WCMS_614088/lang–en/index.htm.

Islam, R. (ed.). 2005. *Fighting Poverty: The Development-Employment Link* (Boulder, CO: Lynne Rienner).

Joffe, A., Kaplan, D., Kaplinsky, R., and Lewis, D. 1995. *Improving Manufacturing Performance in South Africa: Report of the Industrial Strategy Project* (Cape Town: University of Cape Town Press).

Johnson, S., Kaufmann, D., and Zoido-Lobaton, P. 1998. 'Regulatory Discretion and the Unofficial Economy', *The American Economic Review*, 88 (2), 387–92.

Jones, S. and Tarp, F. 2015. 'Priorities for Boosting Employment in Sub-Saharan Africa: Evidence for Mozambique', *African Development Review*, 27, S1, 56–70.

Kalebe-Nyamongo, C. and Marquette, H. 2014. 'Elite Attitudes Towards Cash Transfers and the Poor in Malawi', *DLP Research Paper* 30 (Birmingham: Developmental Leadership Programme, University of Birmingham).

Kamau, P., McCormick, D., Michuki, G., and Gatimu, C. 2013. 'Availability of Technical Skills in Kenya Clothing Industry and its Implications on Competitiveness in the Post-MFA era', Presentation for the UNU-Wider Conference, 25–26 June, Helsinki.

Kanbur, R. 2016. 'W. Arthur Lewis and the Roots of Ghanaian Economic Policy', IDS *Working Paper* (Sussex: Institute for Development Studies), 1–15.

Kaplan, D. 2007. 'The Constraints and Institutional Challenges Facing Industrial Policy in South Africa: A Way Forward', *Transformation*, 64, 91–111.

Kaplinsky, R. and Morris. M. 2006. *Dangling by a Thread: How Sharp are the Chinese Scissors?* Report prepared for the Department for International Development Trade Division, Institute of Development Studies, Brighton, UK.

Kaplinsky, R. and Morris, M. 2009. 'The Asian Drivers and SSA: Is There a Future for Export-oriented African Industrialisation?', *The World Economy*, 32 (11), 1638–55.

Kaplinsky, R., Memedovic, O., Morris, M., and Readman, J. 2003. *The Global Wood Furniture Value Chain: What Prospects for Upgrading By Developing Countries? The Case of South Africa*, UNIDO Sectoral Studies Series (Vienna: UNIDO).

Karshenas, M. 2001. 'Agriculture and Economic Development in Sub-Saharan Africa and Asia', *Cambridge Journal of Economics*, 25 (3), 315–42.

Katjangua, N. 2018. 'Food bank drops 30,000', *The Namibian*, 11 May. Available at: https://www.namibian.com.na/67184/read/Food-Bank-drops-30-000.

Kaufman, B. 2013. 'Sidney and Beatrice Webb's Institutional Theory of Labor Markets and Wage Determination', *Industrial Relations*, 52 (3), 765–91.

Keane, J. and Te Velde, D. 2008. *The Role of Textile and Clothing Industries in Growth and Development Strategies* (London: Overseas Development Institute, Investment and Growth Programme).

Kesper. A. 1998. 'Small Clothing Manufacturers in the Johannesburg Inner City: Facing the Global Challenge', *Urban Forum*, 10 (2), 137–64.

Khanyile, S. 2011. 'More Clothes Plants Meet Wage Target', *Business Report* (23 May).

Kingsley, C. 1850. *Cheap Clothes and Nasty*. Available at: http://www.historyhome.co.uk/peel/economic/sweat.htm.

Kriel, A. 2012. 'Affidavit, 26 March', Case number 5642. High Court of South Africa, Pietermaritzburg.

Krugman, P. 1997. 'In Praise of Cheap Labor', *Slate*, 21 March. Available at: http://www.slate.com/articles/business/the_dismal_science/1997/03/in_praise_of_cheap_labor.2.html.

Kuznets, S. 1955. 'Economic Growth and Income Inequality', *The American Economic Review*, 45 (1), 1–28.

Lazarus, N. and Searll, A. 2004. *Seardel Annual Report for 2004*, Report by the Chairman and Chief Executive Officer.

Lazear, E. 2000. 'Performance Pay and Productivity', *The American Economic Review*, 90 (5), 1346–61.

Le Roux, M. 2009. 'Government abandons bid to save Frame', *Business Day*, 21 July. Available at: http://www.hci.co.za/clothing-textile/government-abandons-bid-to-save-frame/.

Le Roux, P. 2002. 'Financing a Universal Income Grant in South Africa', *Social Dynamics*, 28 (2), 98–121.

Legassick, M. 1974. 'Legislation, Ideology and Economy in Post 1948 South Africa', *Journal of Southern African Studies*, 1 (1), 5–35.

Leibbrandt, M., Finn, A., and Woolard, I. 2012. 'Describing and Decomposing Post-Apartheid Income Inequality in South Africa', *Development Southern Africa*, 29 (1), 19–34.

Lesotho, 2008. *A Practical Guide to Doing Business in Lesotho*, Maseru, Lesotho: Government of Lesotho Ministry of Trade and Industry, Cooperatives and Marketing.

Levinsohn, J. 2008. 'Two Policies to Alleviate Unemployment in South Africa', CID *Working Paper* No. 166. (Boston: Centre for Interational Development, Harvard University).

Levy, B. 2014. *Working with the Grain: Integrating Governance and Growth in Development Strategies* (Oxford: Oxford University Press).

Lewis, D. 1991. 'Unemployment and the Current Crisis', in S. Gelb (ed.), *South Africa's Economic Crisis* (Cape Town: David Philip).

Lewis, W. A. 1951. 'A Policy for Colonial Agriculture', in W. A. Lewis, M. Scott, M. Wright, and C. Legum (eds), *Attitude to Africa* (Harmondsworth: Penguin), 70–104.

Lewis, W. A. 1954. 'Economic Development with Unlimited Supplies of Labor', *The Manchester School*, 22 (2), 139–91.

Lewis, W. A. 1958. 'Employment Policy in an Underdeveloped Area', *Social and Economic Studies*, 7 (3), 42–54.

Lewis, W. A. 1965. 'A Review of Economic Development', *The American Economic Review*, 55 (1/2), 1–16.

Lewis, W. A. 1968. 'Reflections on Unlimited Labour', Development Research Project, *Discussion Paper* 5 (Princeton, NJ: Woodrow Wilson School, Princeton University).

Lin, J. and Rosenblatt, D. 2012. 'Shifting Patterns of Economic Growth and Rethinking Development', *Journal of Economic Policy Reform*, 15 (3), 171–94.

LMC (Labour Market Commission). 1996. *Restructuring the South African Labor Market: Report of the Presidential Commission to Investigate Labor Market Policy*. Available at: http://polity.org.za/polity/govdocs/commissions/fintoc.html.

Loayza, N. V. and Raddatz, C. 2006. 'The Composition of Growth Matters for Poverty Alleviation', *Policy Research Working Paper* WPS 4077. WPS 4077 (Washington, DC: World Bank).

Lombard, A. 2009. 'Union owns stake in sweatshop', *City Press*, 20 September. Republished and available at: http://www.ifashion.co.za/index.php?option=com_content&task=view&id=3083).

Lopez-Acevedo, G. and Robertson, R. 2012. *Sewing Success? Employment Wages and Poverty Following the End of the Multi-fibre Arrangement* (Washington, DC: World Bank).

Losch, B. 2016. *Structural Transformation to Boost Youth Labour Demand in Sub-Saharan Africa: The Role of Agriculture, Rural Areas, and Territorial Development* (Geneva: International Labour Organization).

MacLeod, C. 2015. 'Measuring the Impact of a National Minimum Wage', National Treasury, October.

Magruder, J. R. 2012. 'High Unemployment Yet Few Small Firms: The Role of Centralized Bargaining in South Africa', *American Economic Journal: Applied Economics*, 4 (3), 138–66.

Mahon, R. 2015. 'Integrating the Social into CEPAL's Neo-Structuralist Discourse', *Global Social Policy*, 15 (1), 3–22.

Maree, J., Hirschsohn, P., and Godfrey, S. 2000. 'Industrial Policy-Making in the Auto, Textile and Clothing Sectors: Labour's Strategic Ambivalence', *Transformation*, 41, 55–88.

Marglin, S. and Bhaduri, A. 1990. 'Profit Squeeze and Keynesian Theory', in S. Marglin and J. Schor (eds), *The Golden Age of Capitalism: Reinterpreting the Post-war Experience* (Oxford: Clarendon Press).

Mariotti, C. and Shepherd, A. 2016. 'Getting the Long-Term Macro Development Perspective Right: Diversification of the Economy with Strategic Investment and

Increased Protection from Risks', Pro-Poorest Growth *Working Paper* No. 2 (London: Overseas Development Institute).

Matisonn, H. and Seekings, J. 2003. 'Welfare in Wonderland? The Politics of the Basic Income Grant in South Africa, 1996–2002', in G. Standing and M. Samson (eds), *The Basic Income Grant in South Africa* (Cape Town: UCT Press), 56–76.

Matsilele, T. 2014. 'SACTWU buys Seardel, saves over 2000 jobs', *CNBCA*, 8 April. Available at: http://www.cnbcafrica.com/news/southern-africa/2014/04/08/sactwu-buys-seardel,-saves-over-2000-jobs/.

Mauda, R. 2014. *Performance Metrics for the Garment Industry*. School of Mechanical, industrial and aeronautical engineering, University of the Witwatersrand, final year report.

McKinley, D. 1999. 'Union Investment Strategy: Social Unionism of "Social Capitalism"?', *South African Labour Bulletin*, 23 (6), 85–90.

McMillan, M. and Headey, D. 2014. 'Introduction–Understanding Structural Transformation in Africa', *World Development*, 63: 1–10.

Meer, J. and West, J. 2013. 'Effects of the Minimum Wage on Employment Dynamics', *NBER Working Paper* no. 19262. (Cambridge, MA: National Bureau of Economic Research).

Mill, J. 1848. *Principles of Political Economy with some of Their Applications to Social Philosophy* (London: Longmans). Available at: http://www.econlib.org/library/Mill/mlP.html.

Moll, P. 1996. 'Compulsory Centralization of Collective Bargaining in South Africa', *American Economic Review*, 86 (2), 326–9.

Moll, T. 1991. 'Growth through Redistribution: A Dangerous Fantasy', *South African Journal of Economics*, 59 (3), 181–90.

Morris, M. 1990. 'Unions and Industrial Councils—Why Do Unions' Policies Change?', in N. Nattrass and E. Ardington (eds), *The Political Economy of South Africa* (Cape Town: Oxford University Press), 148–62.

Morris, M. 2011. 'Cooperation, Trust, Power and Predation: Creating and Destroying Industrial Policy in the South African Clothing and Textile Value Chain', Unpublished paper, University of Cape Town.

Morris, M. and Barnes, J. 2009. 'Globalization, the Changed Global Dynamics of the Clothing and Textile Value Chains and the Impact on Sub-Saharan Africa', (Vienna: United Nations, Industrial Development Organisation).

Morris, M. and Barnes, J. 2014. 'The Challenges to Reversing the Decline of the Apparel Sector in South Africa', Paper presented to the International Conference on Manufacturing-led growth for Employment and Equity in South Africa. Johannesburg, 20–21 May.

Morris, M. and Einhorn, G. 2008. 'Globalisation, Welfare and Competitiveness: The Impacts of Chinese Imports on the South African Clothing and Textile Industry', *Competition and Change*, 12 (4), 355–76.

Morris, M. and Levy, B. 2016. 'The Limits of Co-operation in a Divided Society: The Political Economy of South Africa's Garment and Textile Industry', in A. Black (ed.), *Towards Employment Intensive Growth in South Africa* (Cape Town: Juta).

Morris, M. and Staritz, C., 2014. 'Industrialization Trajectories in Madagascar's Export Apparel Industry: Ownership, Embeddedness, Markets, and Upgrading', *World Development*, 56, 243–57.

Morris, M. and Staritz, C. 2017. 'Industrial Upgrading and Development in Lesotho's Apparel Industry: Global Value Chains, Foreign Direct Investment, and Market Diversification', *Oxford Development Studies*, 45 (3), 303–20.

Morris, M., Plank, L., and Staritz, C. 2016. 'Regionalism, End Markets and Ownership Matter: Shifting Dynamics in the Apparel Export Industry in Sub-Saharan Africa', *Environment and Planning A*, 48 (7), 1244–65.

Morris, M., Staritz, C., and Barnes, J. 2011. Value Chain Dynamics, Local Embeddedness, and Upgrading in the Clothing Sectors of Lesotho and Swaziland. *International Journal of Technological Learning, Innovation and Development*, 4 (1/2/3), 96–119.

Myerson, A. 1997. 'In principle, a case for more "Sweatshops"', *The New York Times*, 22 June. Available at: http://www.nytimes.com/1997/06/22/weekinreview/in-principle-a-case-for-more-sweatshops.html.

NAMTAX. 2002 reprinted in 2005. 'Proposal for a Development Grant to the Poor Financed out of a Progressive Expenditure Tax on the Affluent', reprinted in C. Haarmann and D. Haarmann (eds), 2005. *The Basic Income Grant Resource Book.* (Windhoek: DfSD, ELCRN), 19–29.

National Anti-Sweating League (NASL) (ed.). 1907. *Report of Conference on a Minimum Wage.* (London: Co-operative Printing Society). Available at: https://books.google.com/books?id=JTYXAAAAYAAJ&printsec=frontcover&source=gbs_ge_summary_r&cad=0#v=onepage&q&f=false.

National Planning Commission (NPC). 2012. *National Development Plan 2030: Our Future—Make it Work.* Available at: http://www.info.gov.za/issues/national-development-plan/.

Nattrass, N. 1993. 'Economic Aspects of the Construction of Apartheid', in P. Bonner, P. Delius, and D. Posel (eds), *Apartheid's Genesis: 1935–1962* (Johannesburg: Ravan Press and Witwatersrand University Press).

Nattrass, N. 1994. 'Politics and Economics in ANC Economic Policy', *African Affairs*, 93, 343–59.

Nattrass, N. 1999. 'Globalisation and Social Accords: A Comparative Analysis of Sweden, Australia and South Africa', *Labour, Capital and Society*, 32 (2), 159–78.

Nattrass, N. 2000. 'Inequality, Unemployment and Wage-Setting Institutions in South Africa', *Journal for Studies in Economics and Econometrics*, 24 (3), 129–42.

Nattrass, N. 2001. 'High Productivity Now: A Critique of South Africa's Growth Strategy', *Transformation*, 45, 1–24.

Nattrass, N. 2011. 'The New Growth Path: Game Changing Vision or Cop-Out?', *South African Journal of Science*, 107 (3–4), 01–08.

Nattrass, N., 2014a. 'A South African Variety of Capitalism?', *New Political Economy*, 19 (1), 56–78.

Nattrass, N. 2014b. 'Deconstructing Profitability Under Apartheid: 1960–1989', *Economic History of Developing Regions*, 29 (2), 245–67.

Nattrass, N. and Seekings, J. 2015. 'Trade Unions, the State and Casino Capitalism in South Africa's Clothing Industry', *Review of African Political Economy*, 43 (147) (November), 1–18.

Nattrass, N. and Seekings, J. 2018a. 'Employment and Labour Productivity in High Unemployment Countries', *Development Policy Review*, 36: 769–85, doi: 10.1111/dpr.12313.

Nattrass, N. and Seekings, J. 2018b. 'Trajectories of Development and the Global Clothing Industry', *Competition and Change*, 22 (3), 274–92. Available at: https://doi.org/10.1177/1024529418768608.

Nattrass, N. and Walker, R. 2005. 'Unemployment and Reservation Wages in Working-Class Cape Town', *South African Journal of Economics*, 73 (3), 498–509.

Neak, S. and Robertson, R. 2009. 'Globalization and Working Conditions: Evidence From Cambodia', in R. Robertson, D. Brown, G. Pierre, and L. Sanchez-Puerta (eds), *Globalization, Wages, and the Quality of Jobs: Five Country Studies* (Washington, DC: World Bank), 97–130.

Newfarmer, R., Page, J., and Tarp, F. (eds). 2018. *Industries Without Smoke-Stacks: Industrialization in Africa Reconsidered.* (Oxford: Oxford University Press).

Newman, L. 2005. 'In memory of a mother', *IOL News* (9 August). Available at: http://www.iol.co.za/news/south-africa/in-memory-of-a-mother-1.250406? ot=inmsa.-ArticlePrintPageLayout.ot.

Ngui, D. and Kimuyu, P. 2018. 'Senegal: Prospects for Information and Communications Technology-enabled Services in Kenya: The Case of the Mobile Money Transfer Industry', in Newfarmer, R., Page, J., and Tarp, F. (eds). 2018. *Industries Without Smoke-Stacks: Industrialization in Africa Reconsidered* (Oxford: Oxford University Press), 213–231.

Nicol, M. 1984. 'A History of Garment and Tailoring Workers in Cape Town, 1900–1939', PhD thesis (Cape Town: University of Cape Town).

Nurkse, R. 1953. *Problems of Capital Formation in Underdeveloped Countries* (New York: Oxford University Press).

Odhiambo, O., Ashipala, J., and Mublana, F. 2015. 'Are Public Works Programmes Effective in Reinforcing Social Protection Systems? Evidence from Namibia', *Working Paper* no. 132 (International Policy Centre for Inclusive Growth, UNDP). Available at: http://namibiaatwork.gov.na/images/pdf/works.pdf.

OECD. 2013. *Interconnected Economies: Benefitting from Global Value Chains*. Available at: http://www.oecd.org/sti/ind/interconnected-economies-GVCs-synthesis.pdf.

Onaran, Ö. and Galanis, G. 2013. 'Is Aggregate Demand Wage-Led or Profit-Led? A Global Model', in M. Lavoie and E. Stockhammer (eds), *Wage-led Growth: An Equitable Strategy for Economic Recovery* (Basingstoke: Palgrave Macmillan), 71–99.

Page, J. 2013. *'For Africa's Youth, Jobs are Job One'* (Washington, DC: Brookings Institution).

Paton, C. 2013. 'Union reserves "will replenish lost pension funds"', *Business Day*, 26 April. Available at: http://www.bdlive.co.za/national/labour/2013/04/26/union-reserves-will-replace-lost-pension-funds.

Pauw, K. and Leibbrandt, M. 2012. 'Minimum Wages and Household Poverty: General Equilibrium Macro-Micro Simulations for South Africa', *World Development*, 40 (4), 771–83.

Payne, T. 2011. 'An entrepreneur's fight to survive', *Mail&Guardian* (22–28 July).

Payne, T. 2013. 'Textile labour leader does u-turn', *Mail&Guardian* (1 February). Available at: http://mg.co.za/article/2013-02-01-textile-labour-leader-does-u-turn.

Perry, G. (ed.). 2007. *Informality: Exit and Exclusion* (Washington, DC: World Bank Publications).

Philip, K. 2012. 'The Rationale for an Employment Guarantee in South Africa', *Development Southern Africa*, 29 (1), 177–90.

Philip, K. 2018. *Markets on the Margins: Mineworkers, Job Creation and Enterprise Development* (Woodbridge, Suffolk: James Currey).

Pickles, J. and Woods, J. 1989. 'Taiwanese Investment in South Africa', *African Affairs*, 88 (353), 507–28.

Pickles, J., Plank, L., Staritz, C., and Glasmeier, A. 2015. 'Trade Policy and Regionalisms in Global Clothing Production Networks', *Cambridge Journal of Regions, Economy and Society*, 8, 381–402.

Pickles, J., Smith, A., Bucek, M., Roukova, P., and Begg, R. 2006. 'Upgrading, Changing Competitive Pressures, and Diverse Practices in the East and Central European Apparel Industry', *Environment and Planning A*, 38 (12), 2305–24.

Piketty, T. 2013. *Capital in the Twenty-First Century* (Cambridge, MA: Harvard University Press).

Pillay, D. 1990. 'Pursuing Centralized Bargaining', *South African Labour Bulletin*, 15 (4), 8–12.

Planting, S. 2011. 'The dirty truth about SA's clothing bargaining council', *Moneyweb* (13 July). Available at: http://www.moneyweb.co.za/moneyweb-politicaleconomy/the-dirty-truth-about-sas-clothing-bargaining-coun.

Planting, S. 2012. 'Court to do the job the union's unwilling to do', *Moneyweb* (16 July). Available at: http://www.moneyweb.co.za/moneyweb-industrials/court-to-do-the-jobthe-unions-unwilling-to-do?sn=2009%20Detail.

Polanyi, K. 1944. *The Great Transformation* (Boston, MA: Beacon Press).

Pollin, R., Burns, J., and Heintz, J. 2004. 'Global Apparel Production and Sweatshop Labour: Can Raising Retail Prices Finance Living Wages?', *Cambridge Journal of Economics*, 28 (2), 153–71.

Porter, M. 1985. *The Competitive Advantage: Creating and Sustaining Superior Performance* (New York: NY Free Press).

Porter, M. 1990. 'The Competitive Advantage of Nations', *Harvard Business Review*, 1 (1) (March–April), 74–91.

Powell, B. and Zwolinski, M. 2012. 'The Ethical and Economic Case Against Sweatshop Labor: A Critical Assessment', *Journal of Business Ethics*, 107 (4), 449–72.

Pressly, D. 2007. 'Manuel: Protection can make companies lazy', *Mail&Guardian*, 22 February. Available at: http://mg.co.za/article/2007-02-22-manuel-protection-can-make-companies-lazy.

Pritchett, L., Sen, K., and Werker, E. 2018. 'Deals and Development: An Introduction to the Conceptual Framework', in L. Pritchett, K. Sen, and E. Werker (eds), *Deals and Development: The Political Dynamics of Growth Episodes* (Oxford: Oxford University Press). Available at: http://fdslive.oup.com/www.oup.com/academic/pdf/openaccess/9780198801641.pdf.

Psilos, P. and Gereffi, G. 2011. *Workforce Development in the Global Economy: Linking Skills and Capabilities*. RTI International and Duke Center on Globalisation, Governance and Competitiveness (Durham, NC: Duke University). Available at: http://www.cggc.duke.edu/gvc/workforce-development.

Radovanović, V. and Maksimović, M. 2010. 'Labor Market and (Un)Employment in the European Union and Serbia: Regional Aspects', *Journal of the Geographical Institute Jovan Cvijic, SASA*, 60 (2), 59–75.

Ranchhod, V. 2006. 'The Effect of the South African Old Age Pension on Labour Supply of the Elderly', *South African Journal of Economics*, 74 (4), 725–44.

Ranis, G. 2004. 'Arthur Lewis's Contribution to Development Thinking and Policy', *The Manchester School*, 72 (6), 712–23.

Ranis, G. 2008. 'Labour Surplus Economics', in S. N. Durlauf and L. E. Blume (eds), *The New Palgrave Dictionary of Economics*, 2nd edn. (Basingstoke: Palgrave Macmillan).

Ranis, G. and Stewart, F. 1999. 'V-goods and the Role of the Urban Informal Sector in Development', *Economic Development and Cultural Change*, 47 (2), 259–88.

Rankin, N. A. and Roberts, G. 2011. 'Youth Unemployment, Firm Size and Reservation Wages in South Africa', *South African Journal of Economics*, 79 (2), 128–45.

Raworth, K. 2017. *Doughnut Economics: Seven Ways to Think Like a 21st Century Economist* (London: Random House).

Reed, L. 2012. 'The Changing Dynamics of the South African Clothing Value Chain and the Role for Industrial Policy: A Case Study of the China Quotas', PhD thesis, University of Cape Town.

Robbins, G., Todes, A., and Velia, M. 2004. *Firms at the Crossroads: The Newcastle-Madadeni Clothing Sector and Recommendations on Policy Responses*, Report for the KwaZulu-Natal DEDT and Newcastle Municipality.

Robertson, R. 2012. 'Introduction and Theoretical Foundation and Empirical Approach', in G. Lopez-Acevedo and R. Robertson, *Sewing Success. Employment, Wages, and Poverty following the End of the Multi-fibre Arrangement* (Washington, DC: World Bank), 7–40.

Rodrik, D. 2007. *One Economics, Many Recipes* (Princeton, NJ: Princeton University Press).

Rodrik, D. 2016. 'An African Growth Miracle?', *Journal of African Economies*, 27, 1: 10–27.

Rodrik, N. 2015. 'Premature Deindustrialisation', NBER *Working Paper* no. 20935 (Cambridge, MA: National Bureau of Economic Research).

Rogerson, C. 2004. 'Sunrise or Sunset Industries? South Africa's Clothing and Footwear Sectors', in D. McCormick and C. Rogerson (eds), *Clothing and Footwear in African Industrialisation* (Pretoria: Africa Institute of South Africa), 110–47.

Rogerson, C. 2010. 'Successful SMEs in South Africa: The Case of Clothing Producers in the Witwatersrand', *Development Southern Africa*, 17 (5), 687–716.

Rosenstein-Rodan, P. M. 1943. 'Problems of Industrialization of Eastern and South-Eastern Europe', *Economic Journal*, 53 (210), 202–11.

Roskam, A. 2007. 'An Exploratory Look into Labour Market Regulation', DPRU *Working Paper* No. 07/116 (Cape Town: Development Policy Research Unit, University of Cape Town).

RSA (Swart Commission). 1994. 'Long-Term Strategic Plan for the Textile and Clothing Industries in South Africa', Panel and Task Group for the Textile and Clothing Industries in South Africa, unpublished, March 1994.

Rutherford, M. 2007. 'American Institutionalism and its British Connections', *The European Journal of the History of Economic Thought,* 14 (2), 291–323.

Saito, O. 2013. 'Proto-Industrialization and Labor-Intensive Industrialization: Reflections on Smithian Growth and the Role of Skill-Intensity', in G. Austin and K. Sugihara (eds), *Labor-intensive Industrialization in Global History* (Oxford: Routledge), 85–106.

Saul, J. and Gelb, S. 1986. *The Crisis in South Africa* (London: Zed Books).

Savchenko, Y. 2012. 'The Rise of Small Asian Economies in the Apparel Industry', in G. Lopez-Acevedo and R. Robertson (eds), *Sewing Success? Employment, wages and Poverty Following the End of the Multi-Fibre Arrangement* (Washington, DC: World Bank), 163–96.

Schmidt, V. 2008. 'Discursive Institutionalism: The Explanatory Power of Ideas and Discourse', *American Review of Political Science,* 11, 303–26.

Seardel. 2004. *Annual Report for 2004.* Available at: http://www.seardel.co.za/images/downloads/SeardelReport2004.pdf.

Seardel. 2005. *Annual Report for 2005.* Available at: http://www.seardel.co.za/images/downloads/SeardelReport2005.pdf.

Seardel. 2006. *Annual Report for 2006.* Available at: http://www.seardel.co.za/images/downloads/SeardelReport2006.pdf.

Seardel. 2007. *Annual Report for 2007.* Available at: http://www.seardel.co.za/images/downloads/SeardelReport2007.pdf.

Seardel. 2008. *Annual Report for 2008.* Available at: http://www.seardel.co.za/images/downloads/SeardelReport2008.pdf.

Seardel. 2012. *Annual Report for 2008.* Available at: http://www.seardel.co.za/images/downloads/SeardelReport2012.pdf.

Searll, A. 2008. *Report by the Previous Chairman.* 'Report by the Previous Chairman', in Seardel, *Annual Report for 2008,* page 4. Available at: http://www.seardel.co.za/images/downloads/SeardelReport2008.pdf.

Seekings, J. 2007. 'The Inconsequentiality of Employment Disincentives: Basic Income in South Africa', *Basic Income Studies* [online journal] 2, 1 (June 2007). Available at: http://www.bepress.com/bis/vol2/iss1/art12.

Seekings, J. 2008. 'Deserving Individuals and Groups: The Post-Apartheid State's Justification of the Shape of South Africa's System of Social Assistance', *Transformation: Critical Perspectives on Southern Africa,* 68, 28–52.

Seekings, J. 2016a. 'Minimum Wage Setting by the Employment Conditions Commission in South Africa, 1999–2015', CSSR *Working Paper* 375 (Cape Town: Centre for Social Science Research, University of Cape Town).

Seekings, J. 2016b. 'Building a Conservative Welfare State in Botswana', CSSR *Working Paper* No. 388 (Cape Town: Centre for Social Science Research, University of Cape Town).

Seekings, J. 2017. 'The Discourse of Dependency and the Agrarian Roots of Welfare Doctrines in Africa: The Case of Botswana', *Sozialpolitik.ch,* 2 (2).

Seekings, J. 2018. 'Inequality, Popular Attitudes and Elite Ideology in Africa: The Case of Social Protection', paper for the UNRISD Conference 'Overcoming Inequalities in a Fractured World', Geneva (November).

Seekings, J. and Matisonn, H. 2012. 'The Continuing Politics of Basic Income in South Africa', in M. Murray and C. Pateman (eds), *Basic Income Worldwide: Horizons of Reform: Basic Income Solutions around the World* (London: Palgrave Macmillan), 128–50.

Seekings, J. and Moore, E. 2014. 'Kinship, Market and State in the Provision of Care in South Africa', *Soziale Welt*, special issue, 20, 435–50.

Seekings, J. and Nattrass, N. 2005. *Class, Race and Inequality in South Africa* (New Haven, CT: Yale University Press).

Seekings, J. and Nattrass, N. 2016. *Politics and Policy in South Africa: Why has Poverty Persisted after Apartheid?* (Johannesburg: Jacana).

Sehnbruch, K., Burchell, B., Agloni, N., and Piasna, A. 2015. 'Human Development and Decent Work: Why Some Concepts Succeed and Others Fail to Make an Impact', *Development and Change*, 46 (2), 97–224.

Seiler, E. 1984. 'Piece Rate vs Time Rate: The Effect of Incentives on Earnings', *The Review of Economics and Statistics*, 66 (3), 363–76.

September Commission. 1997. *The Report of the September Commission on the Future of the Unions to the Congress of South African Trade Unions*. Available at: http://www.cosatu.org.za/docs/reports/1997/septcomm.htm.

Serrano, F. and Summa, R. 2011. *Macroeconomic Policy, Growth and Income Distribution in the Brazilian Economy in the 2000s* (Washington, DC: Center for Economic and Policy Research).

Shakya, M. 2011. 'Apparel Exports in Lesotho: The State's Role in Building Critical Mass for Competitiveness', in P. Chuhan-Pole and M. Angwafo (eds), *Yes Africa Can: Success Stories from a Dynamic Continent* (Washington, DC: World Bank).

Skinner, C. and Valodia, I. 2002. 'Labour Market Policy, Flexibility, and the Future of Labour Relations: The Case of Kwazulu-Natal Clothing Industry', *Transformation: Critical Perspectives on Southern Africa*, 50 (1), 56–76.

Sorkin, I. 2015. 'Are There Long-Run Effects of the Minimum Wage?', *Review of Economic Dynamics*, 18 (2), 306–33.

South Africa, Union of. 1926. *Report of the Economic and Wage Commission, U.G. 14 of 1926* (Pretoria: Government Printer).

Southall, R. 2007. 'Ten Propositions about Black Economic Empowerment in South Africa', *Review of African Political Economy*, 34 (111), 67–84.

Southall, R. and Tangri, R. 2006. 'COSATU and Black Economic Empowerment', in S. Buhlungu (ed.), *Trade Unions and Democracy: COSATU Workers' Political Attitudes in South Africa* (Cape Town: HSRC Press), 115–42.

Spence Commission. 2008. *The Growth Report: Strategies for Sustained Growth and Inclusive Development.* Available at: http://cgd.s3.amazonaws.com/GrowthReportComplete.pdf.

Standing, G. and Samson, M. (eds). 2003. *A Basic Income Grant for South Africa* (Cape Town: University of Cape Town Press).

Staritz, C. 2010. *Making the Cut? Low-Income Countries and the Global Clothing Value Chain in a Post-Quota and Post-Crisis World* (Washington, DC: World Bank Publications).

Staritz, C. and Morris, M. 2011. 'Local Embeddedness, Upgrading and Skill Development: Global Value Chains and Foreign Direct Investment in Lesotho's Apparel Sector', *Better Work Research Conference: Workers, Business and Government: Understanding Labour Compliance in Global Supply Chains*, 26–28 October.

Staritz, C. and Whitfield, L. 2017. 'Made in Ethiopia: The Emergence and Evolution of the Ethiopian Apparel Export Sector', *Working Paper* no.3 (Roskilde: Centre for African Economies, Roskilde University).

StatsSA. 2010. *Manufacturing Industry: Financial Report No. 30-20-30* (Pretoria: Statistics South Africa). Available at: http://www.statssa.gov.za/publications/Report-30-02-03/Report-30-02-032008.pdf.

Stewart, F. 1977. *Technology and Underdevelopment* (London: Macmillan).

Stewart, F. 2006. 'Do We Need A New Great Transformation? Is One Likely?', *Research Paper* no. 2006/36 (Helsinki: UNU-WIDER)., United Nations University.

Steyn, L. 2012. 'Textile union opts for compliance over wage increases', *Mail&Guardian* (20 July). Available at: http://mg.co.za/article/2012-07-20-textile-unionopts-for-compliance-over-wage-increases.

Stiglitz, J. 2002. *Globalisation and its Discontents* (New York: W. W. Norton).

Stiglitz, J. 2006. *Making Globalization Work* (New York: W.W. Norton).

Stiglitz, J. 2012. *The Price of Inequality. How Today's Divided Society Endangers our Future* (New York: W. W. Norton).

Stockhammer, E. 2015. 'Rising Inequality As a Cause of the Present Crisis', *Cambridge Journal of Economics*, 39 (3), 935–58.

Strauss, I. and Isaacs, G. 2016. 'Labour Compensation Growth in the South African Economy: Assessing its Impact Through the Labour Share Using the Global Policy Model', *Working Paper* no. 4 (Johannesburg: National Minimum Wage Research Initiative, University of the Witwatersrand). Available at: http://nationalminimumwage.co.za/wp-content/uploads/2016/08/NMW-RI-GPM-Model-Final.pdf.

Sugihara, K. 2013. 'Labor-intensive Industrialization in Global History: An Interpretation of the East Asian Experience', in G. Austin and K. Sugihara (eds), *Labor-intensive Industrialization in Global History* (Oxford: Routledge), 20–64.

Tajgman, D. and De Veen, J. 1998. *Employment-Intensive Infrastructure Programmes.* (Geneva: International Labour Office).

Tangri, R. and Southall, R. 2008. 'The Politics of Black Economic Empowerment in South Africa', *Journal of Southern African Studies*, 34 (3), 699–716.

Tejani, S. and Milberg, W. 2016. 'Global Defeminization? Industrial Upgrading and Manufacturing Employment in Developing Countries', *Feminist Economics*, 22 (2), 24–54.

Tewari, M. 2005. 'Post-MFA Adjustments in India's Textile and Apparel Industry: Emerging Issues and Trends', *Working Paper*, (New Delhi: Indian Council for Research on International Economic Relations).

Thomas, S. 2015. 'Clothing industry: Taking on China', *Financial Mail*, 12 February. Available at: http://www.financialmail.co.za/fmfox/2015/02/12/clothing-industry-taking-on-china.

Thorbecke, E. 2007. 'The Evolution of the Development Doctrine, 1950–2005', in G. Mavrotas and A. Shorrocks (eds), *Advancing Development Core Themes in Global Economics* (Basingstoke: Palgrave Macmillan), 3–36.

Tignor, R. L. 2006. *W. Arthur Lewis and the Birth of Development Economics* (Princeton, NJ: Princeton University Press).

Todes, A., 1998. 'Restructuring, Migration and Regional Policy in South Africa: The Case of Newcastle', PhD thesis, Department of Town and Regional Planning (Durban: University of Natal).

Todes, A. 2002. 'Industrial Restructuring in South Africa: The Case of Newcastle', *Tijdschrift voor economische en sociale geografie*, 90 (4), 379–90.

Tokatli, N. 2008. 'Global Sourcing: Insights from the Global Clothing Industry—The Case of Zara, a Fast Fashion Retailer', *Journal of Economic Geography*, 8, 21–38.

Tokatli, N. 2013. 'Toward a Better Understanding of the Apparel Industry: A Critique of the Upgrading Literature', *Journal of Economic Geography*, 13 (6), 993–1011.

Tokatli N., Kızılgün, Ö., and Cho, J. 2011. 'The Clothing Industry in Istanbul in the Era of Globalisation and Fast Fashion', *Urban Studies*, 48 (6), 1201–15.

Tregenna, F. 2010. *Sectoral Labour Intensity in South Africa*, Report for NEDLAC, Johannesburg.

UNCTAD (United Nations Conference on Trade and Development). 2014. *Trade and Development Report, 2014* (New York and Geneva: United Nations).

Underhill, G. 2012. 'Pinnacle Point Consultant Raked in R4.4 million', *Mail&Guardian*, 5 April. Available at: http://mg.co.za/article/2012-04-05-pinnacle-point-consultant-raked-in-r44million.

UNECA, 2009. *Africa Youth Report 2009* (Addis Ababa: UN Economic Commission for Africa).

UNECA. 2011. *Africa Youth Report 2011* (Addis Ababa: UN Economic Commission for Africa).

UNWTO. 2015. *UNWTO Tourism Highlights, 2015 Edition* (Madrid: World Tourism Organisation (UNWTO)). Available at: http://www.e-unwto.org/doi/book/10.18111/9789284416899.

Vlok, E. 1999. 'Plant Now, Harvest Later: Pressures Facing Union Investment Companies', *South African Labour Bulletin*, 23 (4), 23–9.

Vlok, E. 2011. 'Productivity ploy "pays off" to create stability', *Mail&Guardian*, 4 November. Available at: http://mg.co.za/article/2011-11-04-productivity.

Von Holdt, K. 2003. *Transition from Below: Forging Trade Unionism and Workplace Change in South Africa* (Pietermaritzburg: UKZN Press).

Wang, W., Lu, J., and Allan, W. 2018. 'The East Africa Shift in Textile and Apparel Manufacturing: China–Africa Strategies and AGOA's Influence'. China Africa Initiative *Policy Brief* no. 25 (Washington DC: Johns Hopkins School if International Studies).

Wang, X. and Piesse, J. 2013. 'The Micro-Foundations of Dual Economy Models', *The Manchester School*, 81 (1), 80–101.

Webster, E. and Buhlungu, S. 2004. 'Between Marginalisation and Revitalisation? The State of Trade Unionism in South Africa', *Review of African Political Economy*, 100, 229–45.

Webster, E., Benya, A., Dilata, X., Joynt, C., Ngoepe, K., and Tsoeu, M. 2008. 'Making Visible the Invisible: Confronting South Africa's Decent Work Deficit', Research commissioned by the Department of Labour, South Africa.

Wellisz, S. 1968. 'Dual Economies, Disguised Unemployment and the Unlimited Supply of Labour', *Economica*, New Series, 35 (137), 22–51.

Welz, M. 2015. 'Zuma: White Racists' Stereotype Black', *Noseweek*, January 6–7.

Whelan, S. 2018. 'Rising Minimum Wage Puts Pressure on Cambodia's Garment Export Industry', *The Loadstar*, 8 January. Available at: https://theloadstar.co.uk/rising-minimum-wage-puts-pressure-cambodias-garment-export-industry/.

White, L. 2012. *The Clash of Economic Ideas: The Great Policy Debates and Experiments of the Last Hundred Years*. Cambridge, MA: Cambridge University Press.

Whitfield, L. and Staritz, C. 2017. 'Mapping the Technological Capabilities for Ethiopian-owned Firms in the Apparel Global Value Chain', *Working Paper* no.4 (Roskilde: Centre for African Economies, University of Roskilde).

Williams, B. 2015. 'African Growth and Opportunity Act (AGOA): Background and Reauthorization', Washington, DC: Congressional Research Service.

Wisman, J. 2013. 'Wage Stagnation, Rising Inequality and the Financial Crisis of 2009', *Cambridge Journal of Economics*, 37, 921–45.

Woolard, I. and Leibbrandt, M. 2013. 'The Evolution and Impact of Unconditional Cash Transfers in South Africa', SALDRU *Working Paper* no. 51 (Cape Town: Southern African Labour and Development Research Unit, University of Cape Town).

World Bank. 2006. *World Development Report 2007* (Washington, DC: World Bank).

World Bank. 2016. *World Development Report 2016: Digital Dividends* (Washington, DC: World Bank).

World Bank. 2017a. *World Development Report 2017: Governance and the Law* (Washington, DC: World Bank).

World Bank. 2017b. *Future Armenia: Connect, Compete Prosper: A Systematic Country Diagnostic* (Washington, DC: World Bank). Available at: http://documents.worldbank.org/curated/en/716961524493794871/pdf/Armenia-SCD-in-Eng-final-04192018.pdf.

World Bank. 2017c. *Western Balkans Regular Economic Report Number 12: Job Creation Picks Up* (Washington, DC: World Bank). Available at: https://openknowledge.worldbank.org/bitstream/handle/10986/28883/121417-WP-PUBLIC.pdf.

World Bank. 2018. *The State of Social Safety Nets* (Washington, DC: World Bank). Available at: https://openknowledge.worldbank.org/bitstream/handle/10986/29115/9781464812545.pdf?sequence=5&isAllowed=y.

World Commission on the Social Dimension of Globalisation (WCSDG), 2004. *A Fair Globalisation: Creating Opportunities for All* (Geneva: International Labour Office).

Xu, L. 2017. 'On the Edge of Capitalism: African Local States, Chinese Family Firms and the Transformation of Industrial Labour', Doctoral Dissertation, Harvard University.

Young, A. and Lawson, R. 2014. 'Capitalism and Labor Shares: A Cross-Country Panel Study', *European Journal of Political Economy*, 33 (C), 22–36.

Zalk, N. 2014. 'Industrial Policy in a Harsh Climate: The Case of South Africa', in J. M. Salazar-Xirinachs, I. Nübler, and R. Kozul-Wright (eds), *Transforming Economies. Making Industrial Policy Work for Growth, Jobs and Development* (Geneva: International Labour Organization), 327–54.

Zhang, X., Yang, J., and Wang, S. 2011. 'China has Reached the Lewis Turning Point', *China Economic Review*, 22 (4), 542–54.

Index